Indonesia and the Philippines

Indonesia and the Philippines

American Interests in Island Southeast Asia

Robert Pringle

Columbia University Press
New York · 1980

Copyright © Robert Pringle 1980
All rights reserved.

Printed in the United States of America

Columbia University Press
New York   Guildford, Surrey

Library of Congress Cataloging in Publication Data

Pringle, Robert, 1936–
  Indonesia and the Philippines.

  Includes bibliographical references and index.
  1. United States—Foreign relations—Indonesia.
2. Indonesia—Foreign relations—United States.
3. United States—Foreign relations—Philippine
Islands.   4. Philippine Islands—Foreign relations
—United States.   I. Title.
E183.8.I5P74   327.730598   80–13474
ISBN 0–231–05008–9
ISBN 0–231–05009–7 (pbk.)

For Jamie and Anne

Who Enjoyed the Island World
from Their Own Perspective

Contents

Preface

This study was originally conceived as an effort to define the scope and content of American national interests in the Southeast Asian island world, drawing on material from Indonesia and the Philippines. But it did not require much exposure to the rather sterile academic literature on the concept of national interests to conclude that such an effort would inevitably lead either to diffuse generalities or to a more interesting but necessarily subjective discussion of issues. So the original plan was reversed; rather than pretending to define interests I assumed them, and went on to talk about costs, capabilities, and, in some cases, blind spots. Individual essay topics were selected because they have direct and obvious bearing on the interest categories which are briefly set forth in the opening chapter.

My assumptions about American interests in post-Vietnam Southeast Asia are the result of two different kinds of experience, as a student of Southeast Asian history, and later, after joining the U.S. Foreign Service, as a junior political officer at two American embassies, in Jakarta (1970–74) and Manila (1974–77). My Foreign Service career has inevitably included periods when it seemed that U.S. official energies were in one way or another being misspent; that I was writing cabled reports about topics which were essentially insignificant or transitory, while other issues which would surely matter to future generations of both Americans and Southeast Asians were ignored. The project which led to this book provided a rare opportunity to step outside the constricting circumstances of daily official routine for a year, and to offer my own thoughts on policy issues. Opinions expressed are personal and do not reflect the views of the Department of State or other U.S. government agencies. The relatively few areas of serious disagreement, such as the Philippine base question, will be apparent to the reader. In general, the essays do not propose radical new courses of action. But they do attempt to illustrate the need for a reorientation of our foreign policy process away from its traditional preoccupation with crisis, in order to deal more effectively with the "low politics" issues of trade, technology, development, and environment which are now of primary importance in U.S. relations with most countries of the Third World. The final chapter dwells at some length on bureaucratic reform and the need for enhanced analytic capability, because in my view these are the fundamental prerequisites for more effective policy-making in a noncrisis (or precrisis) environment.

My official background requires a word of explanation about sources. The essay topics were selected without regard for political sensitivity, in the conviction that important foreign policy issues can be discussed intelligently on the basis of public sources, including interviews, and that the outside scholar can usually compete on terms of equal authority with the official despite lack of access to classified material. What the outsider may lack in raw material is often more than outweighed by analytic continuity and area expertise, plus a little creative exploitation of the government itself. I believe this expectation was borne out by my experience. In only a few cases have I been aware, on the basis of previous official access, of key facts or arguments which are concealed by official secrecy. In no instance was this information of critical importance for purposes of analysis or judgment. The facts presented are drawn entirely from unclassified sources indicated by the notes. My opinions, however, have obviously been affected by previous experience, by my own perceptions while serving in Indonesia and the Philippines as well as by the views of many Foreign Service colleagues and friends in the academic world.

These essays are about *island* Southeast Asia, the

world's greatest archipelago, and I have at times used the expression "the island world." Many of the generalizations in the political chapters would have to be qualified were they to be applied to the entirety of Southeast Asia, including the mainland areas of Burma, Thailand, and Indochina (Vietnam, Laos, and Cambodia). Confusion is possible on this score if only because the American military services, during the Vietnam conflict, habitually used the term "Southeast Asia" when in fact they were talking about Indochina.

In addition to Indonesia and the Philippines, island Southeast Asia is usually defined to include two states, Singapore and Malaysia, which are historically, geographically, and ethnically part of the island world. Malaysia shares with Indonesia the great island of Borneo and the Straits of Malacca, as well as a common cultural heritage between Sumatra and the Malayan peninsula. Malaysia and Singapore are members of the Association of Southeast Asian Nations (ASEAN) and, despite a unique British cast to their modern polities, demonstrate many of the authoritarian political characteristics which are found among its other members, including Indonesia and the Philippines. For these and other reasons, some of the generalizations in the pages that follow *do* apply to Malaysia and Singapore, including those bearing on environmental issues. I decided to exclude Malaysia and Singapore from the essays partly because I lack recent experience in these two countries, but more because addition of a third variation on common themes would have made comparative discussion awkward if not impossible. Ethnic Malay-Chinese issues dominate the political and economic life of Malaysia to a far greater extent than is the case in Indonesia or the Philippines. This factor demands separate analysis at every turn, as does Singapore's unique city-state configuration.

The essays are occasionally critical not only of the U.S. policy process, and the fundamental bureaucratic and cultural assumptions which support it, but also of Southeast Asian governments and customary attitudes toward the United States. I am aware that some of the judgments expressed may offend some old friends in both Indonesia and the Philippines. I ask only that they understand the underlying assumption, that since the nations of Southeast Asia have achieved maturity and increasing self-reliance, we can and must discuss mutual concerns with complete candor and without the false pretense that all our objectives, much less our cultural values, are shared. The need for more candor is particularly compelling in the case of U.S.-Philippine relations, where an emotional residuum of colonial mythology continues to impede rational intercourse.

This book was made possible by a grant from the Rockefeller Foundation's International Relations Program. Implementing assistance, including office space, was provided by the Carnegie Endowment for International Peace from October 1977 through the end of 1978. Without the Endowment's generous support I would never have been able to make adequate use of the Rockefeller grant within the relatively short time (one year) available. David Yang, a Carnegie student intern, assisted me throughout most of the project. Much of chapter five, including its tables, is the result of his efforts. The Carnegie Endowment library staff, particularly Jane Lowenthal, provided constant assistance. I have presumed heavily on old friendships at the Cornell Southeast Asia Program, most notably in seeking the advice of Professors George McT. Kahin and Frank Golay. Elsewhere, Fred Bunnell, Donald Emmerson, Milton Osborne, Peter Stanley, and David Wurfel were among those who gave generously of their time in commenting on various chapters. I have at several points borrowed from the thinking of others to an extent perhaps not adequately conveyed by the footnote references. Some of my more conspicuous benefactors include J. A. C. Mackie on international relations and Java development issues; Selig Harrison on "detachment" (chapter two); and Frank Weinstein on contract operations at the Philippine bases (chapter three). In addition, I owe a more generalized intellectual debt to Francis T. Underhill, formerly U.S. Ambassador to Malaysia, whose analysis of Southeast Asian politics over the years has combined wit, perception, and the willingness to state unfashionable truths in the highest tradition of Foreign Service reporting. Both the opinions expressed and any errors of fact are, of course, my own responsibility.

The views expressed in these essays are those of the author and do not necessarily represent the policies of the Department of State or any other part of the U.S. government.

Washington, D.C.
January 1980

Chapter One

U.S. Interests in the Philippines and Indonesia: Context and Content

Like variations on a theme, Indonesia and the Philippines are similar enough to be discussed together, yet different enough to make comparison interesting. They are neighbors and were fashioned from related geographic and cultural materials; but the historical experience of the two nations has been radically different, particularly during the colonial period, as has their relationship with the United States. While American acquisition of the Philippines in 1899 stimulated continuing national debate, Indonesia under Dutch rule remained on the extreme periphery of our national awareness. Now, however, thirty years after the end of the colonial era, once dissimilar patterns of interaction with us are converging. Our relations with both countries are friendly, marred by minor friction over human rights and differing positions on some aspects of the more general north-south debate. Isolated from each other until recently, the two are now quasi-allies, as key members of the Association of Southeast Asian Nations (ASEAN). Yet despite the trend toward similarity, the heritage of the past still exerts great influence, not least in U.S.-Philippine relations. This introductory chapter will first compare salient aspects of Indonesian and Philippine culture, resources, and relations with the United States. Then, against this background, it will state certain assumptions about the nature of U.S. interests in the two countries, which are further illustrated in the six chapters that follow.

Geography and Culture of an Island World

The world's greatest archipelago, shaped like a shallow triangle, peaks at the island of Luzon, pointing toward Taiwan, the South China Sea, and Japan. The Philippines forms the apex of the triangle, while Indonesia constitutes most of its body and base. Across this vast area, roughly the same dimensions from east to west as the continental United States, warm, often shallow seas are constantly interspersed with islands. Land areas range from coral reefs which barely emerge at low tide to the world's second largest island, Borneo, bisected by rivers more than 700 miles long. Settlement patterns include teeming cities like Manila and Jakarta, some of the world's most densely settled agricultural land on Java, and the virtually uninhabited coastal peat swamps and highlands of Borneo, Sumatra, and West Irian, the Indonesian half of New Guinea. Major islands are often within sight of each other, land masses are rugged, and the seas consequently serve as much to unite as to divide populations. Not surprisingly, most island Southeast Asians are conditioned to think of both elements in territorial terms. The Indonesian phrase for motherland is *tanah air*, perhaps best translated "homelandwater," reflecting an attitude of considerable consequence for the modern controversy over law of the sea.[1]

In the past, island Southeast Asia has been a zone of political and cultural diversity between India and China. From the sixteenth century until World War II it was a cockpit for contending European powers. In the eyes of the greatest imperial power of all, Britain, the island world was important primarily because it lay across the India-China trade route. In more recent years the principle interisland straits—Malacca, Sunda, Lombok, Surigao, San Bernardino, and others—have retained a high degree of geopolitical significance for the global actors of the moment. Today, for example, virtually all of Japan's imported Middle Eastern oil transits narrow passages through the archipelago.

Tropical Agriculture

The archipelago is highly volcanic. Tapping geothermal energy may, in the long run, be a major factor in the development of both Indonesia and the Philippines. Already, omnipresent volcanoes contribute to popular welfare and GNP by spreading soil-enriching effusions to some areas, but not to all.

Of all the fallacies inherent in the Western notion of the tropical paradise, none is more misleading than the myth of fertility. Unfortunately for romance, most tropical soils are subject to rapid depletion, the result of constant high temperature and heavy rainfall. The nutrients contained in decaying vegetable matter are leached away at a far faster rate than is the case in temperate climates. Unless soils are renewed by occasional coats of volcanic ash, or supplemented with river sediments, the end result is likely to be either the bright red soil known as laterite or the equally sterile, dirty-white podsolic variety.

The same conditions explain the signficant dichotomy between upland, slash-and-burn agriculture and the more intensive irrigated farming of the lowlands. Throughout the upland areas the mature natural vegetation is hardwood forest. Huge trees are able to subsist on shallow (sometimes nonexistent) topsoils because every leaf that falls is rapidly recycled through elaborate root systems. Clearing the forest and burning the debris enriches the soil, but fertility is soon exhausted, usually by one or two sparse crops of rice. The farmer must move on to a new area, and forest reinvades the plot. No permanent damage results as long as sufficient time is allowed for forest regeneration, but if the slash-and-burn technique is repeated too often in one place, usually as a result of population pressure, soil may be completely destroyed and nothing will grow except tough, virtually ineradicable grasses. The end product of forest destruction in the tropics is humid desert.

But on land sufficiently flat to catch and hold water there is an alternative. If nutrient-laden groundwater or even rainfall can be trapped, it creates a mineral and biologic stew rich in algae and other plant food. Under such conditions the fertility of the soil is a much less critical factor. As a result, irrigated rice can be grown in the same spot for generation after generation. Furthermore, wet rice agriculture is almost infinitely responsive to refinements of various kinds—including "inputs" of fertilizer, pesticide, improved irrigation techniques, and better seeds—always leading to increased per-acre production. Only when Southeast Asians had mastered the technique of wet rice agriculture were they able to generate economic surplus in sufficient volume to support the kingdoms which existed on Java and elsewhere before European rule.

A few regions, such as Java and central Luzon, are fortunate enough to have both volcanic soils and good irrigation potential. Unfortunately, the resulting productivity has tended to encourage human as well as vegetable fecundity. After modern medicine brought epidemic disease under control the result was severe overpopulation in restricted areas.

The exploitation of tropical uplands, increasingly profitable in the short run, risks long-range ecological disaster. The colonial powers discovered that some tree crops, notably rubber, flourish in some nonirrigable ecosystems. But the more remote land areas of both the Philippines and Indonesia—more than half the total land mass—remained under magnificent hardwood forest until recently. During the last decade the destruction of this resource has proceeded at an accelerating pace, a phenomenon of perhaps global significance discussed in chapter seven.

Mineral and Maritime Resources

From the days of the spice trade onward the exotic products of the archipelago excited foreign interest. In recent years minerals have played the major role. The island world is a significant source of tin, copper, nickel, aluminum, and to a lesser extent gold. Indonesia (although not the Philippines) is an oil exporter, supplying about 8 and 18 percent of U.S. and Japanese import requirements, respectively,[2] and major natural gas resources are under development. Further expansion of mineral production throughout the region is possible since much of the subsurface, both on and off shore, is unexplored. But here again the image of a bountiful tropical paradise may be seriously misleading. For it is likely that peak productivity of some key commodities—notably Indonesian oil—has already been reached. Without rapid development of renewable energy sources such as solar and geothermal power, both Indonesia and the Philippines are likely to face growing deficits as local consumption increases. Both countries are already seriously lacking in some key resources. Neither, for example, has the mineral base to support a major steel industry, nor would total economic integration of the ASEAN countries solve the problem.

The seas, like the uplands, offer opportunities and pose ecological risks. The extensive coral reef systems that predominate in many coastal and interisland areas have already suffered considerable damage as a result of population expansion and the use of explosives for fishing. Along some low-lying coasts, mangrove swamps may become productive with the right technologies. Almost everywhere deep-water fishing resources have barely been tapped by local fishermen, although some are being exploited under joint ventures with the Japanese.

Patterns of People

The cultures of island Southeast Asia, including Malaysia, are highly diverse, yet from a distance there is a kaleidoscopic symmetry to the overall pattern. Languages vary from island to island (in some cases from river to river), yet all belong to the same Malayo-Polynesian language family. Broad cultural affinity typifies the entire cycle of traditional activity at the village level, from child rearing to rice planting. The Indonesian national motto, "Unity in Diversity," reflects the prevailing theme of variation within limits.[3]

All dominant Southeast Asian societies are characterized by a high degree of syncretism, or the successive adoption and interlayering of religious and cultural elements. In Indonesia and the Philippines the syncretic process was similar, but the ingredients syncretized were radically different. Beginning in about the fifth century A.D. the preliterate village-level societies of Indonesia were exposed first to Hinduism, which brought with it the political concept of kingship and much else, and, a thousand years later, in some areas to Islam. These external influences impacted variously on different regions and touched some not at all. The Philippines began with a similar cultural base but received only a trace of the Hindu influence that saturated much of the rest of Southeast Asia, while Islam took root only in the far south. Instead the two analogous forces were Catholicism, which arrived with Ferdinand Magellan and Spanish rule, and, much later, what might be described as secular Americanism. In contrast to Indonesia, the most significant cultural changes in the Philippines took place after the advent of colonial rule, and were more uniformly and thoroughly impressed on the population. Only a relatively small minority of Muslims and upland tribal peoples—together comprising between 5 and 10 percent of the population—resisted or avoided the Spanish impact. As a result, Philippine society is today *relatively* homogeneous, and the more significant recent additions to the syncretic whole have been derived from the West, as opposed to India or the Middle East.

Historical Divergence

The colonial experience and its aftermath were profoundly different in the two countries.[4] Despite elements of genuine enlightenment, Dutch rule in Indonesia was overwhelmingly economic in motivation. The Dutch created a smoothly functioning machine for the production and export of tropical produce. They discovered that it was politically convenient and economically profitable to preserve certain traditional institutions, but natives were generally denied access to the modernized superstructure of the colonial apparatus. The most striking illustration was the sugar industry on Java, where peasants supplied the raw material, growing cane in the same paddies where they grew rice, and then provided labor for the mills. There was no need for foreigners to own land—indeed, Dutch law prevented them from doing so. However, from the mill onward the operation was completely in non-Indonesian hands. In other sectors of the economy ethnic Chinese played a well-delineated intermediate role. Like the British in India, the Dutch in Indonesia erected an elaborate, multilevel political structure, featuring a mixture of directly ruled territory and theoretically independent states under Indonesian rulers. It was accompanied by a complex legal system with differing codes for "natives," Chinese, and Europeans. A key operating principle of Dutch colonialism was that different ethnic groups have different economic and political roles. In practice, this reinforced existing cultural divisions and strengthened the plural nature of Indonesian society.[5]

Relatively large numbers of Dutch and Indo-Europeans, treated legally as Europeans, came to regard the Indies as home, and Holland developed a major emotional as well as economic stake in the perpetuation of colonialism. Not surprisingly, the Dutch bitterly resisted nationalism and decolonization, and the Indonesians achieved their independence only after a protracted struggle. The consequences of the 1945–49 anti-Dutch revolution were enormous and lasting. It forced the development of a national ideology and a functioning national language (Indonesian) based on the ancient lingua franca, Malay, and it heavily damaged the economic infrastructure built by the Dutch. It gave the Indonesian army a charter role in the birthing of the nation and a philosophy of economic and political involvement which today can be invoked to assert the legitimacy of military rule and military business activities. Because the revolution was partly directed at the traditional Indonesian rulers, who had been part of the colonial system, as well as against the economic institutions of Dutch rule, it took on overtones of class struggle and social revolution, and left an anticapitalist heritage sympathetic to socialist or statist economic policies.

The Philippine colonial experience contrasted with that

of Indonesia at nearly every point. Unlike the neighboring Dutch system, Spanish rule was primarily religious in motivation, resulting in the only Christian nation in Asia. Economic exploitation was a major theme, as in all colonial systems, but the benefits flowed primarily to local Spanish clergy, and to a local mestizo land-owning elite. For more than two centuries Manila was little more than a trading post where the Spanish exchanged Mexican silver for silks and porcelain from China via the famous yearly Manila galleon. The development of a major export sector did not start until the nineteenth century. Export commerce was never as well developed as in the Dutch East Indies, but when it did come the Filipino land-owning elite shared to a far greater extent in the transformation, and they rapidly developed entrepreneurial attitudes and business interests.

From the beginning the Spanish were anxious not to repeat their earlier excesses in Latin America, and Spanish colonialism in the Philippines was more enlightened than is suggested in most American accounts. During periods of liberal rule in Spain, islanders were represented in the Spanish parliament, and although education left much to be desired, as early as 1843 there were proportionately more literates in the Philippines than in Spain itself.[6] By creating a wealthy landlord class Spanish colonialism deepened economic and class distinctions in Philippine society, a failing which has received much attention. However, it is of equal significance that Spanish colonial society placed less emphasis on ethnic categories than was the case in Indonesia, and its impact, on balance, was more integrative than divisive. At the highest economic levels mestizoization resulted in a mingling of Spanish, native, and overseas Chinese cultures and laid the basis for modern Philippine society,[7] a process with no parallel in Indonesia. Chinese cultural elements as well as Chinese blood were injected into the mestizo Philippine elite, perhaps one reason why, in later years, Filipino capitalists have been able to compete with "pure" overseas Chinese in the world of business. The mestizo phenomenon did not extend to the rural areas, but even at the lowest economic levels of society the Catholic religion exerted a unifying, culturally leveling effect quite unlike anything in Indonesia. The major exception to this trend was the Muslim south, which bitterly resisted both Spanish rule and Catholicism, and which has remained badly isolated from the rest of the Philippine nation to this day.

In short, the cultural transformation which accompanied Spanish rule encouraged the formation of a well-integrated, Western-educated, privileged indigenous class, originally agrarian but with increasingly capitalist inclinations, long before the same phenomenon occurred anywhere else in Southeast Asia. The inevitable result, aggravated by the heavy-handedness of the Spanish in dealing with the consequences of their own presence, was the emergence of the earliest nationalist movement in the region. American intervention first encouraged, then repressed, then absorbed the independence movement. Many of its members were drawn from the upper class, or *ilustrado* elite, and easily accommodated to the new colonial regime. More radical elements resisted through two years of bitter guerrilla struggle which served to aggravate the reservations of those Americans—an idealistic but not inconsequential minority, including such curious radicals as Andrew Carnegie—who had bitterly opposed acquiring the Philippines in the first place.

The full irony and ambivalence of American rule in the Philippines is rarely appreciated. No greater contrast with the Indonesian situation can be imagined. The United States never fully adjusted to its role as an Asian overlord, and weighty American interests, both ideological and material, constantly pressed for early withdrawal. The specific content of American colonial policy fluctuated radically depending upon which political party was in power. Beginning with Wilson's Governor General, F. B. Harrison, the Democrats opted for rapid "Filipinization" as a prelude to independence, but subsequent Republican administrations stressed continuing obligation to shoulder the White Man's Burden. Meanwhile, despite what in British and Dutch eyes seemed a bumbling and unprofessional brand of colonialism, certain American values, conveyed through the powerful medium of widespread English-language public education, rapidly penetrated to the heart of Philippine culture, by no means replacing older value systems but adding enduring elements of great significance. These included faith in the possibility of upward economic mobility, heightened respect for the accumulation of wealth, and the enshrinement of democratic political forms, if not democratic substance.

Such elements were assimilated precisely because they accorded with the emerging aspirations of the Filipino elite, and on balance the impact of American rule was socially conservative. By opening economic and political vistas, the United States provided new opportunities for the old landowning class, hastening it along the path toward both capitalism and professionalism, and in the process, bolstering its power. Quite in contrast to Indonesia, the indigenous leaders were not cut off either from the modern world or from a significant economic role. Particularly noteworthy is the fact that William Howard Taft applied the U.S. Chinese Exclusion Act to the Philippines, over the strenuous protests of would-be plantation developers who wanted to import the same, cheap, industrious coolie labor enjoyed by their counterparts in Malaya and elsewhere.[8] By preventing the kind of massive Chinese influx that was then taking place in the rest of Southeast Asia this policy did much to preserve the relativity well-integrated mestizo system and to preclude the eventual development of a dominant, discretely Chinese capitalist class.

Thus it was that reluctant, inconsistent colonialism evoked an unusually sympathetic response. But in the long run this seemingly benign phenomenon proved to be less than a blessing for the Philippine nation. Much of the creative force of Philippine nationalism, instead of being steeled in colonial adversity, as was the case in Indonesia, was lulled against the unresisting, alluring bosom of Columbia. Many Filipinos realized that an insidious process of co-optation was under way, but what could they do? "Damn the Americans!" exclaimed Manuel Quezon in a rare moment of frankness, "Why don't they tyrannize us more?"[9]

As World War II approached, those forces in the United

States which had always opposed Philippine coloniza-
tion—particularly organized labor and American-owned
Cuban sugar interests—gained strength. Since 1899 the relatively inefficient Philippine sugar industry had become dependent on access to the U.S. market. At the same time, Japanese imperialism was becoming a threat. Rapid progress
toward complete independence thus threatened not only economic ruination for a major portion of the Filipino elite, but
also delivery to the uncertain mercies of Tokyo. The foremost
Filipino politician of the day, Quezon, was forced to match
his political competitors' public demands for "immediate"
independence, while in fact he was working furiously behind
the scenes to delay and qualify it. In 1934, Congress finally
legislated Philippine independence, to be preceded by a ten-
year Commonwealth period. Two years later Quezon moved
into what had been the Governor General's palace as the first
President of the Philippines.

During World War II Filipinos were the only Southeast
Asians who fought enthusiastically on the Allied side. An estimated one million died and the country was devastated.
Manila is said to have been more heavily damaged by the war
than any other city in the world except Warsaw. In 1946 the
Philippines obtained independence on schedule, but rehabilitation aid and continued duty-free entry to the United States
for Philippine sugar were conditional on the extension of
equal economic rights—"parity"—to American citizens.
Under the terms of the 1934 independence legislation, the
United States also retained major military bases in the Philippines.[10]

Whatever degree of national malaise may have resulted
from failure to indulge in revolution might have mattered
little had American friendship been less obviously flawed in
Filipino eyes by selfishness and lack of gratitude for wartime
sacrifice. While only a minority of nationalist intellectuals
deeply resented the continuance of close U.S.-Philippine ties
into the postwar period, many felt that "parity" and the other
conditions imposed by the United States in return for its assistance were a humiliating let-down. Filipinos did not lose

their love for Americans and things American, but many were convinced that the United States neither fully comprehended them nor returned their affection in fair measure.

To summarize, as the course of colonialism in Indonesia and the Philippines varied, so did its lasting consequences. Both countries achieved independence with a relatively favorable ratio of population to resources, qualified by rapid population growth. Both suffered heavy physical destruction, a result of war in one case, revolution in the other. The Philippines had more experience with self-government and a more homogeneous, better-integrated indigenous elite, including a substantial and growing class of entrepreneurs. Where the Philippine national ethos was buoyantly capitalistic, Indonesian experience encouraged socialism or statism. Geographic and ethnic cleavages were less significant in the Philippines, but, partly for that very reason, the former American colony failed to develop the kind of tolerant, multicultural political ideology expressed in the Indonesian doctrine of *pancasila* (the five basic principles of the Republic, vaguely theist but deliberately non-Islamic) and the national slogan "unity in diversity." If the Philippines was economically more mature, Indonesia was in some respects politically more sophisticated, especially in the handling of minority problems. Indonesia's nationalism was more self-confident and her sense of identity firmer, in part because her independence, no matter how its costs might otherwise be measured, was unqualified by continuing close association with the ex-colonial power.

Relations with the United States

The pattern of postwar American relationships with Indonesia and the Philippines is, not surprisingly, another study in contrast. The Philippines progressed from colony to firm ally, rarely questioning, until the Vietnam War, the validity of American leadership in a global struggle against communism. American rights to bases in the Philippines were reaffirmed in 1947, and the U.S.-Philippine security relationship was further strengthened by a mutual defense treaty in August 1951 and a military assistance agreement in June 1953. In 1954 Manila hosted the conference that resulted in the formation of the Southeast Asian Treaty Organization (SEATO), a key component of U.S. containment policy, of which the Philippines and Thailand were in fact the only Southeast Asian members.

Throughout the fifties and early sixties, the United States exerted major influence in Philippine internal affairs through investment, economic aid, sheer weight of presence, and semiclandestine interventions. In what U.S. strategists long regarded as a model of effective anticommunist operation, the CIA's General Edward Lansdale provided critical support for Defense Secretary Ramon Magsaysay's struggle against communist Huk guerrillas in central Luzon. Magsaysay went on to be perhaps the most successful Philippine president in history until his tragic death in a plane crash in 1957. But despite the apparent solidarity of a cold war alliance, Philippine-U.S. relations were contentious in many ways. The Philippines continued to agitate for a more favorable economic relationship, and the U.S. military bases were a focus of nationalist resentment and a source of constant irritation from the early 1950s onward. Although the Philippines sent a battalion of troops to Korea in 1951, American pressure on Manila to participate actively in the Vietnam War met stubborn evasion. In the end President Ferdinand Marcos did agree to send a civic action group of army engineers, but only in return for substantial financial reimbursement. However, the Philippine government successfully resisted use of the bases for combat operations against Vietnam. The bases' role, valuable though it was to the conduct of the war, was restricted to transportation, logistics, and other support functions.[11] In short, the U.S.-Philippine relationship remained intimately postcolonial, fraught with conflicting strains of irritation and affection, marked by dependence on one side and all too often by condescension on the other.

American relations with Indonesia have been more distant and orthodox. In the immediate postwar period the United States regarded Indonesia as the territory of a beleaguered European ally and helped supply the Dutch against the revolutionaries; but as the struggle dragged on, American sympathies shifted to the Indonesians, and American mediation helped achieve a settlement in 1951. During the next decade the United States was increasingly alarmed by Sukarno's drift toward radical nonalignment and earned a degree of Indonesian ill-will by a clumsy and abortive attempt to support antigovernment forces in the Outer Island rebellion of 1958. We continued to provide small amounts of military and economic aid, and, in the early days of the Kennedy Administration, Ellsworth Bunker mediated a settlement of Indonesia's claim to West Irian, the western portion of New Guinea. The solution was favorable to the Indonesians and deeply offended the Dutch, who had stubbornly refused to relinquish the last vestige of their eastern empire.

Even those American officials who were convinced that Sukarno was a dangerous crypto-communist eventually recognized that there was no practical way to challenge his popularity with the Indonesian people. Nevertheless, following the brief honeymoon at the beginning of the Kennedy Administration, U.S.-Indonesian relations resumed their gradual downhill slide. As Indonesia became polarized between the largest Communist Party in the world and the army, economic deterioration and political tension sharply accelerated. Sukarno, archetype of the aging revolutionary, attempted to retain control by resorting to foreign policy adventurism aimed at the West. In late 1962 he launched a campaign of armed confrontation against his northern neighbor, the newly formed Federation of Malaysia, asserting that it was a tool of imperialism. In March 1964 he told the United States to "go to hell with your aid," and in early 1965 he took Indonesia out of the United Nations. However, thanks partly to the Malaysia struggle and partly to the efforts of an extraordinarily tolerant U.S. Ambassador, Howard Jones, Indonesian wrath remained largely focused on the British. Although Indonesia was hardly receptive to foreign investment at this period, the two major American oil companies in the country were able to renew their agreements in 1963, relinquishing concession rights but retaining full control of operations.[12]

If American relations with the Philippines were characterized by conflicting familial emotions, our dealings with Indonesia were marked by the less intense kind of misunderstanding that prevails between strangers, and antagonism was more typically qualified by respect. Despite severe misgivings, our policy for the remainder of the Sukarno era remained noninterventionist, a stance of increasingly gloomy disengagement.

More recently, both Indonesia and the Philippines have experienced critical shifts to authoritarian, single-center systems of government. In Indonesia elements of the Communist Party, perhaps with assistance from Sukarno, attempted a putsch which backfired in October 1965. In the months that followed the army crushed the communists, relegated Sukarno to the sidelines, and, under the leadership of General Suharto, assumed a position of political dominance. In the Philippines, after a period of increasing disorder, some of which may have been provoked by the government, President Marcos declared Martial Law in September 1972, and has ruled by decree ever since.

The causes and consequences of both transitions remain controversial.[13] Marxist commentators have concluded that the emergence of so-called authoritarian-dependent systems was, in both cases, the result of collusion between the United States and indigenous "comprador" elements, part of a global conspiracy to insure that future national development would serve the interests of foreign investors and the free market system. In its more extreme variants this view hardly does justice to the skill or nationalist credentials of the present generation of leaders. However, although there is no evidence of direct U.S. involvement in either case, it is also clear, particularly in the Philippines, that American acquiescence, expressed through bilateral and multilateral aid, provided the new regimes in both countries with legitimation and material support.

The events of 1965 in Indonesia and 1972 in the Philippines marked watersheds in many ways, not least in relations with the United States. Since the Coup and Martial Law, and despite the persistence of many unique postcolonial elements in the Philippines, the respective patterns of interaction with us have become similar in content, although not in style. Today both countries are important trade and investment partners, regarding us as a major market, a leading foreign aid donor, and a preferred source of both military technology and private bank loans. In both, authoritarian systems have generated human rights problems, and although the two regimes have made economic development a key objective of national policy, progress is slowed by deficiencies in bureaucratic capacity and popular participation. Both have a tremendous stake in agricultural exports, and hence in the attainment of commodity price stabilization on favorable terms

Table 1.1 Key Indicators

	Indonesia	Philippines
Area (000 square miles)	735	115
Population (1978—millions)	143	46
Population growth rate (1978, estimated)	1.7%	2.6%
Population per physician (in thousands)	16.9	2.7
Literacy, adult (% total)	62	72
Life expectancy (years at birth)	48.1	58.5
Physical quality of life index[a]	50	73
Per capita GNP (1978 estimate, U.S.$)	240	450
Average annual per capita GNP growth rate (1970–75)	3.5%	3.7%
Real growth in GNP (1977)	8%	5%
Percentage of total trade with U.S. and Japan (1973–75)	60%	70%
Public external debt (1977—billion U.S.$)	15.9	5.6
Military expenditure as percent of budget (1978)	15–16%[b]	15%
Percentage of national income received by highest 5% over lowest 20% of population	33.7/6.8	24.8/3.9

[a]Formula based on average index ratings for life expectancy, infant mortality and literacy, devised by the Overseas Development Council. See John Sewell et al, *The United States and World Development Agenda 1977*, (Washington, 1977)

[b]Does not include "nonbudgetary" expenditures which provide 40 percent or more of military support in Indonesia.

SOURCE: Remaining data are drawn from various sources, including World Bank, *World Bank Atlas* (Washington, 1977), World Bank, *World Economic and Social Indicators* (Washington, 1978) and U.S. Agency for International Development, *Annual Budget Submission, Indonesia and the Philippines, FY 1980* (Washington, 1979). For source of external debt figures, see table seven in chapter three.

for the producer. The Philippines is already heavily affected by U.S. and Japanese import restrictions on the product of nascent industries, and Indonesia may be in the same position before long. Finally, for both governments anticommunism is a major legitimizing principle, and both are therefore worried about what they are inclined to perceive as American loss of will in the wake of Vietnam.

Indonesia and the Philippines are key members of the five-nation ASEAN group. Indonesia, the acknowledged *primus inter pares* of ASEAN by virtue of size, sees the organization partly as a means to exert responsible regional leadership. For the Philippines, traditionally beset with identity crisis, ASEAN provides a long-sought opportunity for full-fledged membership in an unequivocally Asian club, plus expanded opportunities for the employment of relatively advanced entrepreneurial skills. Both countries are fully aware of ASEAN's growing value as a vehicle for dealing with the outside world.

U.S. Interests

If discussion is kept at a sufficiently abstract level, it is easy to agree on definitions of U.S. national interest in Southeast Asia or any other region. Such definitions usually start from the basic requirement of American survival and involve some division between broadly political (or security) and economic (or prosperity) components.[14] But it is difficult to proceed much further without entering the controversial realm of capabilities, costs, and priorities: how best to achieve economic and political well-being, which perceived problems are most important, and which are amenable to practical solution. Interest definition is more difficult when, as in the case of Southeast Asia, American survival is clearly not threatened in any direct or immediate sense.[15] Moreover, it is often easier to agree that certain issues are somehow relevant to U.S. interests than to agree on the nature of the relevance.

For the purpose of this study I have assumed certain

categories of national interest, elaborating them in this
chapter only slightly beyond the barest fundamentals. Six
essays then discuss issues which are obviously relevant to
the various interest categories. This approach is explicitly
subjective. The primary purpose of the exercise is to explore
the issues themselves. The discussion is also intended to illustrate the degree of conflict between different interests, if
any, the validity of commonly held derivative assumptions,
and the extent to which national interests can, in fact, be le-
gitimately disaggregated at the country or regional (as opposed to global) level. My conclusions suggest that the
weight of U.S. interests in Southeast Asis is evolving away
from the short-term and simple, toward the long-term and
complex, and that the current pattern of crisis-oriented
policymaking is increasingly irrelevant to a new and less
easily perceived brand of challenge.

What, then, are the broad categories of American interests in island Southeast Asia? I would divide them into three
areas—security, economics, and ideology, plus a few that
defy easy categorization.

Security interests mainly involve interaction among the
great powers. We must remain concerned that no hostile
power control the region to our disadvantage or exclude us
from it, unlikely as that possibility may seem at this time.
Similarly, the United States has a clear interest in avoiding
great power friction which might lead to generalized war,
even if the conflict does not immediately involve us. Sino-
Soviet rivalry remains the most obvious source of danger, as
dramatized by recent events in Indochina. Many observers
combine these two related interests by emphasizing the desirability of maintaining a balance, or equilibrium, among the
great powers in the region. In an article written before the
end of the Vietnam War, William P. Bundy gave the equilibrium concept its most imaginative twist to date by asserting
that America's only *vital* geopolitical interest in Southeast
Asia is that it should remain an area where *none* of the super-
powers, including ourselves, regards its interests as vital.[16]

Our security interests would suffer in some degree
should we become the target of violent hostility by ASEAN

generally or by those individual archipelago states (including Indonesia, Malaysia, and the Philippines) which could deny us the use of critical waterways, including the Straits of Malacca. As the history of Suez suggests, however, it should not be too easily assumed that U.S. or Japanese access to Malacca or other specific sea lanes is a vital interest. According to one expert, use of alternative routes around Australia would impose serious military and economic inconvenience but nothing more.[17] As a final category of international security interest, the United States has a clearly defined stake in the maintenance of good relations between our Australian allies and their Southeast Asian neighbors.

We also have certain security interests relating to internal conflict or insurgency. As the American public clearly perceives,[18] we must not be drawn once again into an Asian conflict contrary to the national aspirations of local populations, as we were in Vietnam. But even if we remain adequately cautious about involvement, we should be concerned about massive internal conflict, particularly if communal factors such as anti-Chinese sentiment are involved, since such conflict could spread across borders and eventually attract great power intervention.

Even this brief list suggests the rapidity with which any intelligent discussion must turn to capabilities and costs, rather than interests per se. Security interests are discussed in the first two essays below. One essay questions the extent to which the internal political stability of Southeast Asian nations should be a concern of American policy. The second examines the most important security issue facing us in the region, the future of two large American bases in the Philippines, in the context of U.S.-Philippine relations and the evolving regional détente.

Economic interests include growing levels of trade and investment plus access to some important natural resources, including oil and minerals. But this is only the beginning. Our concern should extend well beyond these traditional categories to a generalized desire for the progressive economic betterment of the Southeast Asians themselves. We share with them an interest (which in our case is admittedly political as well as economic) in the more rapid solution of north-south problems involving trade, stabilization of commodity prices, and mutually acceptable patterns of resource transfers. If our economic involvement is to prosper it must be compatible with local aspirations; it follows that the kind of capitalism we export should be enlightened rather than rapacious. Finally, Americans, as members of the global community, stand eventually to lose or gain according to the wisdom or folly with which Southeast Asians manage their environmental problems, the most significant of which have implications for global welfare. We share with the archipelago nations a particularly critical interest in the achievement of an international agreement on the rational development of seabed resources.

Three essays bear on various aspects of our economic interests in Southeast Asia. One is an effort to measure levels of U.S. trade and investment in Indonesia and the Phillippines, with a short supplementary discussion of north-south issues. The second looks at the developmental problems of Indonesia and the role of foreign assistance. The third considers a range of problems and opportunities related to the tropical environment, with emphasis on forestry.

The third category of American interests, which I have termed *ideological,* is the most subtle and controversial. We want to live in a world which, insofar as possible, is compatible with what we regard as universal human rights, including political freedom. The extent to which others genuinely share our enthusiasm for such standards, regardless of what they may say in public, is of course open to debate. In another sense our ideological interest is inner directed. It involves what an Australian scholar has termed "our need to recognize purposes beyond ourselves," [19] whether through enlarging our understanding of the human condition or in exerting our leadership to help meet the social and economic aspirations of a significant proportion of humankind. Although it has traditionally been reflected in activities aimed at changing the conditions under which others live, such as missionary efforts and aid programs, the spiritual fulfillment that we seek is in the final analysis our own.

Ideological interests are central only to the chapter on human rights policy in Indonesia and the Philippines, but the other five essays are all, to some extent, attempts to define equitable as well as practical solutions. For as Vietnam demonstrated, persistence in any course that does not accord with fundamental American values risks disaster, one reason why realism carried to extremes usually turns out to be unrealistic. The reader may, for example, perceive a degree of ethical concern in the argument for a termination of our post-colonial relationship with the Philippines which is to some extent a theme of the entire work.

The United States has some other generally recognized interests in Southeast Asia which do not fall easily into economic, security, or ideological pigeonholes. One of these involves our ally Japan. To the extent that the Japanese economy depends on Southeast Asia, we have an economic interest in a healthy Japanese relationship with Southeast Asia. Collective hostility to Japan would embarrass us politically if only because it might well precipitate a more general xenophobia. The major hazard facing the Japanese is one of overexposure. Should they achieve a position of regional economic hegemony it could well attract nationalist reaction. If they also attempt to play a major security role, perhaps in response to an American military withdrawal and conceivably with American encouragement, the likelihood of such a reaction would be very much increased.

The United States has a clear and generalized interest in the further development of ASEAN. To an increasingly discernible extent this five-nation grouping represents a regional projection of the national aspirations of its individual members. The evolution of a collective political will involving 300 million people, no matter how slowly it takes place, must demand sympathetic attention. American policymakers are already cognizant of ASEAN's value in the north-south dialogue, as an influential group which has up to now supported moderate solutions. Beyond this, ASEAN could become a testing ground to determine whether or not such issues can be dealt with, through special trade and aid relationships, at the regional level.

Together Indonesia and the Philippines comprise well over half the territory and population of ASEAN, and although the organization as such is not the major subject of any of the essays, its potential role is a factor in several of them. If we take ASEAN seriously, for example, its cherished goal of regional neutralization must be considered in our planning for the Philippine bases. And regional technical cooperation under ASEAN auspices could add a useful dimension to our efforts to stimulate both economic development and enlightened environmental policy.

The views offered above do not support Lord Palmerston's assertion that a nation's interests, in contrast to her allies, are eternal. The massive impact of population growth and new technologies, both civil and military, have in fact revolutionized the pattern of American interests in Southeast Asia since World War II. Fundamental international relationships have continued to evolve, as witnessed by the growing political role of ASEAN since the fall of Vietnam and the consequent waning of American inhibitions, which until recently were wholly justified, about stifling the organization through excessive friendship. Further sea changes may result should the present metamorphosis of China bring that country onto center stage as an international economic force. It is staggering to imagine the regional consequences of a resurgent China drawing on Japanese capital and overseas Chinese human and financial resources. Even more profound interest shifts have resulted from nuclear stalemate, serious if localized food deficits, and the ever-growing demand of northern economies for the primary products of what, up to now, has been a resource-rich area with large regions of near-wilderness.

The task of creative foreign policy is to recognize shifting interest patterns and make the necessary adjustments. Our record in this respect leaves something to be desired, so far as Southeast Asia is concerned. The reasons are well known. Bureaucracies created to meet the challenge of the previous generation are difficult to reorient, as are the perceptions that both nourish and are nourished by the prevailing way of doing things. The military-industrial complex remains the worst offender in encouraging misallocation of foreign policy resources, but we also suffer from an inadequate national capacity for identifying, analyzing, and publicizing long-term problems, a point which will be the subject of the concluding chapter.

Chapter Two

The Stability Shibboleth

The truly helpless society is not one threat-
ened by revolution but one incapable of it.
—Samuel P. Huntington,
Political Order in Changing Societies (1968)[1]

A few months before the fall of Sukarno, Yale University historian Harry Benda initiated a debate on decolonization in Indonesia. Benda differed with the thesis advanced
by an academic colleague, Herbert Feith, that the waning
years of the Sukarno era represented the decline of constitutional democracy.[2] He argued that Indonesia should not be
measured against such specifically Western norms. With all
its flaws, he reasoned, Sukarno's "Guided Democracy"
signified the difficult readjustment of Southeast Asia's largest
country to its own identity. He observed that the tendency to
seek traditional Javanese solutions was true not only of
Sukarno, but also of such "outwardly modern *dramatis
personae* as the Indonesian officer corps."[3]

On a more fundamental level, Benda asserted that the Indonesian state was emerging from a long and unnatural
period of foreign dominance. He used the image of a great
river sweeping away transitory obstacles:

Whatever Guided Democracy may be—and it has had more than its
full share of adulation at home and vituperation abroad—at least it
is undeniably Indonesian, for better or worse. One by one, most of
the artificial dams, economic, political, but above all psychological,
of foreign overlordship are breaking down. The Indonesian river is
flowing more and more in an Indonesian bed; the game being
played is, once again, Indonesian. This, though it may smack of
historicism, may well be the true meaning of the first phase of
decolonization in Indonesia.[4]

It was Benda's assumption that Indonesia—and the other nations of Southeast Asia—would fulfill the terms of their own national destinies, guided as Western nations had been primarily by internal forces. It was a point of view which came naturally to a historian of enormous erudition, but it was not shared at the time by many other observers of Southeast Asia even in academia, much less in officialdom or among the public at large. In general it was, and still is, more normal to regard the region as a political low-pressure area buffeted by external forces, tender grass for elephantine great powers to trample, characterized above all by endemic instability.

The current condition of Southeast Asia suggests that Benda's emphasis on the strength of national forces is more valid than ever. If so, American capability to influence local events is likely to remain limited, as it proved to be in Vietnam. This chapter suggests how U.S. policy might further adjust to this problem in the political realm. Specifically, it discusses the internal politics of Southeast Asian states as they relate to U.S. interests, with emphasis on Indonesia and the Philippines. It looks first at potential sources of instability, including regional as well as national trends, and then weighs some possible consequences and costs of future revolution.[5] In conclusion, it advocates a more considered official posture of detachment from the internal affairs of Southeast Asian states. Such a policy would not imply more general disengagement or lack of interest in other areas of mutual concern, which, I argue elsewhere, are growing in number and importance.

This proposal may appear superfluous to those who assume that since Vietnam, American willpower has waned to the point where we are unlikely to keep formal treaty commitments, much less to intervene in the affairs of others. But our conventional military capability in the region remains awesome, and debate early in the Carter Administration over events in Africa and elsewhere suggests that our future propensity to act or not to act may hinge to an unhealthy degree on highly politicized perceptions of Soviet intentions. Partly for this reason, and partly because the occurrence of revolution could pose some very real threats to broad as well as sectoral U.S. interests, it is worth pausing now, with crisis out of the picture, to examine the local political terrain.

Island Southeast Asia has remained generally free of conflict since the end of the Vietnam War. Hostilities on the mainland, including the Vietnamese conquest of Cambodia and subsequent Sino-Vietnamese war, have not spread beyond Indochina, although they still pose a threat to regional peace. Elsewhere there has been a pattern of continuity; of conservative, authoritarian regimes stressing anticommunism and committed to mixed economic systems. Viewed collectively, these governments have achieved a remarkable record of cohesion in national leadership—a record which would certainly have astonished those who, ten years ago, espoused the domino theory.[6] It suggests that Americans have generally underrated the strength of Southeast Asian polities and the durability of Southeast Asian leaders.

Nothing in sight is likely to break this pattern during the next two or three years. But beyond that the future remains unclear. Expert opinion does not shed much light. Scholarship on Southeast Asia reflects the more widespread schism between neo-Marxism and an array of non-Marxist thought ranging from liberal to conservative. In general, the left now argues that Benda's vision of successful decolonization has remained a vision. Advocates of dependency theory believe that Indonesia, the Philippines, and others are still in thrall to external forces, and often posit the inevitability of revolution.[7] Non-Marxists do not accept this view in its totality. However, it is noteworthy that they do share, to a significant degree, the perception that violent political change, if not revolution, iş likely although not inevitable if present trends continue. Often, debate centers not around whether violent change will occur but on questions of timing, dynamics, the relative likelihood of right- or left-wing radicalism, and the probable depth of social upheaval.

There is considerable agreement about the underlying conditions in contemporary Southeast Asia which are cause for pessimism. Foreign investment and the growth process have helped solidify existing elites, which are now more than ever insulated from the kind of social mobility that characterized the often chaotic period directly following independence. Economic growth has occurred all too often without sufficient distribution or accompanying social change. Investment-created enclaves are still dominated by primary producers with little or no backward or forward linkage, or "trickle down." Recent events in both Indonesia and the Philippines have strengthened the position of small upper classes relative to the poor majority. Leaders (if judged by what they do, not say) are interested in family and personal enrichment to a most unhealthy degree. One need not be hypnotized by Marxist emphasis on economic predetermination to believe that such conditions will prove destabilizing in the long run.[8]

The Specter of Insurgency

Post-Vietnam prophets of disaster feared that the moral repercussions of American defeat, plus, perhaps, an outpouring of secondhand arms from Hanoi, would raise Southeast Asian insurgency levels to unprecedented heights. Although this prediction proved to be empty, local insurgencies are still an important fact of political life, and their significance is subject to legitimate debate. They remain, in the eyes of one experienced Western diplomat, "like Malaria—low level, debilitating, but not fatal; endemic to the region." Like the disease, they are a major cause of human suffering. Southeast Asian leaders are well aware of the persistent, low-level nature of most insurgency, but as long as they depend on anticommunism as a legitimizing doctrine they will continue at times to exaggerate the immediate political threat.

Generally speaking, there are two types of insurgency in Southeast Asia. The first is clearly linked to ethnic or religious minorities (Burma's horseshoe-shaped assemblage of perpetual hill tribe revolts offers several classic examples).[9] The second type appeals to a dominant ethnic group and aspires to be national in character. Making good on a claim to nationalist credentials guarantees success, or a good chance thereof, to any insurgent movement, but thus far in modern times this critical linkage has been made only in the case of anticolonial struggles. The latter point cannot be sufficiently emphasized.

The present low level of insurgency in Southeast Asia is directly attributable to automatic limiting mechanisms which apply to these two types of unrest. In the case of ethnic insurgencies it is a relatively simple matter for governments to exploit nationalist sentiment against insurgents, especially when, as is usually the case, there is widespread awareness of the contagious, never-ending quality of ethnic separatism. Would-be national rebellions are faced with the equally formidable dynamic of elite self-preservation—formidable as long as elites are unified, possess monopoly control of mass communications and weapons, and can make credible claims to be the heirs of the anticolonial struggle.

The current status of insurgency in Indonesia and the Philippines illustrates the situation. In Indonesia there has been recent insurgent activity in West Irian and in Timor. In West Irian, Papuan tribal peoples, ethnically distinct from other Indonesian societies, lived under Dutch control until 1960 and have never fully accepted rule from Jakarta. Their disaffection is complicated by a land border with independent Papua New Guinea. While Irianese insurgency is an extreme example of geographically restricted ethnic revolt, in a remote and underpopulated province, it is likely to be sustained by pan-Papuan sentiments and the relative proximity of Port Moresby.[10] Armed dissension on Timor, now reduced to embers, is the result of very special international circumstances (discussed in chapter four).

The Indonesian government regards the Islamic religion as a potential agent of insurgency second only to communism. The reasons for this attitude are complex but fundamental to an understanding of Indonesian politics. Statistically the national population is about 90 percent Muslim. However, there is a significant cleavage between a minority whose political views are dominated by Islam and a probable majority composed of non-Muslims and nominal, syncretic Muslims, the latter concentrated on Java. The cleavage is reinforced by class and regional distinctions. In general, politics have been dominated by the syncretic (abangan) Javanese, heavily represented in the traditional nobility and in the modern army, whose primary cultural adherence is to an older, pre-Islamic, animist-Hindu tradition.[11] Not surprisingly, tension has persisted between the syncretist element and more devout (or "fanatic") variants of Islam, and will undoubtedly persist in the future. Muslim insurgency was a serious problem in the early days of the Republic, when some of today's senior generals cut their teeth in combat against Darul Islam rebels in West Java, and there have been enough signs of recrudescence in recent years to keep the security forces on edge.[12]

The Indonesian Communist Party (PKI), once the world's largest, shows no signs of revival following the devastating reverses it suffered a decade ago. Having become an overt political movement during the Sukarno era, it proved quite unable to survive as a covert insurgency for reasons which, leaving aside the skill of the Indonesian Army in repressing it, remain obscure. In its Sukarno-era guise, Indonesian communism was in many ways a religious phenomenon, falling neatly into the overall Muslim versus non-Muslim pattern, with tremendous appeal to the poor peasantry of Java, for whom it offered both radical programs and a seemingly powerful vehicle for the syncretist world view. But the same cultural factors that gave it strength on Java aroused violent hostility among Muslims throughout the country, and it remains doubtful whether in fact the PKI could ever have ruled Indonesia without precipitating national disintegration. It is true that the Indonesian Communist Party has risen from the grave twice before, after unsuccessful rebellions in 1926–27 and 1948.[13]

In the Philippines there are two active insurgencies. In the South, Muslim rebels tie down about forty battalions, approximately two-thirds of the government's maneuverable forces, in a dirty and protracted struggle. The Marcos regime has attempted both military and diplomatic solutions. A major motivating factor has been the possibility that sympathetic Islamic nations might restrict the flow of Middle Eastern oil on which the Philippines remains dependent for most energy needs. This concern is the main reason why, as late as 1977, the government emphasized Middle Eastern mediation, including the good offices of Libya's Qadhafi, rather than seeking to place more reliance on Indonesian mediation in the ASEAN context.[14]

On the whole, the Philippine government has appeared remarkably unmoved by the domestic political implications of this civil war, to a point which suggests that it may be useful as a justification for Martial Law. There is, however, a less sinister and more valid explanation. The secessionist rebellion in Mindanao is a classic case of traditional ethnic unrest, with antecedents stretching back three centuries. It was here that the Spanish tried and failed to pacify and Christianize the same "Moros." It was here that our own General Pershing won his spurs in counterinsurgency, making many of the same mistakes (e.g., attempting to confiscate firearms) that Filipinos have made in recent years.[15] Americans who are inclined to be critical should remember that until the end of U.S. rule a pair of gunboats, inherited from the Spanish, was stationed on Lake Lanao and employed to shell "insurgent" villages. Generations of anti-Muslim struggle are reflected in Christian folklore, to the point where most Filipinos regard bloodshed in Mindanao as a normal state of affairs. The fact that modern weapons are now being used does not make the situation more threatening or destabilizing in their eyes.

The second Philippine insurgency, that of the Communist New People's Army (NPA) does aspire to a national goal, the overthrow of the Marcos regime and the establishment of a communist state. Thus although it is militarily insignificant compared to the Muslim problem, requiring (as of 1978) the attention of less than two battalions of troops plus regular provincial constabulary forces, it has some long-range potential. But again it is essential to view the insurgency in its complex historical context. Philippine communism is a melange of ideological, regional, and ethnic elements shot through with acute contradictions. It draws on a powerful tradition of rural unrest, sometimes "agrarian" in the classic sense, but frequently strongest in remote marginal areas, particularly along the isolated east coast, where it is often religious and messianic in character. There is nothing new about such insurgency; it persisted throughout the Spanish period and, as a result of economic depression, may have been almost as serious in the 1930s as it is at present.[16]

Today in northern Luzon the NPA also attracts upland tribal minorities alienated by the government's continuing inability to practice multicultural politics with the same skill generally shown by the Indonesians.[17] Further to the south, in the great rice plain of central Luzon, communist "rebels" draw on a complex tradition of mingled agrarian insurgency, ward politics, and gangsterism. It was here that the old Huk movement, to which the NPA is heir, degenerated from insurgency to running vice rackets in Angeles City, fueled then as now by the nearby American military complex at Clark Air Base.[18] There is inconclusive evidence that, even under Marcos' "New Society," a symbiotic relationship continues between local leaders (now usually military commanders rather than senators) and these "rebels."[19] Last but not least, the NPA continues to reflect schizoid tendencies which are the natural result of a post–Martial Law infusion of upper-class ex-student elements, the restless offspring of the Manila Forbes Park oligarchy, whose romantic revolutionary idealism is often genuine, but whose social antecedents make for difficult accommodation with peasants. It may be that in view of these rather fundamental problems the NPA is, for the moment, no more powerful than a strong authoritarian government would have it, given its value as the only credible manifestation of the communist menace.

In the past the government has underlined the importance of outside aid—Libyan and Malaysian in the case of the Muslims, Communist Chinese in the case of the NPA. Chinese assistance, never significant, halted after Manila recognized Peking in 1975. In the south, Malaysian involvement, complicated by the Philippine claim to part of Malaysian Borneo, has ceased under the influence of ASEAN good will, while the influx of Qadhafi's Qurans (the equivalent of Beecher's Bibles) has apparently slowed to a trickle.[20]

To summarize, there is little about the currently active

insurgencies in either the Philippines or Indonesia to suggest that they pose serious threats to existing regimes. Some are little more than nuisances, while others serve the useful function of demonstrating "crisis" and the existence of communism. In general there appears to be waning opportunity for external forces (aside from neighboring cross-border ethnic relatives) to intervene successfully on behalf of rebels. Insurgency will persist, however, and for reasons outlined below it could be a contributing although not a causative factor in future revolutions.

Instability Scenarios

The short-term prognosis for national governments in Southeast Asia is more, not less, stability, authoritarianism, and perhaps repression. In the early postcolonial era, elites were fragmented and competitive. Today they have pulled together, and the trend is toward even greater elite consolidation. Political leaders have profited handsomely from economic growth and have close relationships not merely with foreign investors but also with overseas Chinese capitalists, an apparently happy development which, in Indonesia, involves considerable long-term political risk. The ethnic Chinese themselves are, at least for the moment, more content and prosperous than at any time since World War II. Against a dwindling subversive threat, both Philippine and Indonesian rulers can mobilize experienced, well-equipped security forces.

It is impossible for anyone to state with certainty how long this situation will continue. The most sophisticated intelligence system in the world cannot get inside the brain of one man, and perhaps for this reason the great powers continue to display a singular inability to prejudge political shifts in the authoritarian Third World. In discussing political trends it is necessary to begin by acknowledging that the variables are too numerous, and regime politics too opaque, to allow of anything but humility. Nevertheless some generalizations can be made.

Revolution is unlikely to start from below, via spontaneous mass action or insurgency. Indeed, we may take as axiomatic that if it comes it will start from above, through competition among elites. Given the force of elite preservation as a restraining motive, the resulting change is likely to be limited to ruling circles. But even the most seemingly innocuous colonels' coup is not without risk. Everywhere there are reservoirs of social disconent to nourish more widespread upheaval. There is always the possibility that the competitors in an intra-elite contest may try to gain advantage by reaching down and mobilizing mass support. It is precisely this kind of possibility that makes the Indonesian government so unabashedly sensitive to rumors of division in the military leadership. That such fears cannot be dismissed as groundless was demonstrated in January 1974, when, amid talk of conflict between Generals Murtopo and Sumitro, the urban poor of Jakarta took to the streets, allegedly in demonstration against the visiting Japanese Prime Minister, and for a time appeared to be on the brink of precipitating something far more widespread and serious.[21]

The most obvious source of intra-elite conflict is the absence of clear-cut succession mechanisms, a failing endemic among authoritarian regimes. In Indonesia the key question is whether the military can agree on a successor to President Suharto before his term expires in 1983. Failure to do so, and to make the choice explicit, would risk precisely the kind of escalating sub rosa competition that became apparent during the January 1974 affair, only on a much more dangerous scale. The fact remains that the Indonesian Army's record of cohesion and demonstrated sense of self-preservation are both excellent. In the Philippines there is no equivalent institution which can be counted on to work for a peaceful transition should Marcos leave office. Despite more than five years of Martial Law, something of a misnomer for what is really Marcos family rule, it is by no means clear that the military will assert itself to play more than its traditionally secondary political role in a succession contest, unless forced to do so by turmoil. The President has repeatedly referred to the existence of a secret decree naming his successor, but its value once he is gone seems highly dubious.

The middle ranks of either government could, at some point, produce a radical-nationalist coup following Ethiopian or Libyan precedent, led by a group dedicated to the end of corruption and the expulsion of foreigners. In Indonesia there are at least two possible breeding grounds for such a reaction, the middle-level military and the ranks of disaffected Islam. Observers have long speculated on the possibility of smoldering resentment among majors and captains against the wealth and corruption apparent at senior levels. (Similar sentiment attracted some officers to the PKI before 1965.) Because the army's political cast is anti-Islamic, a military-based reaction would probably appeal primarily to conservative, syncretic Javanese tradition, and there is little likelihood of a Qadhafi- or Khomeini-style apostle of Koranic reform emerging from the barracks.

As noted above, Indonesian governments have been preoccupied for decades with the problem of Islamic subversion. Such concern has not produced policies capable of curing the underlying malaise, and indeed since independence governments have tended to alienate the activist Muslim minority at every turn. Islam might, at some future point, initiate a more general political upheaval, an Iranian scenario. It could conceivably shed its traditionally conservative character in favor of a radical-socialist mode, and thereby capture the leadership (if only momentarily) of a class-based revolution. At the moment, however, such a denouement seems remote given the prevalence of powerfully anti-Islamic traditional social forces in Indonesia. It appears more likely that the ruling generals, like their predecessors in the Dutch and Sukarno periods, will continue to "manage" the Muslim threat by a combination of repression and co-optation, plus skillful exploitation of the Catch 22 factor in Indonesian politics—the fact that while all political factions are quasi-religious, all religions are functional minorities, leaving as the ultimate and inevitable referee the military.

Partly because of historical factors mentioned in chapter one, Philippine political tradition is radically different from that of Indonesia. Most significant is the fact that the country has never experienced social revolution. Rather, the *ilustrado* elite class has progressively enhanced its position since Spanish times, and Philippine independence was the product of American rather than Filipino decisions. But it should not be overlooked that the very durability of the Philippine elite has resulted in part from a relatively high degree of social mobility—high enough to absorb energies that might otherwise have turned against the system.[22]

Other factors behind the nonrevolutionary Philippine tradition include a blending of Chinese and Malay values resulting from mestizoization, and the success of Filipino entrepreneurship. American rule contributed mass education, a dash of self-help ideology, and lingering emigration opportunities for the middle class. The widespread practice of godparenthood ("compadre kinship") provided a mechanism for individual social elevation through the patronage of the poor by the powerful, thereby contributing to a national ethos of optimism. Until recently, survey research conducted among the more deprived classes in the Philippines revealed persistent belief that despite the dismal present, the future would be better. It may be significant that this faith now appears to be waning.[23] logically or not, in Philippine society bourgeois aspirations have penetrated far beyond the economic confines of the middle class, blurring and softening what otherwise might have evolved more easily toward harsh class conflict.

Two other aspects of Philippine political culture are worth mentioning. For some Filipinos, Catholicism provides a vehicle for opposition sentiment in much the same way that Islam does in Indonesia. Unlike its Indonesian counterpart, moreover, Catholicism is a genuine majority faith, highly organized and with relatively good channels of communication to the outside world. There is thus a possibility that Catholicism, or a folk variant, could in future provide the unifying force, as well as the revolutionary élan, for major political change.[24] But given the serious political divisions within the Philippine church and the preeminently conservative cast of the current hierarchy, such a development is not imminent.

The second factor is a cultural context which encourages

the individual, romantic revolutionary. The Malay *amok* and the Spanish intellectual-cum-hero (José Rizal was such) are both familiar characters in the Philippines. The romantic impact is most keenly felt among the upper classes, one reason why the communist movement has often attracted the offspring of the oligarchy. The pattern suggests that in times of turmoil, Philippine society could produce charismatic, revolutionary leaders of rather unpredictable characteristics, conceivably on the order of a Fidel Castro or a Che Guevera.

The decisive factor bearing on the political evolution of the Philippines may be the longevity of Marcos family rule. As things stand, there is a fair chance that the end of the present regime would bring a restoration of something approaching the old decentralized system—perhaps under a politician such as the imprisoned Senator Benigno Aquino. However, as time goes by the institutions and individuals who comprised the previous system will inevitably lose strength relative to the military. At the same time, continuing repression or worsening economic conditions will encourage the merger and revitalization of communist and leftist-Christian radicalism and rural insurgency. Considering these factors, political scientist David Wurfel has described the possibility of an initial transfer of power to an indecisive civilian regime, arousing exaggerated expectations among rural revolutionaries that, in turn, would force the harsh intervention of the military and lead to a general escalation of conflict. This scenario is based on shrewd appreciation of factors behind the rise of the Huk movement in the early postwar Philippines, and suggests the extremely uncertain situation which a long-delayed transition is likely to bring.[25]

For Americans, the most significant aspect of Philippine political culture is the disproportionate place still occupied by the United States. Continuing political ties, pervasive American cultural influence, and, above all, residual feelings of guilt and inadequacy resulting from the failure, to date, to achieve a convincing break with the colonial past—all these factors make it likely that if revolution does come to the Philippines the United States will be an inevitable target. The implications of this for our major military facilities in the islands will be discussed at greater length in the next chapter.

In conclusion, one can only speculate with little assurance and no precision that revolution in either Indonesia or the Philippines is unlikely in the next few years but remains a possibility over the long run. It may be that Benda's decolonization process has already ended; that we stand on the verge of a generation or more in which Southeast Asian rulers will continue to practice the politics of stasis, sure of their own hold on the levers of power, untroubled by significant external threat, and essentially unmoved by their own rhetoric about popular welfare. It is by no means certain that deteriorating social and economic conditions will produce proportionately mounting political pressures, nor is it by any means a foregone conclusion that present development efforts will fail.[26] But it is also possible that liberal assumptions about the cyclical connection between repression and revolution will hold true, and that what we are now witnessing is the peace and order of a boiler with the safety valve tied down.

The U.S. Interest in Stability

How should Americans evaluate the prospect of revolution in Southeast Asia? Obviously it depends to some extent on the depth of an upheaval. Shallow interelite coups would probably be of little significance one way or the other. The less likely prospect of massive social upheaval, perhaps with strong ideological overtones, carries costs which are bound to concern the United States.

The most critical danger would be that of great power intervention, discussed below, but there would be other hazards as well. Ethnic struggle could easily spread across borders, e.g., from Indonesia to Malaysia. The understated but significant ASEAN concord might be shattered by revolution in Indonesia, if not in other member states, all the more so if new and insecure leaders decided to try the age-old ploy of cementing domestic support by generating foreign crisis.[27] It may not be without reason that Indonesian doctrine, increasingly shared by other ASEAN governments, posits a direct connection between national resilience, or "ability to endure" (ketahanan), and regional, Southeast Asian "ability to endure."

In other respects the internal cost of widespread social revolution would be high, with no certainty that the result would be more favorable to long-term development, more enlightened, or more humane than present regimes. Revolution involves much violence and suffering and the destruction of scarce physical and intellectual capital. Revolution is, to put it mildly, bad for the economy. What is most worrisome here is that experimental capitalism with a high degree of social return and a low rate of raw profit—tree plantations in the Outer Islands of Indonesia, for example—is more vulnerable than orthodox investment (e.g., oil), whose returns may be essential to the survival of new leaders, and which is thus more likely to survive undamaged under conditions of ideological, perhaps Marxist, hostility. Such costs cannot be contemplated lightly. But they should not obscure the more fundamental certainty that if social revolution occurs it will be driven by internal, national forces and that there will be little that external opposition can accomplish, other than to aggravate whatever antiforeign sentiment may be involved.[28]

At the same time, however, awareness of the *possibility* of revolution is a force of considerable social and political utility. The assumption that poor performance will inevitably breed radical reaction has become international conventional wisdom to such a degree that all rulers must, to some extent, be concerned lest it prove true. As noted above, the countervailing tendency toward complacency may in fact be more typical. To the extent that it is not, the idea of revolution can be a more significant agent of social change than revolution itself.[29] For this reason it is not in the U.S. interest to oppose or denigrate either the idea or the ultimate possibility, any more than in our own internal affairs, we should refuse to face the possible consequences of social unrest.

Regional Instability

The international relations of post-Vietnam Southeast Asia are often described in terms of great power "balance" or "equilibrium."[30] The concept is somewhat misleading for a number of reasons. To be sure, the nuclear balance of terror constrains great power behavior in Southeast Asia as it does elsewhere. Within the region itself, however, there is no discrete Southeast Asian "balance." Despite withdrawal from Vietnam, U.S. conventional military power remains without serious rival. The Chinese are almost wholly a continental power, the Japanese are not in the act militarily, and the Vietnamese are unlikely to provoke new quarrels, leaving aside the resentments aroused by refugee exodus, so long as their ancient problems with Cambodia and China persist. Although growing, the Russian naval threat remains more potential than real at this writing. The Soviets have little amphibious capability, and their occasional maneuvers in Southeast Asian waters have consisted to date of antisubmarine and other activities which are part of a global (anti-American) rather than a regional game. Other areas, including both Northeast Asia and the Indian Ocean, are likely to remain of greater strategic interest to them. If they decide to deploy additional conventional naval strength, as they could at any time they choose, they will probably discover (as we did in Vietnam) that naval power does not translate easily into influence in Southeast Asian waters. Indeed such an effort would probably do little more than confirm the distaste and suspicion with which they are currently regarded by many local leaders. In general, recent efforts by the Soviets to enhance their position in noncommunist Southeast Asia, whether by diplomacy, aid, or subversion, have met with an almost pathetic lack of success.[31]

Of all the factors that could aggravate great power conflict within the region, Sino-Soviet rivalry is the most critical. As long as the states of island Southeast Asia remain under well-established regimes with good nationalist credentials, there is little opportunity for the rivals to back opposing factions or otherwise engage in hostilities by proxy. With little military presence involved, the behavior of the communist superpowers has been less a balancing act than a display of mutual paranoia. Given the primarily psychological dimensions of this confrontation, it is no wonder that they appear to have reached common ground in acquiescing to the continuance of U.S. bases in the Philippines, if only for their utility as symbols of a status quo in which neither Chinese nor Russian force is dominant. Conflict such as the current Vietnam-Cambodia-China friction naturally increases the danger of active Sino-Soviet collision, all the more so since the Vietnamese have, for the moment at least, aligned themselves firmly with the Soviet Union.

Revolution in Indonesia or elsewhere might prompt great power intervention, especially if violence spread to neighboring states. Recent events in Vietnam suggest that serious persecution of ethnic Chinese, a likely by-product of revolution, would attract the attention of Peking despite the latter's general policy of aloofness from overseas Chinese affairs. A Philippine conflagration sufficiently violent to endanger the U.S. bases would almost surely prompt U.S. intervention, thereby perhaps provoking Soviet reaction. Other theoretical possibilities that could result in great power conflict range from the disintegration of China, with rival warlords recruiting allies among the southern barbarians, to the possibility (which appears less likely with every passing month) of a violent Indonesian-Vietnamese competition for the leadership of Southeast Asia.[32]

Any reasonably fertile imagination can fill pages with similar alarming possibilities, none of them wholly incredible. But to do so is to overlook the current trend toward great power disengagement, a fact (not a hypothesis) which may be of far greater significance. Underlying this trend is a general awareness, prompted by the American experience in Vietnam, that regardless of what may happen in Africa or elsewhere in the Third World, the day has passed when great powers can profitably intervene in Southeast Asian affairs. Distance and island geography may encourage this perception, but it derives mainly from the political maturity of the region, evidenced by the national leadership continuity of the past few years. Nor do present superpower activities in the region automatically lead to rising tension. Leaving aside Sino-Soviet rivalry, none of these activities are obvious zero-sum games. One minor but illustrative example has been the dramatic growth in Soviet merchant shipping, regarded as most alarming when it commenced a few years ago. It is now viewed by both Southeast Asians and Westerners as a primarily commercial phenomenon, good for the Southeast Asians (who welcome Soviet competition with Western and Japanese shippers) and, as the Russians increasingly play by international conference rules, somewhat less disturbing to the shippers.[33]

The further progress of regional détente depends on great power restraint and respect for the potential of ASEAN, which in island Southeast Asia has already effectively ended or reduced to quiescence intraregional squabbles, such as the Philippine claim to Sabah, that might invite outside intervention. As the paramount military power in the area, the United States bears a special responsibility to use its strength in a way which will encourage and not uproot this tender growth. We should, for example, actively encourage future efforts by the Vietnamese to achieve a genuinely nonaligned stance which would decrease the danger of Sino-Soviet rivalry in the region. Nothing could do more to alarm national leaderships and disrupt the current trend toward tranquillity than a Vietnam driven under Russian pressure to play the role prematurely ascribed to her by Deng Xiaoping as the Cuba of the East.[34]

U.S. Policy: Containment to Nation-Building to Stability

Throughout most of the postwar period, anticommunism was a more typical objective of U.S. policy than stability per se. In some cases we actively promoted the instability of what were judged to be left-leaning regimes. As is now well-known, the United States intervened in the Indonesian Outer Islands rebellion of 1958, lending initial support to Muslim rebels. The policy was abandoned when it quickly failed, and we suffered out the remainder of the Sukarno regime in unhappy, and (for that era) unaccumstomed inactivity. (The main reason may have been that American energies were being progressively absorbed in Indochina.) Other examples of potentially destabilizing involvement included our support for Chinese Nationalist (KMT) irregulars in Burma and years of intense meddling in the affairs of Laos. Our Vietnam struggle, including its Cambodian subchapter, was the most destabilizing of all, certainly in terms of lives lost and permanent (if hardly welcome) alterations in the political map.[35]

So far as friendly governments were concerned, however, our mission was not only to stabilize, but to invigorate and construct. A Council on Foreign Relations study on Southeast Asia published in 1963 nicely expressed the assumption that intervention was nothing to be ashamed of:

We must at least frankly recognize what it is that we are trying to do. It is to prosecute a constructive manipulative diplomacy in the interests of nation building. To pretend that the new diplomacy is less than interventionist is not only hypocritical but imposes a psychological inhibition that may prove disastrous to the elaboration of successful policy.[36]

The United States routinely channeled clandestine assistance to friendly governments in the hopes of improving the "nation building" capability of enlightened elements, thereby making them more effective agents in the mortal contest with communism. Contrary to more recent conventional wisdom, we did not always back losers. American support for Philippine Secretary of National Defense Magsaysay, never much of a secret in Manila, came to be regarded in Washington as a classic cold war success story, although by powerfully perpetuating the postcolonial U.S.-Philippine relationship it involved long-run costs that have not yet been fully calculated.[37]

The Shanghai Communiqué, the Nixon Doctrine, and final withdrawal from Indochina destroyed the rationale for the incessant political activism of earlier years. Events since the fall of Saigon have amply confirmed the position of those who argued that the end of the war would if anything strengthen America's position in Southeast Asia beyond those areas of Indochina still directly threatened by Vietnamese hostility, e.g., Laos and Cambodia. Having anticipated the direst consequences, we now find that our influence, writ large, has never been more widespread. American material culture, and the English language, are pervasive. We are more welcome than ever as purveyors of foreign investment, technological change, and management techniques, and of course as purchasers of Southeast Asian products. The recent lag in American investment, largely the result of global recession, has been lamented, not cheered, by Southeast Asian leaders. Our only close competitors in terms of total presence are the Japanese, but we have long since recognized, as discussed in chapter five, that their economic role is rather fundamentally in our own broader interest. Meanwhile the influence of our erstwhile "enemies" is at an all-time low. As former U.S. Ambassador to Malaysia Frank Underhill has expressed it, "Who in Southeast Asia would buy a Russian computer, consult a PRC economist, or send a student to the Patrice Lumumba School of Business Administration?" Orthodox communist doctrine, which two decades ago was a major source of inspiration to radical youth, has largely lost its appeal. The growing popularity of neo-Marxist dependency theory among Southeast Asian students is only one of many indications that the West (or at least its universities) has eclipsed Moscow and Peking even as the mother lode of voguish radicalism.[38]

Deriving from this situation, the attitudes which underlie current U.S. policy are clear. Most of the countries in the region are friendly and ideologically compatible with us. They are now in charge of their own fates; we can at best help them to help themselves. Political intervention of the old variety is no longer viable, and military intervention, even to fulfill treaty obligations, might risk grave congressional reaction. Nevertheless, we remain inclined to assume that the internal stability of friendly countries is a proper concern, however vague, of U.S. policy. Revolution, except in communist or hostile states, is definitely bad. American aid programs are, it is believed, still the most significant means of expressing friendship and support. All too often the consideration of "supportiveness" threatens to outweigh the merits of the aid itself.

Official public utterances on Southeast Asia routinely list security and stability (both regional and of individual friendly countries) as U.S. interests and as primary rationales for military and economic aid.[39] Formal policy documents usually add the qualification that stability may not be in the U.S. interest unless it is accompanied by development, equity, and due concern for human rights. In theory it is generally accepted that the United States runs long-term risks by appearing to be the major prop of a dictatorial regime. But in the messy world where policy happens (it is rarely "made" in any systematic fashion) our more fundamental bias in favor of stability is inevitably reinforced by many factors. Responsibility to protect American lives and investments abroad, and pressures from specific U.S. interests ranging from the farm lobby to the Pentagon bureaucracy, often reinforce a tendency toward clientism. Human nature being what it is, the mere process of contact with foreign rulers breeds desire to be helpful, to see those we know personally succeed. This is nowhere more true than in Southeast Asia, where personal charm is endemic and hospitality has been developed to a fine art.

Nevertheless, a correct American policy demands a systematic effort to achieve a posture of political detachment dictated by respect for the political maturity of the region as well as realistic apprehension for problems that may lie ahead. There is room for a more conscious application of the principle that Southeast Asians have the same right to revolution and civil war that we did, and that upheavals may not only be inevitable but could conceivably be part of the national growth process. Absolute detachment is impossible for obvious reasons. A great power cannot have an active, multifaceted relationship with a much poorer, weaker state without conveying some degree of political support. The only complete solution would be total isolation, hardly an attractive or possible alternative. But detachment can be pursued as a goal, a policy theme, much as the pursuit of stability and political influence has been a theme up to now.

With this in mind it should be possible to vet bilateral programs so as to minimize direct political content. Clearly, political content varies according to local circumstances. In the Philippines, because of our emotion-laden relationship, virtually any official interaction with Americans has high political content—a major reason why the present amalgam of "special" ties, ranging to the Filipino stewards who still serve the White House Mess in Washington, should be systematically reduced as rapidly as possible. In Indonesia, American assistance does not convey anything like the same degree of legitimizing political support, and it is easier to co-operate without co-optation.

It is equally clear that some types of aid are inherently more political than others. Direct aid to internal security forces, along the lines of the old "public safety" programs, or the training supplied before Martial Law to the Phillippine Presidential Security Guard,[40] is understandably interpreted as a clear signal of U.S. interest in preservation of the regime. It should be an established policy not to revive such programs in the future.

Nowhere, as Selig Harrison has pointed out, is the need for caution and detachment greater than in the area of military aid.[41] Arms aid to a much weaker country inevitably conveys a high degree of political support. This is often the main reason why it is so eagerly sought by governments, including those of the Philippines and Indonesia, whose only security threat derives from insurgencies and (perhaps) civil disorder. From a purely military point of view such aid is usually redundant, since any government can be counted on to take care of its own vital security requirements as a matter of highest priority, without outside help. Its real significance is often more symbolic than material, but nonetheless important for that.

At this writing, grant military aid has been virtually phased out in Indonesia, although government arms sales credits and training assistance are continuing. In the Philippines all three categories of military aid were included in the informal compensation scheme for the bases agreed upon in January 1979.[42] In one form or another, supportive military assistance is likely to remain a tool of U.S. policy in Southeast Asia, even though such assistance is not (as in the Middle East) relevant to major problems of regional or international security, and the sums of money at stake are small. Thus when Vice President Mondale visited Jakarta in May 1978 he announced, as an obvious political plum, sale of a squadron of A-4 Skyhawks, a ground-support aircraft of no conceivable use except against insurgents and as a symbol of military modernization.[43]

Military training can be a particularly vexing problem, as the Indonesian case amply demonstrates. The United States maintained a small training program throughout the most hostile years of the Sukarno regime. In view of what happened in 1965, it is temptingly easy to see the program as an example of successful influence-building at very low cost. The reality was more complicated. There is no evidence to support the assumption that the behavior of the Indonesian military in crushing the Communist Party was swayed by trips to the United States or by a few shiploads of small arms. Indeed, three of the relatively few senior officers who joined the *communist* side during the Coup had attended American service schools, and there is evidence elsewhere that others who experienced U.S. training were not always favorably impressed.[44] The Indonesian Army's anticommunism had its origin in far more profound factors, including ideological incompatibility, memories of the communist-led Madiun revolt of 1948, and an ongoing "us or them" rivalry for power which had been developed over many years. Experience in Ethiopia and Libya (whose present ruler was British trained) should by now have taught us something about the tenuous connection between foreign military training and political friendship.

For the future, it is argued, military training is one of the few means at our disposal to maintain contact with a professional organization which will probably continue to run Indoensia even in the event of radical change. As in the days of Sukarno, Indonesians might tend to interpret such training as assistance for the army as an institution, not support for the army as a ruling class. But it is doubtful that this distinction occurs to a wide range of civilians, especially among Muslims and students, who are restive under indefinitely prolonged military rule. Another argument for military training is based on the fact that according to Indonesia's "dual function" doctrine, military men are deeply involved in civil administration. To some extent, even the most purely development-oriented aid program requires cooperation with the army, and the military constitutes a significant pool of technical skills. Although this argument has validity, it all too easily slides into self-fulfilling prophecy: the military are essential as agents of development, hence foreigners give them aid (support); hence they are made even more capable relative to others—and strengthened in a position of privilege and power.[45]

Other forms of military assistance, such as arms sales and credits under the government Foreign Military Sales (FMS) program, are equally problematical. Government sales on nonconcessional terms may be preferable to direct commercial transactions insofar as they allow a greater degree of public accountability and control. (Progress toward more general reduction in commercial arms transfers, while highly desirable, seems hopelessly remote.) On the other hand, many forms of U.S.-government standard weapons and munitions much in demand in Southeast Asia are available only through the FMS program, and to some extent it conveys the same kind of official benediction which has been so conspicuous a feature of the grant program.

In short, significant levels of security assistance to governments faced primarily with internal disorder often serve mainly to identify the United States as a proponent of the status quo. Although most other consequences of such aid are debatable, there is no doubt that the act of giving it encourages other outsiders to practice similar interventions. Finally, as noted in a later chapter, arms aid tailored to coun-

terinsurgency (usually the only variety of any practical value)
makes flagrant hypocrisy of the most modest human rights
policy. These are compelling arguments in favor of restraint,
yet in my view it would be wise not to be dogmatic about assistance to military recipients. Some security functions may
be so closely tied to nonmilitary requirements as to warrant
minor exceptions—for example, the need for small boat coast
guard and marine surveillance capability to patrol archipelago seas. The ultimate test should be whether aid (military or
other) supports national development, or is primarily intended to produce the most perishable of all tropical commodities, political influence.

I am suggesting little more than a logical underpinning
for the existing American relationship with Southeast Asia.
A policy of political detachment would affirm the fact that
under current circumstances we have no more will or ability
to intervene with profit in the internal political affairs of
Southeast Asians than they do in ours. It may be, of course,
that many Southeast Asian leaders devoutly wish for greater
"stability," not to mention predictability, in Washington. The
difference is that we are not only much more powerful but
also inclined to see them as volatile and manipulable, and
that this assumption, unless exorcised for good, could at
some future point lead us into further misadventures. A new
and more relaxed stance would in one sense compliment
Southeast Asian leaders, while at the same time it would establish our awareness that we cannot help them postpone the
consequences of misrule.

Since genuinely impartial relations cannot be achieved
overnight, given the residue of the past and a continuing, if
altered, high level of U.S. involvement, it is all the more important that the goal should be clearly enunciated in public
statements, in lieu of the old litany of support for stability.
There is, in my view, little danger that Southeast Asians will
regard such a stance as a harbinger of withdrawal. They will
continue to judge our presence or lack thereof on more pragmatic grounds. In the meantime, to the extent that detachment is achieved, it will begin to minimize the emotional

content—ranging from fear of subversion to dependency cravings—which currently confuses our relations. This in turn will facilitate frank speaking and rational cooperation in pursuit of answers to the complex development issues which it is in our most essential mutual interest to solve.

mance in Shanghai, might have been widened. As it was, his remarks alarmed the Philippine government, and he partially retracted them on his departure. At this writing the "special relationship"—an amalgam of security connections, historical ties, and emotional hangups—is alive and well. Its linchpin is a military alliance with three components—two large American bases in the Philippines, a mutual defense treaty, and a military aid program.

This chapter examines the U.S.-Philippine military alliance, renewed and amended in 1979, as it relates to political considerations, both regional and bilateral. It concludes that as presently constituted, questionable and decreasing security benefits are outweighed by the costs and long-term risk involved in perpetuating the pathological character of our connection with Manila. Reforming the alliance, primarily through a program of Filipinizing the logistics and maintenance functions of the bases, could further reduce our anachronistic role as actor and adversary in Philippine politics. At the same time it would enable the United States to maintain an effective military presence on terms more compatible with the trend toward regional détente and with the ASEAN goal of Southeast Asian neutrality, since the bases themselves would become progressively less "foreign." Given complex administrative and political hurdles, such a policy would necessarily be implemented in stages. While it would strain our limited capability for long-term planning and execution, the alternative of continued drift could at some future point involve us on the wrong side of revolution.

Why So Special?

In 1965 the British Deputy High Commissioner in Sarawak, East Malaysia, an eminently eligible widower, wanted to marry a local Chinese girl of good family and considerable means. But the idea was not popular in Sarawak, which had ceased being a British Crown Colony only a year earlier. As rulers, the British had favored the Malay component of the multiracial population. For the Queen's representative to as-

Chapter Three

The U.S.-Philippine "Special Relationship" and the American Military Bases

> Dr. Spock should be the Ambassador in Manila. The U.S. has a father image in the Philippines, and like most fathers we do not understand the problem.
> —unnamed American official, quoted in Symington hearings, 1969

> Manuel Quezon was faster on his feet, and Sergio Osmena was shrewder in his tactics, than most of their American opponents; and since they were basically playing our game, it was easier to humor them than to risk having to make a major commitment in opposing them. Ferdinand Marcos is playing the same game with equal brilliance under a slightly revised set of rules.
> —Peter Stanley, "Why Didn't the Americans Tyrannize Them More?"

> As I come to the Philippines in this brief stay I hope that we can initiate a new era in Philippine-American relations, not returning to the old special relationships—because the winds of change have swept away these factors—but building a new relationship. . . .
> —Richard Nixon, statement on arrival in Manila, July 26, 1969[1]

President Nixon never pursued his pledge, made on arrival at the Manila airport in 1969, to reduce the "special relationship" between the United States and the Philippines. Had he done so, his paradoxical niche in history as an architect of progressive Asian policy, assured by his later perfor-

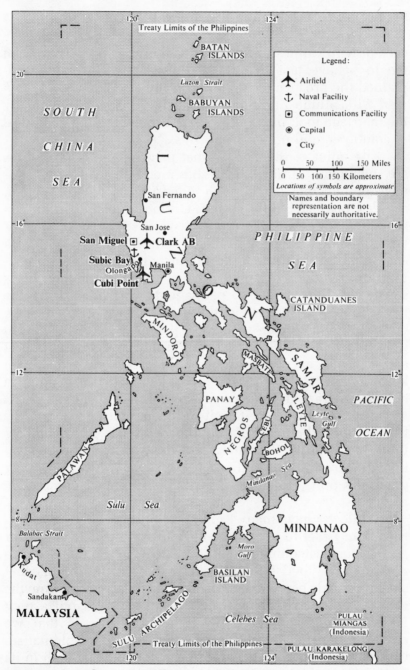

Major U.S. Military Installations in the Philippines

SOURCE: U.S. Senate, Committee on Foreign Relations, *United States Foreign Policy Objectives and Overseas Military Installations*, 96th Cong., 1st sess., p. 148.

sociate with Chinese was thus doubly *infra dig.* "They want me to behave just like the old Governor General," complained the prospective groom, "a symbol of the Crown, covered with plumes, no human behavior allowed." Eventually the marriage took place anyway, but not without a good deal of emotional and professional stress.

The point of the story is that postcolonial relationships are inevitably difficult, all the more so when the ex–metropolitan power, through good luck or wise policy, avoided being forcibly ejected. Orthodox relations between sovereign states are like those between strangers or friends. Postcolonial relations are familial, and may be fraught with emotional complications. To the extent that the ex–colonizing power retains a large presence in the ex-colony, he is somewhat like a parent permanently established in the household of a married child, revered but resented. Now imagine a situation in which the parent, a powerful person with many other interests, absentmindedly forgets his past and expects the child to behave just like any other hotel keeper. The latter can hardly be blamed for developing a degree of paranoia. He expects favorable treatment and reacts with resentment when it isn't forthcoming. He wants to be free but fears the effect of total independence. His neighbors think it is odd for the parent still to be hanging around, although they are too polite to say so. The child senses peer group disapproval, and reacts with boastful and insecure behavior.

While we have many "special relationships" with countries from Israel to Korea, the Philippines is the locus of our only major postcolonial presence. The resulting malaise cannot be understood without looking behind the myths that cloak mutual perceptions of the colonial period, myths which to this day mislead and sometimes antagonize both Filipinos and Americans. Myth number one is that we created democracy in the Philippines; that our colonialism was more enlightened than European colonialism, both in its motivations and in its consequences. In fact, American rule bolstered a preexisting landed elite, encouraging it to express itself through representative forms. The result was perhaps as "democratic" as Mississippi in 1900. The forms were there, but the substance was *sui generis*. Myth number two is that Filipino political leaders struggled for their independence and that we graciously acceded, extending it to them short of revolution, thereby confirming our superiority to other colonialists. In fact, as noted earlier, we decided for reasons of self-interest to divest ourselves of the Philippines before local leaders wanted full independence, under conditions (world depression and looming war) which bid fair to destroy the Philippine nation, and nearly did.

In short, the American self-image of colonial benevolence is not fully warranted. It has encouraged us to assume falsely that the Philippine nation owes us a degree of gratitude and will behave in a manner that we can understand. But even more enduring problems arise from the fact that the "Fil-Am" mythology, like most mythology, also contains some potent strands of truth. Filipinos did react to American tutelage—particularly to such genuinely enlightened elements as free public education—with unparalleled affection, as their pro-Allied record in World War II proved. In their eyes, we responded with niggardly postwar aid, hedged with infringements on Philippine sovereignty. The most unspeakably sensitive aspect of the U.S.-Philippine colonial experience is that, having waved the American Dream before the Philippine nation, we then snatched it away. *In the end they realized that we would never let them become part of us.*

Unrequited love is not a pleasant phenomenon, but it is persistent. In one sense we are still enormously popular in the Philippines. A fifty-first state movement claimed three million members until it was outlawed after Martial Law.[2] Of all this the vast majority of Americans are blissfully unaware; many, by now, could not locate America's only major former colony on a map. Yet, at the risk of historicism, I think it is likely that the complex political attitudes which are the enduring product of our earlier association may still be the most important, as well as the least understood, determinant in U.S.-Philippine relations.

The Residuum of Postcolonialism

Today some of the principal legal provisions that contributed to the special relationship have ended. Most prominent was the Laurel-Langley Agreement, terminated in 1974, which had continued the parity provision of the earlier Philippine Trade Act of 1946 and extended other special privileges to American business firms. Since the dismantling of the U.S. sugar quota system in 1974, that major Philippine crop no longer receives preferential treatment, and sugar exports are being diversified to new markets, including the USSR and China. There have been reductions in the American military presence since the tremendous Vietnam War peak, and two minor facilities, including Sangley Point, a symbolically significant installation in Manila Bay, have reverted to Philippine control. Moreover, it has been some years since the Philippines obediently followed the U.S. lead in international affairs.

Nevertheless, the emotional core of the special relationship remains well preserved. It is perhaps best symbolized by the frequent arrivals, five years after the fall of Saigon, of American military helicopters at the U.S. Embassy (formerly the U.S. High Commissioner's residence) in Manila. They roar in parallel to the old Dewey (now Roxas) Boulevard, the premier avenue of the capital city, a momentary diversion for the hundreds of Filipinos who gather every morning outside the embassy seeking visas to the promised land.

Immigration plays a special part in the special relationship. The first major outflow of Filipinos, almost all from President Marcos' home province, Illocos, went to Hawaii as plantation workers in the 1920s. The majority of postwar migrants have been middle class, including thousands of doctors and nurses to staff inner-city American hospitals. Revision of U.S. immigration law in 1965 to favor relatives greatly stimulated outflow from the Philippines. In 1976 the embassy in Manila issued 30,652 immigrant visas, more than any other U.S. Foreign Service post in history, and Filipinos consistently run second to Mexicans in legal immigration to the United States.[3]

Today there are between 500,000 and one million Filipinos and naturalized Americans of Filipino descent in this country. To put it another way, about one of every forty ethnic Filipinos is an American. In general they have been highly successful as skilled workers, professionals, and entrepreneurs. They have also succeeded in transferring a lively cross-section of pre–Martial Law Philippine political life to the United States. Much but not all of the present politicking is anti-Marcos in tone, and the premier exile opposition group—Movement for a Free Philippines (MFP)—is headquartered in Washington. (The Hawaiian Filipino community, an exception to the general rule, has remained loyal to fellow Illocano Marcos.)

American Filipinos support half a dozen newspapers, including one, The Philippine News (San Francisco), which is the last survivor of the old Lopez family Manila media empire. As is the case with Greeks and others, ethnic Filipinos are vocal lobbyists on Philippine-related issues, exerting pressure on the Congress out of proportion to their numbers. The significance of the exile community for domestic politics in the Philippines is difficult to judge. Opponents of Marcos like to believe that it will prove analogous to the pre-1898 Filipino community in Spain, which produced the foremost hero of Philippine independence, José Rizal. Prominent Filipino politicians in the United States include MFP leader and former Foreign Minister Raul Manglapus, various scions of the Lopez and Osmeña families, and former Executive Secretary Rafael Salas, now with the United Nations. Some of these individuals could return to major political roles at home. It goes without saying that this situation does nothing to diminish the residual suspicion of the present Philippine government—further discussed below—that the U.S. government might revert to playing a covert role in island politics.

The impact on Philippine society of out-migration to the United States has been extraordinary, at least on a par with the situation in Greece or Poland. Kinship networks are such that there is hardly a middle- or upper-class family in the country that does not have family ties in America. The effect is perhaps most keenly felt in the provinces. Many rural Southeast Asians naturally look toward their capital city as a locus of upward mobility, but in the Filipino aspiration pattern, Manila is often only a way station on the road to New York or Chicago. The lure of emigration motivates thousands of youths who throng to Manila for training as nurses, accountants, and engineers. This process unquestionably helps to sustain the dynamism of the Philippine urban middle class, but the rural areas are correspondingly deprived of motivation and talent. In addition to a draining of brains, there is a hemorrhaging of vitality and ambition. The government encourages the export of skilled labor, professedly to generate foreign exchange but perhaps also out of awareness that the phenomenon may act as a political safety valve.

As befits the special relationship, the U.S. Embassy in Manila is the largest in the world. It has more the spirit of a federal building in an American city than of a conventional diplomatic post. Because Manila has long been a comfortable and convenient place for Americans to work, it serves as a regional headquarters for almost every conceivable agency, from the FAA to the IRS, with operations in the Far East. Extraordinary facilities are the rule rather than the exception. There is, for example, a sophisticated International Communications Agency regional printing plant, the only one of its kind in the world. Among other tasks it prints the Russian-language magazine *Amerika,* which is forwarded to Moscow via Vladivostok and the Trans-Siberian Railroad. From a huge transmitter site north of Clark Air Base, the Voice of America relays broadcasts to points throughout Asia.

Embassy-based officials administer major residual colonial responsibilities, such as paying pensions to Philippine veterans of the U.S. armed forces and overseeing a large veterans' hospital in the Manila suburbs. With payments from the Veterans' Administration, social security, and the Railroad Retirement Act included, U.S. pension disbursements in the Philippines amount to more than $120 million yearly, almost double the size of a bilateral economic aid program, which is itself (in per capita terms) the largest in Southeast Asia.[4] Pensions are small by American standards but go a long way in the rural Philippines, where recipients can often be identified by their solid, prosperous-looking homes. Recent U.S. congressional criticism of the pensions,[5] which Filipinos regard as a legal obligation to those who fought with MacArthur, is bitterly resented.

Filipinos continue to serve in the U.S. Navy under a special agreement. Traditionally most have been stewards. To this day they are employed in Washington as waiters at the White House Mess and the Vice President's residence, and one accompanied President Ford throughout his visit to the Philippines in 1976 as a personal servant. Including civilians and employees at the bases, the navy employs more than 40,000 Filipinos worldwide.[6]

The community of American citizens in the Philippines, numbering at least 65,000, is equally special. Apart from Panama, Manila is probably the only city in the world with an American colon society, including second-generation residents who can recall what the Army-Navy Club was like before Asians were admitted, and who suffered together in the infamous Santo Tomas prison camp during World War II. U.S. investment in the Philippines is considerable in amount, but it may be more significant that such investment is highly diversified and visible, and that its owners and managers are a prominent and well-entrenched feature of Manila social life. Some major Filipino firms are in fact American, the most notable being the multinational Soriano family conglomerate (San Miguel beer, etc.). The Sorianos were Spanish until World War II but have since for the most part taken U.S. citizenship.

Missionary connections are deep and influential. The most prestigious private university in the country (Ateneo de Manila) was founded and is still partially staffed by American Jesuits. The presence of almost 500 American priests and nuns in the Philippines—many of them active in the "liberal" anti-Marcos wing of the Church—guarantees an unusually keen and critical interest in Philippine affairs in

American Catholic circles. In recent years Protestant fundamentalist missionaries have also arrived, primarily to work with local hill tribes, in sufficient numbers to justify a large, fully equipped American-style boarding school for missionary children near Manila.

Under such circumstances, and despite the establishment since 1975 of Chinese, Soviet, and Vietnamese embassies in Manila, the special aura which surrounds official American behavior lingers on. In the past the director of the U.S. aid mission was virtually a member of the Philippine cabinet. Special U.S. assistance was expected and received in such times of emergency as the 1972 Luzon floods, which resulted in an abnormal increase in American aid levels during the first year of the Martial Law regime. (President Marcos rejected similar assistance following a disastrous earthquake in Mindanao in 1976, but he did so only after the American press reported that U.S. officials were hoping to exploit the relief effort to gain leverage in the negotiations over the U.S. bases.)[7] American aid officials normally work on terms of unusual intimacy with their Philippine counterparts. As late as 1976, for example, the U.S. AID Provincial Development Program ran what amounted to a school for governors, who gathered periodically in Manila classrooms like obedient pupils to be lectured by American experts on correct accounting techniques, tax reform, and the proper methods of motor pool maintenance.

The most enduring aspect of the postcolonial relationship is the matrix of reactive, contradictory emotions and unrealistic expectations which it has engendered among both Americans and Filipinos. Both parties want more from the other than reality warrants. The myth of shattered Philippine democracy, for example, encourages instant American criticism of human rights violations which would be accepted with relative equanimity in the case of countries such as Indonesia. ("How can my child be behaving like that?") On the Philippine side, as a recent Senate staff committee report noted, many people continue fervently to believe that the United States "is the ultimate power . . . that nothing has happened or could happen without at least tacit U.S. approval."[8] Filipino opponents of Marcos, such as former President Diosdado Macapagal, have unblushingly asserted that it should be an *American* responsibility to terminate the Martial Law regime.[9] ("Why doesn't father come and rescue me?") Building on the same Freudian foundations, President Marcos has tried to play on nationalist sentiment by charging that the CIA is supporting his incarcerated rival, Senator Aquino.[10] In the United States, the exile opposition eagerly publicizes similar tales in the hope that they will discredit Marcos by proving the end of American support for him.[11] In the atmosphere of the special relationship, such charges are never wholly incredible to many Filipinos, whether pro- or antigovernment.

Emotionalism pervades all aspects of U.S.-Philippine relations, from visa transactions to base negotiations. Special treatment is expected, slights and insults are magnified, motives are suspect. There is much warmth and frank talk in the relationship, but they yield quickly and unpredictably to alienation and misunderstanding. The Philippine attitude toward the United States, conditioned by years of postcolonial dealing, has been characterized as a neurotic, manipulative, psychically crippling dependency. As long as the pattern is encouraged by an extraordinary American presence in the Philippines, managed along traditional lines, the United States will remain an inevitable priority target for future outbursts of nationalism. Given the uncertain long-range potential of the Philippines for revolution, discussed in the previous chapter, this consideration alone is cogent cause for eradicating postcolonialism as soon as possible.

Security Ties

Whether judged in terms of symbolic significance, of dollar expenditure, or of legal commitment, security ties are the most potent single factor in the U.S.-Philippine relationship. There are three pertinent formal agreements: the

Military Bases Agreement dating to 1947 (but built on colonial foundations); the Mutual Defense Treaty of 1951, originally part of John Foster Dulles' cordon of containment; and the Mutual Defense (military aid) Agreement of 1953. From either a U.S. or a Philippine perspective, the bases are by far the most important element. There are two big ones, Clark Air Base and Subic Naval Base, plus half a dozen smaller supporting facilities.

Subic, home to eight separate U.S. Navy commands, is primarily a forward base and repair/logistics facility for the Seventh Fleet. It is the largest naval supply depot in the world and the site of Cubi Point Naval Air Station which, independent of the facilities at Clark, would still be a major air base, capable of handling the largest aircraft (C-5 Galaxies) in the American arsenal. Clark, headquarters of the Thirteenth Air Force, and the largest overseas American airbase, serves two tactical fighter wings (currently equipped with aging Phantom jets) and one utility transport squadron ("ash and trash"). It is a key link in a worldwide air force communications network, complete with its own orbiting satellite. Clark also has a big military hospital and almost infinitely expandable airlift facilities for both personnel and cargo.

There are approximately 5,000 American servicemen at Subic (not counting sailors who regularly disembark in lots of several thousand from visiting ships) and 10,000 at Clark, plus a total of almost 25,000 dependents. Both bases, but especially Clark, have training facilities which contribute to the readiness of U.S. forces in Northeast Asia (Japan and Korea). Until the reversion of unused territory in 1979, Clark sprawled over 129,000 acres (almost the size of the State of Singapore) in the central Luzon plain north of Manila. Of this vast acreage only a small amount was ever utilized, and much of the arable area was regularly farmed, quasi-legally, by Filipinos, who in the mid-seventies produced about $5 million worth of sugar cane there annually. Subic is located on a magnificent harbor, an indentation on the South China Sea flank of the Bataan Peninsula, which encircles Manila Bay on the west. It was originally the site of a Spanish naval station and has considerable future potential for civilian industrial development.[12]

Subic can perform a full range of repair jobs on virtually any ship in the U.S. Navy at much less expense than alternative American or Japanese facilities. The Subic Ship Repair Facility (SRF), the most indisputably valuable element in the entire Philippine base complex, has imparted industrial skills to thousands of Filipinos, and its trained graduates are (somewhat to the discomfort of the U.S. Navy) beginning to be much in demand in the Middle East. Directly and on contract the bases currently employ more than 40,000 Filipinos. Base-related expenditures, including liberty spending by servicemen, pump an estimated $200 million or more a year into the Philippine economy. The U.S. government estimates that, with a multiplier, this amounts to about 5 percent of the Philippine GNP.

Such bland figures do not tell the whole story. Clark and Subic remain conspicuous enclaves of American affluence and technological prowess. To enter them is to enter a different world, one which can only remind Filipinos of their own material and managerial shortcomings. The surrounding communities, including the usual accretions of bars and brothels, are, of course, dependent on the foreign presence. Black-marketing, pilfering, and scavenging are major occupations. Quantities of PX goods, still bearing dollar price tags, are diverted into a gray market which circulates them throughout the islands, where they encourage the fatalistic assumption that anything imported is inherently superior to anything Filipino. This lucrative operation has traditionally been a bone of contention among local politicians and generals; there is theoretically nothing illegal about it as long as the gray marketeers pay a modest sales tax on the ex-PX goods. The base-based societies are a gaudy, often violent demimonde, where, even more than elsewhere in the Philippines, cynicism and corruption are rife and things are rarely what they seem. For years in the 1960s the communist Huks ran the rackets of Angeles City, near Clark, turning an estimated $1 million in annual gross income.[13]

The Bases in Philippine Politics: Playing on Two Strings

The bases have been a target of intermittent nationalist attack and a source of constant irritation reflected in negotiations which have been virtually unceasing throughout the postwar period. The late Senator Claro M. Recto, who died in 1960, most eloquently enunciated the antibase position, arguing for a policy of total self-reliance in international affairs. This uncompromising position never spread far beyond the bounds of a small but influential intelligentsia.[14] Although there can be no proof, it is likely that most Filipinos regard the bases primarily as a source of jobs and only secondarily as a source of humiliation. On a more fundamental level, the bases are desired, with love-hate ambivalence, because they are the most important embodiment of an American presence which only a few are ready to reject. For President Marcos they represent tangible evidence of American support, which in the Philippine context still has legitimizing force.[15] The revision of the agreement in January 1979 may have enhanced his prestige, if not his popularity, as well as the longevity of his regime. The fact that in the past Marcos' opponents were reluctant to attack him on this issue is the most eloquent testimony to the sentimental and financial attraction of the bases,[16] although as noted below this reluctance may be waning.

The Philippine government has shrewdly exploited the full range of ambivalent attitudes toward the bases. They serve as a multipurpose bargaining tool, one that can be used in many ways to extract concessions and remind the United States that the Philippines still matters. Before a domestic audience they can be exploited to demonstrate continuing American transgressions against Philippine nationalism—the Tagalog equivalent of waving the bloody shirt. Since the 1979 revision the regime can reassure Third World leaders, who are in any case collectively drifting away from radical anti-Americanism, that the old, outdated relationship with Uncle Sam is on the way out. At the same time, it can reassure the Chinese, the ASEAN allies, and anyone else who wants a strong and continuing U.S. presence, that nothing has changed.

Our massive military presence has generated a variety of specific controversies, most of which are by now hoary with age. Filipino leaders have for years charged that the United States unjustly retained "sovereignty" over the bases, even though the 1947 agreement provided for rights of use, not ownership. Although he need not have done so, then Vice President Nixon underlined the point during a 1956 visit by ordering all deeds to the base properties returned to the Philippine government, an act which did not end the criticism.[17]

Another ancient bone of contention involves criminal jurisdiction over American troops. Krag-wielding American soldiers and barefoot Filipino guerrillas had barely stopped shooting at each other in 1902 when an ambiguous regulation led to controversy on this subject. A U.S. Supreme Court decision failed to resolve it a few years later. The jurisdiction problem flared again during the Commonwealth period when G.I.'s began to bring automobiles to the islands. The imperious Manuel Quezon suddenly announced that local courts should have jurisdiction over traffic accident cases involving U.S. military personnel. The American High Commissioner, who overruled him in 1937, thought he had settled the issue.[18] But it has continued to flourish, probably the hardiest perennial adjunct of the special relationship.

Since at least 1965, criminal jurisdiction arrangements in the Philippines have in fact been substantially the same as those which govern U.S. bases in the NATO countries and Japan. Why, then, does the endless bickering continue? First, because criminal disputes are by definition inflammatory and hence at times useful to the government in Manila. But there is a parallel and less cynical motive. Any foreign military presence does involve some derogation of sovereignty, as, for that matter, does the presence of an aid mission or even an embassy. Such considerations do not bother the British, Japanese, or others who feel equal to Americans. But Filipinos, haunted by a sense of inequality, simply cannot believe that they are not the victims of contempt and neglect, that they are not somehow still getting the Little Brown Brother treatment. As a result, they react to imagined infringements with hypersensitivity. It is pertinent that in both the NATO countries and the Philippines, offenses committed by U.S. military personnel while off duty are subject to the jurisdiction of local courts. A survey conducted in 1976 revealed that the NATO allies waived their jurisdiction in 90.5 percent of such cases. The equivalent percentage in the Philippines was only 0.5 percent.[19] For some years dispute has centered on the American right to determine what is "off duty," a right we claim worldwide.

The Bases' Role in History: What Is Past Could Be Prologue

Our Philippine bases have played three clearly discernible roles in the past. They began in the colonial period as garrisons and to provide for the external defense of an American possession. Fort Stotsenburg (now Clark), originally a cavalry post, was an airfield by the 1930s. Heaviest U.S. military expenditure was devoted to Manila Bay fortification, including the island redoubt of Corregidor, which absorbed millions of pre-depression dollars.

Unfortunately, the bases proved unable to defend the Philippines against the Japanese. On December 8, 1941, Formosa-based aircraft virtually wiped out the small American air force on the ground at Clark, despite the fact that eight hours had elapsed since the Pearl Harbor attack.[20] The great fortifications on Corregidor and elsewhere, deemed impregnable, were no impediment at all; the Japanese simply landed on Bataan Peninsula instead of making a frontal assault into Manila Bay, as they were apparently supposed to do. In the end, Filipino ground troops made perhaps the most effective contribution to their own defense, during the hopeless Bataan campaign. Nationalists of the Recto school have not neglected to draw the obvious conclusion that while the American military presence served to attract outside aggression, it was unable to protect Filipinos against the consequences, which were indeed unpleasant. General

MacArthur's return to the Philippines took place as promised, but it also brought terrible devastation and suffering, leaving Manila the second most heavily damaged city of World War II, after Warsaw. In today's nuclear world nationalists see heightened danger that the bases might again serve as a magnet for great power attack.

The third and most recent phase was Vietnam. Out of sensitivity for Philippine concerns (and because under the Bohlen-Serrano Agreement of 1959 it would have required consultations) the United States did not stage combat operations against Indochina from the Philippine bases. Instead B-52 raids were flown from Guam and from new facilities constructed in Thailand.[21] However, the Philippine bases served as an invaluable logistics and support facility, and it is generally believed that without them the struggle would have been more expensive than it was.

Present Function of the Bases

Although obsolete, the following exchange from 1969 Senate hearings is instructive precisely because it underlines the often transitory nature of threat perceptions which have served to justify the bases:

SENATOR SYMINGTON. You said in your statement, Admiral, that it was agreed the chief problem was—I will read what you said— "The Board considers the principal threat to the Philippines to be Communist China with possible assistance from internal dissent groups."

What is the capacity from the military standpoint of the Red Chinese today in the Pacific to menace the Philippines from a military standpoint since this is a military board?

ADMIRAL KAUFFMAN. I would say at the moment, sir, very small.

SENATOR SYMINGTON. General, what would you say?

GENERAL GIDEON. Very small, very small.

SENATOR SYMINGTON. But you say it is the principal threat.

ADMIRAL KAUFFMAN. Of the threats that exist, I would say it is the principal threat; yes, sir.

SENATOR SYMINGTON. What you two are actually saying, militarily speaking, is there is no threat to the Philippines, are you not?

ADMIRAL KAUFFMAN. If, by the word "threat"——

SENATOR SYMINGTON. I am only using your word, not my word.

ADMIRAL KAUFFMAN. I think I was using it as a longer term implication perhaps, sir, than perhaps just right now.

SENATOR SYMINGTON. What do you mean exactly?

ADMIRAL KAUFFMAN. Well, I would say when the Chinese Communists have perfected the use of a nuclear weapon that the threat would increase.[22]

Today the Chinese threat is no longer credible. Instead Chinese support for a continued antihegemonic American presence is a major rationale for the status quo. As Congressman Nix rightly observed at another hearing in 1974, "new missions can be thought of for old bases."[23]

Present justifications for the bases fall into several categories:

—*The bases are part of our global force structure*, an essential link in a chain of facilities which enables the United States to project its conventional forces worldwide. It is not argued that they have any relevance to our strategic nuclear deterrent. Polaris submarines use facilities in Guam, not the Philippines, and there are no ICBMs, IRBMs, or B-52 bombers based in the Philippines. From time to time it is argued that the bases could be an essential link in a "back door" route to the Middle East, via Diego Garcia, in the event that U.S. access via Europe is denied as was the case during the Yom Kippur War. Similarly, the bases could aid in the projection of conventional forces to the Persian Gulf, the Horn of Africa, the Indian Ocean, or anywhere in South Asia. (It has never been claimed by anyone that the Philippine bases contribute directly to the defense of the American mainland against strategic nuclear attack, either by ICBM or by submarine-launched missile.)

—*The bases help maintain great power equilibrium in Southeast Asia and U.S. force readiness throughout the Far East.* Subic provides a home for the Seventh Fleet which is both more convenient and less expensive than alternate bases in Japan, at Pearl Harbor, or on the West Coast. Both the fleet and the bases help deter Soviet interference with the Straits of Malacca and other sea lanes to Japan which transport that country's supply of Middle Eastern oil. As noted in chapter one, alternate routes are available around Australia, but they would add travel time and an increase of up to 11 percent in the cost of some Japanese imports.

The bases would be necessary should the United States ever again wish to deploy military force in Southeast Asia itself, as in Vietnam. Clark provides irreplaceable training facilities for U.S. forces based in Japan and Korea—most notably a spacious bombing and gunnery range—thereby contributing to American military readiness in Northeast as well as Southeast Asia.

—*The bases are required to meet our obligation under the Mutual Defense Treaty of 1951 to defend the Philippines.* This argument has diminished (but not vanished) insofar as the only credible threat to the Philippines may derive from the possibility of revolution, a point discussed at greater length in the preceding chapter. There are enough unpredictable elements in the regional political environment to make the U.S. defense guarantee valuable in Philippine eyes. Vietnam's 1978 invasion of Cambodia and her more recent expulsion of thousands of ethnic Chinese refugees sent political shock waves through the region and raised severe doubts about the competence, much less the benign intentions, of the aging revolutionaries in Hanoi. China's future behavior is another question mark, one which will remain of particular interest to Manila, especially in light of the strong possibility that Taiwan, a strategic stone's throw from northern Luzon, will at some point reunite with the mainland. What air defense capability the Philippines has is at present largely dependent on the American facilities.

—*Transferring existing facilities elsewhere (e.g., the Marianas) would be enormously expensive.* Capital expenditures might run as high as $5 billion plus $300 million yearly in additional operating expenses.[24] Congress would certainly refuse to countenance additional expenditure at such levels, and even to replace the present facilities on a more modest scale might prove politically impossible given budgetary constraints. As things stand, the bases are not exactly cheap; in 1972 they cost about $300 million yearly in operating costs alone,[25] and today the expense is presumably much greater, certainly more than the total amount we spend on economic assistance in Southeast Asia.

—*The bases are a hedge against the unknown and the unpredictable* (for example, the political disintegration of China) and a means of combatting incidents of piracy, such as the 1975 Mayaguez affair.

—*Finally, the bases symbolize American determination to remain a Pacific power.* Closing them would upset not only the Chinese, who fear Soviet encroachment, but also the Japanese, who might feel compelled to build up their own defense forces in the region, yet would rightly fear the political reaction that such a move would be likely to provoke among the Southeast Asians. Any precipitous decline in U.S. military presence would also be disturbing to the ASEAN powers, whose leaders have assured us privately that they want the bases to stay. Out of deference to the ASEAN goal of neutrality, discussed at greater length below, only Lee Kuan Yew of Singapore has offered such assurances in public.[26] In fact the other four ASEAN countries view the entire subject of foreign bases with some ambivalence, and since they tend to assume that we will, in any case, remain on the scene militarily, they generally prefer to say as little as possible on the subject.

While most of these rationales have merit, several of them are questionable, and the relevance of others will probably diminish over time. To begin with the equilibrium argument, it is doubtful how much the bases contribute to military balance, if only because it is arguable whether, in Southeast Asia, such balance exists in isolation at the regional level (see chapter one). American deterrent power rests fundamentally on strategic nuclear weapons and is global in character. It is embodied in the Polaris submarine, invisible at sea, not in the painfully exposed drydock at Subic Bay. The absence of major Soviet bases closer than Vladivostok, combined with the assertion that Soviet naval force is a real and growing menace in the region, suggests that the relationship between local bases and genuine military power is questionable. Moreover, so long as the U.S. bases remain, they pose an open invitation to ambitious security bureaucrats in the Soviet Union or elsewhere to build their own bases (perhaps on the territory of their Vietnamese ally) or their own Seventh Fleet to match ours. To the extent that this is true, as Dwight Perkins has pointed out, foreign bases attract rather than deter hostile activity and are a destabilizing factor.[27]

The most obvious utility of massive conventional facilities would be in the event of large, World War II–type non-nuclear conflict. Under such circumstances the bases would indeed be required to protect the sea lanes against Soviet interdiction. But it strains credibility to posit a conventional war with the Russians in the Pacific, if only because we would presumably be unwilling to engage on terms so clearly disadvantageous to us. Hence, any incident or scenario sufficiently serious to warrant the full-scale use of the bases in a superpower confrontation would swiftly invoke the more fundamental nuclear sanction. The Russians know this as well as we do, and it is therefore unlikely that they will interfere with shipping in the Malacca Straits unless they have already decided to go to war.

Vulnerability is another problem lightly glossed over by those who believe in the continued high utility of the bases. Even in conflict with a second-rank military power, such as China, it seems altogether obvious that the sprawling facilities, like their rusting ancestor on Corregidor, would prove vulnerable to surprise attack, e.g., by submarine-launched missile. It is easy to infer that the only practical combat (as opposed to logistical) role of the bases would be the time-tested one of projecting conventional U.S. power into Southeast Asia, implying Vietnam-style involvement in the internal affairs of states which have no serious offensive capability and can in no way pose a threat to the United States. But even this function may be obsolete. The development of cheap, highly portable, precision-guided antiship missiles casts doubt on the future practicality of naval blockades and other instruments of "coercive diplomacy" against underdeveloped countries, as even the advocates of such a capability are aware.[28]

Assumptions about the utility of the Philippine bases in the event of Third World crises, whether in Southeast Asia, the Middle East, or elsewhere, tend to ignore proven political constraints as well. The suggestion that Clark could be part of a "back door" route to the Middle East, for example, was perhaps calculated to generate congressional support by establishing a linkage between the Pacific facilities and our commitment to Israel. However, modern aircraft, such as the C-5 Galaxy, can reach the Middle East nonstop through the transatlantic "front door" with aerial refueling, thereby eliminating the problem posed by denial of European transit rights during the Yom Kippur War. Furthermore, the Filipinos, sensitive to the sentiments of the Muslim majority in ASEAN, and dependent on the Middle East for the bulk of their own energy supply, would be most unlikely to stand idly by while their territory is used as a springboard to Israel.

When the Philippines opened diplomatic relations with socialist Vietnam in 1976, both countries pledged "not to allow any foreign country to use one's territory as a base for direct or indirect aggression and intervention against the other country or other countries in the region."[29] Since that time, and despite the language barring "indirect aggression and intervention," President Marcos has repeatedly assured the United States of "unhampered military operations," implying no new restrictions vis-à-vis the rest of Southeast Asia.[30]

In attempting to evaluate these seemingly contradictory commitments to Washington and Hanoi one need only recall that even at the height of the Vietnam War, with the Philippine government still set in a rigorously anticommunist course, the United States was inhibited from using the bases for combat operations by the realization that it would strain our relations with Manila. Regardless of present assurances, it is likely that any further use of the bases against a Third World target would prove even more embarrassing. Perceiving the problem, we would again fail to press the issue. Already, awareness of such political limitations, which are bound to strengthen with time, is reflected in growing American reluctance to deploy weapons systems that really matter—such as the Polaris—to Philippine territory.[31]

With combat functions increasingly dubious, the rationale for the bases depends on their support role; on their value as symbols of U.S. political will, both to remain in the region and to resist possible Soviet encroachment; and on a variety of comfort, convenience, and economy factors. The support function is of tremendous importance, but if the combat role is no longer viable, two questions need to be asked more frequently: *how much* support is really necessary, and *for what?* The point is underlined by the present situation at Clark, with its 17,000 Americans and only two squadrons of fighting aircraft. The additional function of the bases as part of a system designed to support global deployment of conventional forces, plus their role as a hedge against the unknown, does not quite obscure the fact that, here as elsewhere, major overseas "support" facilities are largely engaged in supporting each other.

The amphibious landing beaches at Subic and the bombing and gunnery ranges at Clark contribute to the readiness of our forces in Japan and Korea. But it is not clear why this training needs to be carried out in the Philippines. Surely if such readiness is vital to the defense of Northeast Asia the Japanese and Koreans, whose primary interests are at stake, should be able to provide the required ground and air space closer to the scene of the action. Failing this, similar training facilities exist in the United States, although their use would require more expensive rotation of combat-ready personnel across the Pacific.

By far the most persuasive argument for the bases is political and symbolic, not military. Without doubt, Japanese, Chinese, and Southeast Asian anxieties would be aroused by sudden withdrawal. Moreover, beginning in early 1976, U.S. public opinion added another dimension to the political/symbolic justification. Negative reaction to the Korean troop withdrawal served notice to policymakers that the first phase of post-Vietnam disillusionment, which had stimulated the "never again in Asia" tone of the Guam and Pacific doctrines, was over. In the second phase, fear of excessive retrenchment, manifest during the Panama Canal debate, appeared to overtake fear of excessive commitment. The thrust of congressional concern was further modified by perception of President Carter as irresolute, and for a time it appeared that he and his security advisers were being thrown back into a posture, somewhat reminiscent of the 1950s, of defensive reaction against charges of being "soft" on external enemies. As a result of the altered political climate the new administration quickly dropped its initial consideration of a major military retrenchment in the Philippines and strenuously pursued the status quo. Since that time there has been little inclination to challenge such constant factors as bureaucratic convenience and the natural desire of professional military men to retain highly developed facilities in glamorous overseas locations. No one who has gazed across Subic Bay, crammed with the magnificent paraphernalia of naval power, can fail to appreciate the weight of sentiment involved.

During the 1969 Symington hearings, Senator Fulbright observed that, as a consequence of our interest in the bases, "We will always resist any serious change in political and social structure of the Philippine government, which is very likely to be, in the long run, a detriment to the people of the Philippines."[32] The actual situation is more complex than this conventional criticism would suggest. As our recent human rights initiatives indicate, American policy toward the Philippines is by no means always hostage to the bases; rather it is perpetually ensnared in an emotional, reactive relationship in which the bases are the most powerful active ingredient. Although the relationship is often manipulated by the Philippine government, it has acquired a dynamic of its own. It is not amenable to consistent control by anyone, which is precisely why it is dangerous.

The most obvious risk involves three elements: the continued dominance of the United States in Philippine political perceptions, the uncertain potential of the Philippines for revolution, and the existence of rural insurgency, traditionally powerful in the neighborhood of the bases. As noted in the previous chapter, the insurgency is not very serious at present, but could expand with explosive rapidity in the event of a national political upheaval. Should full-scale revolution envelop the Philippines, the U.S. facilities would be an inevitable target, if only because once aroused, the full force of nationalism is unlikely to be spent until the paramount symbols of the traditional American presence have been removed, or at least assaulted.

Because of their enormous exposure the bases are likely to become quickly involved in a succession crisis or any other haphazard, revolution-from-above situation where competing factions are attempting to mobilize mass support, a possibility discussed in chapter two. Under such circumstances the temptation for rival leaders to play on nationalist sentiment by creating incidents involving the bases could easily prove irresistible. Similarly, a threatened regime might logically hope to see the bases become the object of an insurgent attack, manipulated or otherwise, in order to obtain rapid American assistance. The large American community in the Philippines, with its continuing *colon* ethos, would tend to evoke a Panama-type reaction in the United States, rapidly generating political pressure to protect American lives and property. Our image of the Philippines as a country blessed by American benevolence would guarantee keen resentment of the consequences likely to result from runaway radical nationalism.

It was earlier observed that the absence of past revolution in the Philippines may be reason to fear for the future. While neither probability nor timing can be calculated precisely, the prospects of upheaval are likely to increase with time. Assuredly, the potential cost to us needs to be placed in the balance against the value of the bases under equally hypothetical situations of conflict elsewhere in the world.

The Revised Base Agreement (1979)

Except for World War II, our Philippine facilities have been under almost constant negotiation since the Commonwealth period. The latest round began in 1975 and was intially expected to result in a new treaty to replace the 1947 agreement. Several factors combined to result in a more modest outcome. Although the bases had hitherto been rent free, it was clear that the Philippine government would not enter a new agreement unless it provided for significant compensation. Yet it was unlikely that the U.S. Senate would ratify such an agreement, certainly not without a bruising public debate. On the Philippine side, the political desirability of renewing the American tie steadily increased in proportion to growing domestic and international political uncertainty. The eventual agreement of January 1979 took the form of an exchange of notes renewing the 1947 treaty, with provision for a thorough review in 1984.[33] In effect it reduced the term of the agreement, which does not formally expire until 1991, to five years. The exchange-of-notes formulation required no Senate ratification, and under the Case Amendment became law when the Congress took no action within ninety days.

Thus we obtained reduced but apparently stabilized tenure at the Philippine bases. The United States is guaranteed "unhampered military operations" at "the Philippine military bases known as Clark Air Base and Subic Naval Base" and associated lesser facilities. In return, President Carter promised President Marcos his "best efforts" to obtain congressional approval for a compensation package of $500 million over a five-year period, to include $50 million in grant military assistance, $250 million in Foreign Military Sales (FMS) credits, and $200 million in Security Supporting Assistance. The entire package is contingent on annual congressional authorization and appropriation. Economic aid was not mentioned in the agreement, but if projected at approximately current levels it would result in a five-year grand total in bilateral assistance not far below the $1 billion total aid package offered by Henry Kissinger during an earlier, abortive stage of the negotiations—an offer which at that time (December 1976) was rejected by the Filipinos. In fact, the only element in the compensation package which is not a continuation of previous assistance modes and levels is the $200 million in Security Supporting Assistance, recently renamed Economic Support Funds (ESF), a special category of explicitly politically motivated grant aid hitherto employed mainly in the Middle East, above all for Egypt and Israel.

There were two other significant aspects to the agreement. First, the exchange of notes confirmed and in some respects strengthened the U.S.-Philippine Mutual Defense Treaty, about which more below. Second, it provided for a substantial reversion of unused base territory, mainly at Clark, to full Philippine jurisdiction. Philippine sovereignty over the bases was reaffirmed and symbolized by the appointment of "Philippine Base Commanders." However, the core operational areas of the bases (as well as all U.S. forces) remained administratively distinct, under the command of "United States Facility Commanders." Responsibility for the security of the entire "Philippine base" perimeter, the same as the old base perimeters, was assigned to the Philippine commanders, in the hopes that this would reduce incidents between American security personnel and Filipino intruders. The American commanders remained responsible for the security of the core operational areas, and even within the reverted territory certain regions, known as "depicted areas" are subject to joint management. The latter include portions of Subic Bay and the hilly watershed in back of the big naval base, presently covered by some of the last virgin tropical rainforest on the island of Luzon. This stand of great trees is of more than merely environmental interest. Should invading slash-and-burn squatters destroy it, as has happened virtually everywhere else on Philippine public lands, the water supply upon which the base and its sophisticated ship repair facility depend would be disrupted.

The amended agreement of 1979 was designed above all to preserve the status quo. While this outcome was inevitable under the political conditions prevailing in the United States, it leaves much to be desired. There is a fundamental incompatibility between the two key provisions of the revised agreement—assurance of "unhampered military operations" for the United States, and "Philippine sovereignty" *as perceived by Filipinos*—and this latent but inescapable contradiction assures that the bases will retain their decades-old role as a contentious and volatile element in U.S.-Philippine relations. The formalized, multiyear military aid commitment amounts to a long-term pledge of political support for the present regime and greatly increases the likelihood that the bases will become a focus of anti-Marcos political opposition. The amendment quickly produced hostile commentary from Marcos' arch foe, the imprisoned Senator Aquino, who in the past had maintained a typically ambivalent stance on this tricky issue. (During the March 1978 election campaign he actually supported retention of the bases.)[34]

Assigning responsibility for outer perimeter security to Filipinos may, as intended, reduce the likelihood of American guards shooting or abusing Philippine intruders. But in the past, perimeter incidents have been only one of many sources of friction between American forces and Filipinos. Others have included labor disputes, civilian casualties resulting from training operations, insurgent contact with U.S. forces traveling between facilities, and the activities of American military investigation personnel involved in the policing of off-base criminal behavior by American servicemen, usually involving black marketing or theft and some degree of collusion with Filipinos. Incidents will continue as long as thousands of Americans, including numerous transients, are in intimate contact with a much poorer Asian society.

The Reconfirmed Defense Commitment

The 1979 agreement reaffirmed the 1951 Mutual Defense Treaty, thereby reviewing a source of dangerous misunderstanding with the Philippine nation. From its inception at the height of the cold war this treaty appeared to promise more than the United States was ever likely to deliver, and caused Filipinos to question its sincerity. The treaty states:

Each party recognizes that an armed attack in the Pacific Area on either of the Parties would be dangerous to its own peace and safety and declares that it would act to meet the common danger in accordance with its constitutional process.

Article V further stipulates that an "armed attack" includes:

an armed attack on the metropolitan territory of either of the Parties, or on the island territories under its jurisdiction in the Pacific or on its armed forces, public vessels or aircraft in the Pacific.[35]

Ink on the original treaty was hardly dry before Manila began to object that it did not provide for "automatic" retaliation, as the NATO alliance appeared to do when it stipulated that "an armed attack against one or more of [the parties] in Europe or North America shall be considered an attack against them all."[36] The objections prompted a series of statements, issued by U.S. officials from Dulles onward, asserting that the question was irrelevant, since if an aggressor attacked the Philippines he could not help but simultaneously attack U.S. forces deployed there. At the Symington hearings in 1969 the State Department granted that in fact it might be possible to attack areas of the Philippines beyond Luzon (Mindanao for example) without involving Americans. It was conceded that our response in such situations would not be "automatic."[37]

Although they have continued to express skepticism over the years, Filipino leaders undoubtedly realized that the treaty is in fact comparable to the NATO agreement; both are subject to constitutional processes, nor could it be otherwise. But this misses the point. What has really pained them from the beginning is the fact that our NATO tie carries more political weight than a commitment to our former possession and loyal wartime ally in the Pacific. (They are presumably aware that we have no formal treaty obligation whatever to defend Israel.) Moreover, it is apparent that the political weight of our Philippine commitment has tended to diminish progressively over time, first with the end of the Dulles containment strategy, then with our withdrawal from Vietnam involvement (which as long as it lasted put a premium on the support, no matter how contrived, of other Southeast Asians), and finally with the triumph of trilateralism and its apparent corollary of unconcern for minor allies. Perhaps most important, Martial Law has badly damaged, if not destroyed, the basis of shared political values, admittedly exaggerated in the past, which gave the alliance legitimacy and popular appeal in the United States.

Given these circumstances it is unlikely that any U.S. government would regard the treaty as applicable either in case of clandestine external support for insurrection (e.g., Libyan support for Muslim rebels in Mindanao) or in the event of conflict over the disputed South China Sea islands—a dispute which may be sharpened by recent oil discoveries.[38] A third possibility, hostilities with a neighboring Southeast Asian state, would today be regarded as fit object for ASEAN, not U.S., intervention. It can therefore only undermine American credibility to affirm, as the agreement does, that we regard it as applicable not only to attacks on Philippine territory but also and "of equal validity" to attacks on Philippine "armed forces or public vessels" anywhere in the Pacific, not to mention "island territories under [the] jurisdiction" of either of the parties—a formulation which appears to cover Filipino garrisons in the contested islands.[39] Like the Rusk-Thanat agreement of 1962 between the United States and Thailand, this one will in the end only confuse and irritate those it is supposed to reassure.

What to Do

Despite these problems, there are two features of the amended agreement which offer a basis for future progress. First, the term of the existing agreement has been shortened to five years, with the requirement for "a complete and thorough review and reassessment" in 1984 and on the fifth anniversary of any subsequent modification. Second, the amendment opens the door to a phased increase in Philippine participation in the management of the bases.

The five-year review should include a close reexamination of the Mutual Defense Treaty. It should be revised to cover only major, external aggression, specifying that disputes arising within the ASEAN region would be the initial responsibility of that organization. It might be possible to reach an understanding with the Philippine government to retain, as the basis of alliance, the 1954 Manila Pact, the foundation charter of SEATO. While SEATO is now defunct as an organization, the Pact remains valid.[40] Although presently redundant in the case of the Philippines, it embraces our other ASEAN ally, Thailand, with whom we have no other treaty link. It obligates signatories to "consult immediately" and to "act to meet the common danger" in accordance with their constitutional processes.[41] It does not contain the far more comprehensive definition of "armed attack" found in the U.S.-Philippine bilateral treaty, and would hence be less easily applicable to questionable instances of external support for internal subversion. It could and should be easily redefined to apply only to cases of external, armed aggression. It would then represent a promise that could be kept.

Filipinization: Swords *and* Ploughshares at Clark and Subic?

The more vexing question of the bases themselves remains. Despite the rhetoric of the amended agreement they are still in fact enclaves of American power and wealth. The appointment of Philippine base commanders will have little impact on the situation so long as Filipinos command only a tiny fraction of the resources available to their American counterparts. Real improvement must involve a major reduction in the sheer mass of the U.S. presence. For example, it should be possible to combine the duplicative army and navy terminal facilities at Clark and Cubi Point, either of which, as noted above, can handle the largest aircraft that we possess.

The term "Philippine Base Commanders" suggests a major transfer of operational authority. It thereby risks adding an increment of hypocrisy to an already unhealthy situation, because the one base function in which Filipinos can never share satisfactorily, if at all, is the command and control of U.S. forces and operations. Yet, as we have seen, the real bread and butter of the bases is not operations but logistics and maintenance. Here there are great and unexploited opportunities for partnership which would build on the best elements in the U.S.-Philippine heritage, including the high level of education and keen entrepreneurial aptitude of the Filipinos.

Much of the present maintenance function of the bases could in time be turned over to Filipinos on a contract basis, after an appropriate transition period, to include whatever training might be required. The contract concept was first proposed by a senior Philippine official, Executive Secretary Alejandro Melchor, before he left the government in late 1975. Two variations have been suggested.[42] The first would place primary reliance on Filipino contractors and is known as the "Singapore Model" because it would follow the pattern already in effect at the former British naval base there. The second variant, or "Brooklyn Model," envisions a major U.S. contractor or contractors with primary responsibility for the Subic Ship Repair Facility, similar to the private contractors who presently operate the great Brooklyn and Newport News shipyards in the United States. "Brooklyn Model" firms would, like other multinationals, be subject to Philippine law. At Clark, contract modalities could be used to stimulate the development of an industrial park, perhaps in combination with a free trade zone. Properly promoted by the Philippine government, such a project could attract aerospace and electronics firms from Japan and Europe as well as the United States. Clark is now less than an hour by road from the expanding suburbs of Manila, potentially one of the greatest semiskilled labor pools in Southeast Asia.

The advantages of a gradual shift to contract operations would be several. It would increase Philippine participation, link the bases to a program of national development, and thereby reduce the likelihood that they will become the legitimate focus of nationalist attack. It would signal American recognition that Philippine society, which has already produced some of the most impressive corporate and financial structures in the region, has the clear potential to achieve at least Korean and Taiwanese levels of industrial sophistication. It would prove to Filipinos that the old era of mutual recrimination, condescension, and hyprocisy is over, and that we regard them seriously as adults capable of doing adult work. The transition to contract operations would give American planners a healthy stimulus to consolidate and trim excess base facilities while the changeover is under way. At the same time it would allow us the option of transferring some maintenance work to contractors at locations elsewhere in the region, including Singapore, where labor costs and facilities at presently underutilized shipyards compare favorably with the Philippines.[43] There is no doubt that both the government of Singapore and U.S. aerospace firms already in business there would be eager for the extra business. The result would be to "show the flag" in a more enlightened fashion and on a more widespread basis, as well as to disperse the benefits of U.S. military spending within ASEAN territory. Finally, it would justify a phased termination of military aid in compensation for the bases, except for technical assistance required in connection with Filipinization. Indeed, once the facilities were refashioned to be more responsive to Philippine national needs and relevant to national development, no compensation whatever would be justified.

The type of contract arrangements envisioned would not necessarily affect U.S. military operations at the bases, including training, airlift, and reconnaissance functions. Some critics of the present system believe that all such operations should be simultaneously transferred to U.S. territory in the western Pacific, including Guam and the Marianas, or to Japan.[44] There is obvious and cogent cause for making all combat (as opposed to training) operations fully independent of the political uncertainties associated with the Philippine bases as soon as possible. It is also true that the very considerable facilities on Guam are frequently overlooked by those who claim that Subic is essential. Nevertheless, the inconvenience and expense entailed in rigorous separation and relocation of all operations currently conducted in the Philippines would probably outweigh the advantages to be gained, and create sufficient distress at the Pentagon and in the Congress to imperil the entire concept of Filipinization. For the moment, at least, reductions in operational presence should be geared primarily to perception of American security needs; on these grounds alone, considerable retrenchment is undoubtedly warranted.

There are two additional means by which the Philippine element in the bases might be increased in the years ahead, both of them likely to be controversial. One would involve more joint use of the facilities by the Philippine military, building on their present share in administration, security, and air defense. While increased Philippine use could lead to more anti-insurgency operations from the bases, it will be an inescapable component of genuine partnership. Strict understanding that American forces would not become involved in domestic operations would be necessary and would follow logically from a revised alliance directed solely and unambiguously against the possibility of extraregional aggression. In addition, we should be prepared for the possibility of joint use by other ASEAN states in cooperation with the Philippines. Not long ago such a possibility would have been unthinkable, given the residual fear of invidious comparison with SEATO. This inhibition is likely to diminish steadily in future, and if ASEAN evolves toward more explicit political partnership, a greater degree of defense cooperation is inevitable. While the United States need not promote or encourage such a trend, it would certainly be pointless and indeed retrograde to oppose it.

Filipinization and the Zone of Peace

It should be a major objective of Filipinization to reduce, if not eliminate, the nagging contradiction between our military presence and ASEAN political doctrine, most notably the proposal for a Southeast Asian Zone of Peace, Freedom, and Neutrality.[45] This proposal, formulated with all the great powers in mind, is not a perfect or legalistic concept. Originally and most ardently promoted by the late Tun Razak of Malaysia, it posits the long-term goal of a Southeast Asia free from external interference, including foreign bases. None of the ASEAN states believes that attainment is imminent. Until it is, all of them hope—and, as noted above, expect—that the United States, regarded as the most benign of the super-powers, will maintain a sufficient military presence.

The Zone of Peace deserves more considered American support than it has received to date for at least two reasons. Far more than mere rhetoric, it represents the deep aspirations of every member state. The desire for freedom from great power conflict has become a summation and projection of nationalisms in individual countries, and for this reason alone compels our sympathetic attention. But in addition, the neutrality concept accords with the reality of an existing, thoroughly healthy trend toward decreasing great power competition in Southeast Asia, as discussed in the preceding chapter.

Energetic Filipinization of the bases would serve the spirit of neutrality in several ways. It would reduce the weight of "foreign," American interests relative to Philippine interests. It would accentuate the non-combat-related aspects of the bases, which are already their major justification, suggesting a day to come when the facilities and the skills which they produce may be turned largely to developmental purposes. Finally, it would hold the door open for a future regional defense role for the bases, without pushing anyone through it. With a credible "Philippine" label on the bases the United States could and should formally endorse ASEAN neutrality, thereby giving some further impetus to détente in Southeast Asia and some modest encouragement to ASEAN's embryonic political function, which first became apparent, not by coincidence, in the aftermath of our withdrawal from Vietnam.

The initial reaction of the Philippine government to a program along the lines suggested could not, of course, be taken for granted. The Filipinos, as much as we, are bedeviled by habit and a degree of vested interest in things as they are. As noted earlier, the traditional relationship of su-perficial antagonism with the United States is in many ways useful to Manila. Both the popularity of the bases and their legitimizing function might prompt the present regime to react with suspicion and distaste to a change that might first be interpreted as withdrawal of U.S. support. To avoid such problems, Filipinization would require maximum prior planning and consultation with Manila. Once the Philippine government perceived the policy to be in accordance with long-term national aspirations, including the oft-expressed desire for self-reliance, it is likely that it would be accepted, all the more so if it included legitimate business and employment opportunities.

Switching Symbols

The bases are perhaps already more important as symbols than as functional facilities. They manifest American commitment to the western Pacific; they demonstrate staying power to our allies; they reassure the Japanese, who fear that any derogation of our security stance portends something similar in Korea. These are the present messages, well known, comfortable. What would be the new message, assuming evolutionary changes along the lines suggested above? Suppose that we succeeded in making the bases Philippine in fact as well as word; that this enabled us to endorse the ASEAN neutrality concept, but that the Seventh Fleet and U.S. forces were still patrolling and exercising much as before, and that U.S. military ships and aircraft were being repaired at facilities (including some operated by U.S. and local contractors) in Singapore and elsewhere? Suppose further that we managed to revise our treaty relationship with the Philippines to realistic, unambiguous proportions (i.e., defense against direct aggression) and to disengage base compensation from military aid, thereby calming, at least somewhat, the pro- and anti-Marcos hubbub in America?

I believe it is a safe assumption that the ASEAN countries would appreciate our support for their desire to see the region free of great power conflict. Both they and the Japanese, in line with their own traditions, would perceive subtlety as a sign of strength, not weakness. Assuming adequate consultations, the Japanese would be willing to let us be the ultimate judge of what the details of our military presence in Southeast Asia ought to be. They would, however, be disturbed if they believed that we were retrenching entirely because of American domestic political factors, with no concern for the well-being of Asian allies. Finally, both the Japanese and the ASEAN countries should welcome healthier, less contentious U.S.-Philippine relations, and they would appreciate the technology-transferring accomplishment involved in building contract relationships at the bases.

Conclusion

Filipinization along the lines suggested may not be the only possible solution to the base issue. A strong alternative case can be made for a more complete withdrawal to Northeast Asian facilities or to U.S. territory in the western Pacific, coupled with complete termination of the bilateral U.S.-Philippine treaty relationship. In my opinion this would be too sharp a break with the status quo, easily interpreted as betrayal of trust to an ally. No matter how logical or desirable such a course may seem to those who dislike the Marcos regime, it would probably be bad politics both at home and abroad.

But there is no doubt whatsoever that change is needed, and that it should be grounded on principles which have been habitually ignored. In the spirit of Clausewitz, the bases should be an extension of U.S. policy by other means, not a determining, dominating factor. Military bureaucratic convenience should yield to broader political considerations, and not vice-versa. Above all, the peculiar hazards of postcolonialism require adequate consideration. To continue treating the Philippines as little more than a link in a global chain of facilities, a kind of fixed aircraft carrier, is to invite serious trouble. Emotionalism, lingering dependency, and unfulfilled nationalism are not comparable risk factors when dealing with equal partners such as Japan or West Germany. In the final analysis our policy should either strive to make the

Philippine partnership more equal, or if this is deemed impossible, to recognize that the alliance may be more liability than asset.

The path of rationalization and reform suggested here will entail lengthy planning and phased execution in place of the ad hoc maneuvering that has kept the Philippine bases under almost constant negotiation since World War II, with generally unsatisfactory results. It would severely test our limited ability to anticipate future crises and act before events force us to react. Clearly, the extraordinary effort required will not be made unless there is greater recognition of the hazards involved in the present pattern. Even then the mass of legal and technical obstacles to be overcome will be formidable. But if our civil and military bureaucracies cannot accomplish such a degree of innovation there is all the more reason to doubt that the bases are a net asset in an essentially unpredictable foreign environment.

Former Foreign Affairs Secretary Salvador P. Lopez recently observed that "in the end, American policy makers will have to decide whether it is more important for Americans to keep the bases than to keep the friendship and goodwill of the Filipino people."[46] He may be right, but for the moment there is another choice based on the shared interest of both countries in maintaining regional détente and getting the United States out of Philippine politics. Only the United States can take the lead in finding that middle way.

Chapter Four

U.S. Human Rights Policy in Indonesia and the Philippines

During the first few months of the Carter Administration, human rights was among the most contentious issues in United States foreign policy. A substantial share of the controversy swirled around Indonesia and the Philippines. The components of the problem were familiar; both countries were (and are) major recipients of American economic and military aid, yet neither had hesitated to incarcerate domestic political opponents without trial, sometimes under degrading or inhumane circumstances. Partly as a result of initial overenthusiasm, the Carter human rights policy came to symbolize the freshmen naiveté of the regime, and by late 1978 it seemed to be running out of steam. Yet regardless of whether the issue remains fashionable in official Washington, it will endure as a source of tension and debate as long as there is a gulf in political values between the United States and the authoritarian Third World.

In the wake of disillusionment with Watergate and Vietnam, President Carter reasserted our national faith in American ability to improve the moral character of world society, a faith expressed in the past through doctrines and policies such as the Open Door and Wilson's espousal of self-determination and of the League of Nations. Critics of this tradition have emphasized the accompanying self-delusion, hypocrisy, and lack of realism. They note that the American tendency to moralize has led us into profound misadventures, not least those associated with the crusade against Third World communism which culminated in Vietnam. But Vietnam also demonstrated that a healthy American foreign policy is impossible without public support, and that this in turn requires effective appeal to moral as well as material interests.

This chapter starts from an assumption that emphasis on human rights—an ideological component, if you will—is desirable on its own merits as well as a healthy reflection of domestic political reality. But as the past record shows, it is also a singularly problematic issue, difficult if not impossible to balance against other concerns without risk of disillusionment and destructive reaction. In the pages that follow an attempt is made to examine and compare the implementation of U.S. human rights policy in Indonesia and the Philippines. The record reveals what at first glance appears to have been an anomaly. Although the Indonesian human rights performance is somewhat worse, official U.S. criticism and sanctions have been more forcefully directed against the Philippines. This is true in spite of the fact that the major U.S. military bases in the Philippines might, under the Carter Administration's own policy criteria, have justified a relatively lenient approach. There is really no anomaly here; the apparent inconsistency is largely a result of the U.S.-Philippine special relationship and the presumption, which I believe is pernicious, that the United States has greater leverage in Manila than in most Third World capitals. Although it is too soon to make final judgments, the more modest and muted methods employed in Indonesia appear to have been somewhat more effective. Comparison between the two countries is instructive precisely because it illustrates some of the dilemmas, not all of them insoluble, which lie in the path of a durable human rights policy.

Genesis of U.S. Policy

Congress established the basis of current human rights policy in the waning years of the Nixon-Ford Administration. Critics of Kissingerian Realpolitik began legislating concern for fundamental freedoms by borrowing language which had long been employed in U.N. resolutions. One of the most influential was former Congressman Donald Fraser of Minnesota, whose House Subcommittee on International Organizations subsequently led the congressional drive for human rights. For Fraser this was a new variation on an old theme. In 1966 he had been the author of an influential provision in the foreign assistance legislation, Title IX, which mandated the use of aid funds to stimulate "popular participation" and the development of representative institutions. Broader concern with human rights was then dormant, so much so that the term "human rights" was not even mentioned in a 1973 study of liberal foreign policy doctrines which devoted heavy attention to Title IX.[1]

Between 1973 and 1975 Congress imposed specific human rights restrictions on both economic and military aid. The general congressional policy established in those years, which remains in effect, is, in Fraser's words, that

military aid should be reduced or terminated in a country guilty of a consistent pattern of gross violations of internationally recognized human rights. We define gross violations as those involving the integrity of the person: torture, prolonged detention without charges or trial, and other cruel and inhuman treatment. On economic aid, we state that when a country is engaged in gross violations of human rights, the aid may go forward only if it goes to the needy.[2]

Congress also directed the State Department to establish a Coordinator for Human Rights and Humanitarian Affairs separate from the line regional bureaus. This position has since been elevated to assistant secretary level.[3]

To candidate Jimmy Carter's foreign policy advisers, human rights seemed an ideal campaign theme. Its two distinct subissues—political dissidence and emigration from the USSR, and the more generalized problem of dictatorial regimes—were uniquely appealing to a combination, admittedly unstable, of liberals and conservatives. As Elizabeth Drew has observed, Carter's advisers probably did not anticipate the degree to which the future president would be personally attracted, as the campaign progressed, by an issue which when raised in speeches consistently evoked enthusiastic audience response.[4]

The new administration began with heavy, widely publicized human rights initiatives on both the Soviet and Third World fronts, including the famous Carter letter to Andrei Sakharov and the reduction of security assistance to several Latin American countries, followed by their rejection of all U.S. aid. Since then, the administration has, to a greater extent, tempered concern for human rights with caution lest U.S. security and other interests be damaged. Secretary of State Vance's speech before the Georgia Bar Association on April 30, 1977, called for realism, emphasized "the limits of our power and our wisdom," cited the perils of doctrinaire plans of action, and even warned of "hubris." However, it would not be correct to infer that the administration successfully elaborated a finely tuned policy which balances human rights against other factors. As Indonesia and the Philippines demonstrate, courses of action or nonaction have been routinely determined by conflict and competition, often vituperative, among various segments of the executive branch and between the executive branch and Congress. By Washington standards there has been nothing particularly unusual in this process, except, perhaps, the emotional temperature involved. But whether policymaking by bureaucratic confrontation will suffice in the case of human rights, a naturally fragile subject, remains to be seen.

Human Rights in Indonesia and the Philippines

Human rights are commonly defined in terms of three categories, in the following order: first, freedom from government torture or other cruel and degrading treatment, including arbitrary arrest; second, the right to fulfillment of basic needs, including food, shelter, health, and education; and third, the right to civil and political liberties, including freedom of movement, and the right to participate in government.[5] For Indonesia and the Philippines, international criticism has focused heavily on torture and arbitrary arrest. Authoritarian political systems (Martial Law in Manila, military rule in Jakarta) have been a major issue in the case of the Philippines but much less of one in the case of Indonesia. Both countries have generally been acknowledged to be making honest efforts to meet overwhelming problems in the second area of basic human needs.

The genesis of most internationally recognized human rights problems in Indonesia and the Philippines is similar, deriving primarily from the accession of centralized, authoritarian regimes, governing through the mechanism of sweeping emergency powers.[6] In neither case are other legal and electoral institutions of sufficient strength to deter the rulers from making full use of their emergency powers. In neither case is there any likelihood that these powers will be significantly modified in the foreseeable future, quite possibly not short of a revolutionary crisis. In both countries, the rulers have been trapped in the inevitable dilemma of authoritarian systems: they find it difficult to perceive serious opposition as anything but subversion, and the control measures which this perception entails tend to make the perception self-fulfilling—any serious opponent *must* work underground, in a subversive fashion, to survive. (This observation is somewhat less applicable to the Philippines than to Indonesia.) The logic of such systems powerfully motivates rulers to practice arbitrary, often inhumane methods in times of crisis, whether actual or imaginary. Short of crisis, however, neither the Philippines nor Indonesia is characterized by extremes of brutality. The death penalty is rarely employed as either a judicial or a political tool, particularly in Indonesia where there have been no executions reported since the events of 1965–66. The looseness of both states combined with a generally tolerant cultural ambience softens and diffuses the practical consequences of authoritarianism, both good and bad, at every turn.

In both Indonesia and the Philippines the greatest crisis came at the birth of the present regime, in 1965–66 and 1972, respectively, resulting in the arbitrary detention of large numbers of potential opponents. In both cases there has been relatively little need for repetition, although detention,

usually temporary, has been employed sporadically when-
ever it appeared that opposition might be getting out of hand,
and as a routine form of political deterrence.

The net result of the two systems has, of course, been different, reflecting different traditions and levels of development. In mid-1979, according to Indonesian government figures, Indonesia continued to hold about 8,000 political
prisoners, the remainder of up to half a million members of
the Communist Party and associated front organizations arrested in 1965–66. In addition to this group, about 70 persons
were detained during disturbances at the time of the visit of
Japanese Prime Minister Tanaka in January 1974, and 400
after preelection agitation in early 1978. As of 1979, about 35
of the 1978 detainees were awaiting trial. In recent years political opponents have typically been detained for relatively
brief periods without any accusation of criminal activity except in the case of key figures (mostly students or journalists), who have sometimes been brought to trial under co-
lonial-era sedition statutes which forbid "sowing hate"
against the government. Those found guilty have in most
cases received sentences of several years imprisonment, including time already spent in detention.[7]

Well before the genesis of a systematic human rights policy in the U.S. Congress, international concern was focused
on a large group of 1965–66 detainees, originally about
10,000 in number, on the island of Buru in eastern Indonesia.
These individuals, including a number of prominent intellectuals who were members of communist front groups, were
held without trial, without families, and without newspapers
or radios, compelled to grow rice for their own subsistence.
For years the Indonesian government stimulated criticism by
making vague and frequently contradictory statements about
the number of prisoners and plans for their trial or release.
Confusion has been compounded by the fact that to this day
the government continues to make occasional new arrests of
those suspected of communist involvement in the events of
1965–66. As recently as December 1977 an influential official
repeated earlier suggestions that ex-detainees would (if home
communities proved hostile) be resettled in transmigration

projects beyond Java, allegedly for their own protection.[8] Subsequently, however, the government moved forward with increasing assurance to implement a program first announced in December 1976 whereby *all* of the 1965–66 political prisoners would be released or brought to trial by the end of 1979. It also asserted that there would be no forcible resettlement. Since 1977 it has released more than 29,000 prisoners, mainly of the less dangerous "Category C" variety, but apparently including all from the Buru penal colony except for a few hundred who elected to remain on Buru.[9]

Even the most skeptical commentators, including Amnesty International, believe that the 1977–79 Indonesian prisoner releases represent a major improvement, although it should not be overlooked that the majority of the 1965–66 detainees were held for fifteen years without charge or trial. While the precise number of political prisoners who will remain in Indonesia after the promised releases have been completed is uncertain, it is a safe assumption that future political rumblings will occasion more arrests, of variable duration, from time to time.

In the Philippines, several thousand people were detained, including many prominent noncommunist opponents of President Marcos, immediately after the declaration of Martial Law. All but a few of the politicians, journalists, and teachers were freed over the next year, but other individuals have since been arrested. At this writing, an estimated 400–500 political prisoners are being held, although the government disputes the "political" label, maintaining that all are implicated subversives, hence criminal and not political suspects.[10] International concern has been concentrated on a relatively small number of prominent figures, most notably Senator Benigno Aquino, Jr. But detention has not been the most critical factor in the Philippines. Rather, it has been a continuing flow of reports of torture. In addition, since 1975 there have been approximately 30 reports of cases where torture victims have apparently "disappeared," suggesting that they were murdered to eliminate evidence. As of early 1979 critics of President Marcos feared that such incidents were on the increase. U.S. government observers believed that there had been some decrease over the previous year. There was general agreement that the problem remained serious.[11]

For the Philippines, international criticism (including official U.S. commentary) has linked the problem of arbitrary arrest with authoritarianism by calling for an end to Martial Law and encouraging elections. At least partly in response, President Marcos held limited parliamentary elections in April 1978. They were marked by well-publicized fraud and the subsequent arrest or flight of several opposition candidates, thereby exacerbating both the detention and the political freedom issues.

There is an obvious difference in the quality of human rights information available for Indonesia and for the Philippines which results from a broader difference in the total human rights climate. In the Philippines, the Catholic Church, or, more precisely, a minority of activist, anti–Martial Law elements in the Church, has continuously played an effective ombudsman role, gathering information on a wide spectrum of political cases. This organized effort has provided most of the data for all other detailed assessments of human rights. The Church is able to communicate information independently both to Rome and to parent missionary organizations and others in the United States. Church efforts have been complemented by a limited number of government-tolerated opposition groups and leaders, including former Senators Kalaw, Diokno, Rodrigo, Tanada, and Salonga, and the Civil Liberties Union of the Philippines.

Such institutions and individuals exist in a tradition of widespread literacy and developed legal institutions, part of a cultural context which the Martial Law regime probably could not eliminate completely even if it wished to do so. As it is, President Marcos has allowed considerable freedom of expression to individual opponents, as long as they do not appear to represent any fundamental challenge—as the detained Senator Aquino does—presumably because such a policy demonstrates the "smiling" character of Philippines Martial Law and forestalls even more trenchant international criticism.

The situation in Indonesia is wholly different. There is

no institutional equivalent of the Catholic Church. Islam, by theological dictum, cannot be organized as Catholicism is; there can be no hierarchy or ecclesiastical structure insulated from political attack. As in Iran, the most durable and effective Muslim opponents of the regime have been the most conservative, particularly the adherents of the old Muslim Scholars' Party (Nahdatul Ulama) based primarily in East Java. While conservative Muslims have proved effective at resisting the government on parochial issues (e.g., the legalization of syncretic Javanese sects) they are hardly in sympathy with liberal political principles, especially when the likely beneficiaries would include their mortal enemies, the former members of the Communist Party.

Two courageous lawyers, Yap Thiam Hien and Adnan Buyong Nasution, have over the years, at the price of constant personal risk, attempted to monitor civil and political human rights. But there are only about 500 lawyers in all Indonesia, compared to many thousands in the Philippines. The vastness of the Indonesian archipelago, with its profound ethnic divisions and poor communications, contributes to the relative lack of information. The situation is further complicated by the fact that much of the detailed information coming out of Indonesia is traceable to educated communist detainees and their families. In recent years it has been channeled through an organization known by the acronym TAPOL (meaning "political prisoners") in which a leading role has been played by Mrs. Carmel Budiardjo, a former member of the British Communist Party, herself a former detainee and the wife of a recently released member of the Indonesian Communist Party. TAPOL's reluctance to acknowledge a communist role in the violent events of 1965–66 or to distinguish between the detention of leading PKI members and others, combined with its extreme antipathy to the Indonesian government, has reduced its credibility in the eyes of all but the most severe critics of the Suharto regime.

The less comprehensive nature of Philippine authoritarianism, characterized by the widespread survival of legal institutions and the role of the Church, extends to other areas as well. Thanks partly to a tradition of weak, decentralized local government there is less control over individual movement within the country. The Philippines has nothing approaching Indonesia's structured system of dual civil and military bureaucracy, heavily oriented toward security functions, extending in ordered stages down to the subvillage level. It is generally conceded by his opponents that President Marcos' efforts to organize village-level administrative and youth organizations (the *barangay* system) have thus far been singularly ineffective. Nor should this be seen as simply the result of inefficiency.[12] It has been a leitmotif of Marcos' essentially conservative statecraft not to uproot—indeed to rely upon—traditional kin and community-based elites. Thus he has made only a few replacements and no fundamental systemic alterations in the network of elected mayors and governors, dating to before Martial Law and reflecting a traditional ruling order. While the military presence has grown under Martial Law, it does not yet consistently dominate the old structure, as it does in Indonesia, and appears to be moving only slowly in that direction. The result may not be progressive, but neither is it the engine of a ruthless dictatorship.

Similarly, although Marcos' security apparatus may be brutal at times, it is not very consistent, and its institutional memory often appears to be mercifully short. There is nothing like the Indonesian practice of stigmatizing former detainees, or anyone discovered, even years *ex post facto*, to have been associated with a communist front in the pre-1965 period. In Indonesia, such people are still often routinely denied the papers required to obtain or hold virtually any job.[13] The Philippine intelligence services are fragmented and competitive, no doubt because the President, who has retained a shrewd control over the military, likes it that way. The Philippine system has no equivalent of the powerful and unified Indonesian Command for the Restoration of Security and Order (KOPKAMTIB).

A similar quality of looseness continues to mark the intellectual climate of the Philippines. Comments are warranted in three areas: campus freedom, access by outside observers, and the press. Marcos' policy toward the universities has been to tolerate intellectual dissent, but to deny it access to the mass media. He apparently believes that ideas are not inherently dangerous. Students and faculty may be bitterly critical of the government in lectures and campus newspapers, although not without some danger of harassment and intimidation. In this respect they are in a position similar to that of the Church-based opposition. Although the situation is far from ideal, the contrast with any other country in Southeast Asia is remarkable. A few undisguised Marxists and others bitterly opposed to the current regime and its strong continuing American connection can and do lecture, publish books, and disseminate their ideas among youth. A noteworthy example is the Marxist historian Renato Constantino.[14]

No country in Southeast Asia has been more open to critical outside observers than the Philippines. The Marcos regime has admitted a steady stream of professional, nongovernment human rights analysts, including Amnesty International (late 1975), the International Commission of Jurists (three visits between May 1975 and November 1977), the International Commission of the Red Cross (three visits between 1973 and 1975), and a mission from the United Church of Christ (1977).[15] In addition, many critical American congressmen have visited Manila. In every case the government has tolerated and often facilitated visits to detention centers and meetings with opposition leaders, who have freely described the excesses of Martial Law. The result has been a flood of reports roundly criticizing the Marcos regime. Indonesia's attitude has been far less forthcoming. Amnesty International has been, in effect, persona non grata since 1974, and it was only in 1979, after several years of international pressure, that the government allowed the International Commission of the Red Cross visit East Timor. The United Church of Christ mission, one of the few groups to visit both Indonesia and the Philippines, observed that "It was a very difficult job to get information from the people we talked to in Indonesia. I was afraid. They talked freely in the underground in the Philippines."[16]

Both foreign scholars and reporters enjoy practically

unrestricted access to the Philippines. Scholars can travel and conduct research on almost any topic, including many which would be unthinkably sensitive in most other Southeast Asian countries. The Philippines is the only state in the region which does not even possess a central governmental body to vet and control foreign research. Similarly, foreign correspondents can travel and file stories with minimal restraint. Under Section 9(a) of Philippine immigration law reporters can enter the country without visas for up to sixty days and are generally treated as favored personages. Most of them proceed to write highly critical stories with a gusto which would never be attempted or tolerated in Indonesia, where visas are both required and swathed in red tape. As one newsman with wide experience throughout the ASEAN region put it, "Journalists don't in practice reward the Philippines for being open and penalize Indonesia for being closed." The result has outraged the Marcos family, and in 1976 the government moved against two resident critics. Arnold Zeitlin of the Associated Press was expelled, and Bernard Wideman, a stringer for the *Washington Post*, was allowed to stay only after strenuous intervention by his home office and the U.S. Embassy. But such actions have been exceptional; despite their heart-felt resentment of the Western press, President and Mrs. Marcos have not altered the basic policy of tolerance.[17]

The domestic Philippine press is controlled according to a non-system which is in itself illuminating.[18] At the outset of Martial Law, President Marcos shut down virtually all critical newspapers. Since then, no mass media have been allowed (with a few provincial exceptions) which are not owned and managed either by members of the President's extended family or by close and trusted friends. Under such circumstances censorship is not necessary, and indeed there is no regular mechanism of press control. Editors know what they can get away with and almost invariably err on the side of caution or sycophancy. But once again the entire system is marked by inconsistency. Normally, for example, the press does not print detailed accounts of the fighting against Muslim rebels in Mindanao. But in late 1976 the government felt inspired to assert, as it has from time to time, that the insurgents were cooperating with communists as well as perpetrating banditry. To make this case the Manila *Daily Express* published a detailed and apparently accurate list, in fine type, of virtually all the major incidents in Mindanao over the past three years.[19] Suddenly, for any reader who cared to know, the true scope and political character of the conflict was clearly revealed. Such slips are not infrequent and they do not appear to arouse much if any official concern.

There is an obvious contrast between the Indonesian and Philippine press. The Jakarta papers, between recurrent official crackdowns (e.g., in January 1974 and 1978) have consistently pressed against the limits of the politically possible by resorting to indirection, including feature reporting on social topics, thereby avoiding confrontation with an alert and sensitive security apparatus. Indonesian editors seem to thrive on the narrow edge, exploiting innuendo and the possibilities inherent in covering "foreign" stories, such as the crisis in Iran, which allow clever headlines about such internally taboo topics as corrupt military rulers and Muslim dissidence. In the Philippines, however, there is no tradition of this kind of thing. Prior to Martial Law the press was known for its freedom, often verging on license, but writers and editors were frequently in the service of competing political bosses, and Philippine journalists were not typically attracted to serious social issues. It is hard to avoid the conclusion that since Martial Law, except for underground and Church publications, Philippine journalists have made little real effort to follow the path of implicit criticism which has been so effective in Indonesia under equally difficult circumstances (and which is admittedly easier to admire than to imitate).

Mindanao and Timor

The two major recent cases of armed conflict in Indonesia and the Philippines, the Muslim rebellion in Mindanao and Indonesian intervention in East Timor, have one thing in common: both have resulted in much suffering and widespread violations of human rights. Aside from this, the political and social circumstances are quite different.

The Mindanao rebellion, described in chapter two, has since 1973 resulted in an estimated 10,000 government casualties, plus at least 30–50,000 civilian victims, and generated more than a million refugees.[20] Like most guerrilla wars, the conflict has entailed widespread abuse of civil and personal liberties in the insurgent areas. Despite the scale of the suffering, Mindanao was until recently rarely mentioned in discussions of Philippine human rights.[21] There are at least two reasons. First, as a traditional ethnic conflict with antecedents dating through four hundred years of American and Spanish rule, Mindanao is difficult to blame on the current regime, although its handling of the problem is certainly open to criticism. I have already observed that many Filipino critics of Marcos, both in the Philippines and abroad, are prone to the same culturally induced lack of concern about the Muslim problem which is characteristic of Christian Filipino attitudes generally, and which is indeed a root cause of the problem.

The Timor episode is complicated by violation of international law. Briefly, in 1975, following the end of the Salazar regime, Portugal abandoned her overseas empire, including East Timor, a possession with a population of 650,000. Indonesia, to which the western half of the island of Timor belonged, watched the decolonization process with alarm. When the Portuguese left, military authorities turned over stocks of NATO-standard weapons to an organization known as Fretelin, dominated by a group of Timorese and Eurasian NCOs who were left of center (precisely how far left is not certain) in their political orientation. Fretelin swiftly dominated its political rivals, the most important of which wanted continued union with Portugal.[22] The Indonesians at first professed to favor self-determination for East Timor, an act of politesse which has subsequently haunted them. In fact, there is little if any likelihood that the military authorities in Jakarta would have tolerated a genuinely independent regime regardless of its political hue. Rightly or wrongly they were convinced that an independent state would be weak and vulnerable, a channel for communist penetration of their remote eastern marches. They were initially concerned by the presence of an unassimilated Chinese minority, typical of unreconstructed, "plural" colonial societies, and this concern was aggravated by the apparently leftish character of Fretelin.

By the late summer of 1975, the Indonesians had intervened covertly against Fretelin. The result was a growing civil war. On December 7, 1975, Indonesian Army "volunteers" equipped with American weapons invaded the capital of East Timor. The invasion took place one day after Secretary of State Kissinger and President Ford had visited Jakarta, suggesting official American acquiescence in, if not approval of, the invasion. Although the Indonesians soon controlled all major towns, fighting has continued to smoulder in East Timor down to the present writing. Occurring as it did in naturally poor, arid terrain, the confict has generated starvation and disease on a massive scale. Jakarta formally incorporated East Timor in July 1976. Estimates of total casualties in the 1975 fighting vary from a low of 10,000 (favored by official American analysts) to a high, advanced by an Australian observer critical of Indonesian behavior, of between 50,000 and 100,000.

In the period immediately after the invasion both the U.N. General Assembly and the Security Council called on Indonesian forces to withdraw "without delay" and affirmed the Timorese peoples' right to self-determination. The U.S. formally supported self-determination, but within a short period made it abundantly and publicly clear that it accepted de facto Indonesian control, a point discussed at greater length below.

Comparing the Two Cases

Since no one is perfect, human rights policy inevitably requires invidious comparisons. In absolute terms the Indonesian situation is more serious. There have been greater numbers of political prisoners, and may be even when the currently scheduled releases of 1965–66 detainees are completed. Institutionalized restrictions on the press, individual liberties, and academic freedom have been more consistent and onerous in Indonesia. Outside access and monitoring have been more tolerated in the Philippines, where, as a result, Western standards of reportage have been more strenuously applied and a much more accurate and critical body of information and analysis on human rights violations is available. Only with regard to instances of torture and "disappearances"—admittedly a very serious exception—is the Philippine situation apparently worse, and this judgment must be qualified in view of the limited information available concerning conditions in remote Indonesian prisons.

The U.S. Response

U.S. human rights policy formally takes into account other elements besides the absolute level of human rights. These include other American interests, especially security, and improvement, or retrogression, in the situation. During 1978 U.S. officials twice publicly cited the prisoner release program as evidence of improvement in Indonesia.[23] In the Philippines there has been no such clear-cut trend, and the circumstances surrounding the April 1978 elections suggested regression. Nevertheless, the administration's desire to retain military bases might have prompted a relatively less critical policy. Indeed, Secretary of State Vance specifically linked the Philippines with South Korea as countries where security considerations would be overriding.[24]

In fact, however, the U.S. response has been more demanding in the case of the Philippines. The contrast was strikingly apparent in the respective "country reports on human rights practices" submitted to the Congress on January 31, 1978. The Philippine report castigated Marcos for failing to restore democracy and linked human rights violations with the Martial Law authoritarian system. (". . . No real steps have yet been taken toward the restoration of democratic government or the elimination of the more severe intrusions on individual rights.")[25] By contrast, the Indonesian report makes constant reference to the more alien aspects of Indonesian political culture to justify apparent violations. Under "denial of fair public trial," for example, it was noted that:

Indonesia contains many ethnic groups, all of whom have strong authoritarian traditions. Statutes which permit long detention without trial and which restrict freedom of speech, of the press, and of movement within the country, are deeply ingrained in Indonesian history and tradition, although contrary to internationally recognized human rights.[26]

In the realm of U.S. action the contrast is equally apparent. As early as 1974 the Senate almost voted to terminate Philippine military aid as a result of political detentions.[27] In 1977 the Congress reduced security assistance by 8½ percent ($3.5 million) below the administration's request and, despite continuing base negotiations, a similar cut was legislated in the summer of 1978.[28] On two occasions in 1976 the United States prominently abstained from Asian Development Bank loans for the Philippines not related to "basic human needs." However, since the Harkin Amendment was enacted, the administration has voted in favor of eleven other international financial institutions' ("ifi") loans for the Philippines.

The United States has intervened diplomatically on behalf of human rights victims in the Philippines with an intensity unmatched elsewhere in the region. The best-known case involved squatter organizer Trinidad Herrera, detained and tortured in May 1977.[29] More recently, official U.S. disapproval was made abundantly evident when, following the May 1978 elections, a sharp and very audible debate took place within the State Department between human rights Assistant Secretary Patricia Derian and East Asia Assistant Secretary Richard Holbrooke over the wisdom of including Manila on Vice President Mondale's Southeast Asian trip. According to a "compromise" reported in the New York Times, Ms. Derian lost her effort to have Manila dropped, but only on condition that Mondale emphasize to the Filipinos the administration's concern with human rights violations.[30]

The United States has not made public protestation of comparable intensity in the case of Indonesia, and private representations have apparently been diplomatic in every sense of the word. There have been no cuts in security assistance or abstentions on "ifi" loans for Indonesia. The nearest thing to the kind of public debate that has consistently marked Philippine human rights policy occurred in 1976, when PL 480 food aid loans to Indonesia were suspended while Jakarta supplied a certification, required by law only in the case of "gross violators" of human rights, that the food would really reach the needy.[31] (The Philippines is not a major recipient of PL 480 loans, or it would no doubt have been included in this requirement as well.)

The executive branch has not applied human rights criteria to either Mindanao or East Timor. Although there has been no involvement of American "advisers," the United States has continued to provide both Indonesia and the Philippines with military grant assistance of a specifically counterinsurgent nature (e.g., T-28 and OV-10 aircraft)[32] which as of 1978 was being used in both conflicts. In both cases, the Carter Administration has maintained a policy which assumes that the broader political benefits accruing to us from such aid relationships outweigh whatever human suffering may result, and that other weapons would be used if ours were not.

Our initial response to the East Timor case was probably indefensible on legal grounds. The Indonesians' use of American equipment violated the terms of the extant military assistance agreement, and hence U.S. law. The United States voted for the Security Council resolution of December 22, 1975 which affirmed the right of East Timorese self-determination, but abstained on subsequent measures demanding immediate Indonesian withdrawal. We reacted to Indonesian use of U.S. equipment in the December 7 invasion by subjecting military assistance shipments to "administrative delay" from January to June 1976. However, the suspension was implemented with such exquisite tract that the Indonesians were never aware that they were being chastized, nor was the Congress, and in fact some arms shipments appear to have continued throughout the period of suspension.[33] Subsequently the U.S. government "did not question" the annexation of East Timor into Indonesia, although, according to the State Department legal adviser, "this did not represent a legal judgment or endorsement of what had taken place."[34] A Congressional Reference Service analysis concluded that:

As in the case of Spanish Sahara, the United States appeared to accept the results with equanimity. Indeed, in the case of East Timor the U.S. public stance, as measured by its abstentions from voting on UN resolutions which reproved Indonesia in relatively mild terms, would seem to have been on the side of the government acquiring territory by force.[35]

The Timor issue might have faded entirely away in the United States (it remains a major public issue in Australia) had it not been for Congressman Fraser, who thought it bad precedent for the U.S. government cynically to acquiesce in the swallowing of little states by larger ones. Fraser described Timor as "the most ominous breach yet in the fight for evenhandedness in our human rights policies" and never stopped urging the United States to take a stand, in principle, against the Timor annexation, either by unilateral affirmation, or in the United Nations.[36]

In summary, the broad outlines of our human rights policy toward Indonesia and the Philippines have been similar. The Carter Administration has demonstrated its concern, and there is no doubt that both governments have been made aware that future large-scale human rights violations might affect the level of U.S. cooperation and, at the very least, result in controversy embarrassing to us. However, we have not been willing to make more than token changes in security relations, including concessional military aid, because of human rights violations. Abstentions on "ifi" loans have been symbolic. Within these fairly modest boundaries, the policy has been applied with much more vigor to the Philippines.

Why the Difference

The apparent inconsistency results partly from the judgment of many informed observers, both in and out of government, that Indonesia is making progress on human rights while the Philippine problem remains constant. Moreover, it is a common perception, especially among American liberals, that the Philippines, like Beelzebub, is doubly damned for having fallen from a state of democratic grace. Indonesia after all has had virtually no experience with representative institutions, leaving aside the chaotic postindependence years, and the fact that the events of 1965–66 came in response to a violent communist challenge inclines us to sympathize with the authoritarian result. Military rule in Indonesia is further perceived, not wholly without reason, as a natural if not inevitable mechanism for coping with extraordinary hazards of ethnic and regional conflict.

The United States has also been tougher on the Philippines because of certain special relationship factors discussed at greater length in the preceding chapter. The human rights issue has naturally been amplified and exploited by the anti-Marcos forces in the American Filipino community, including exiled political leaders like Raul Manglapus. They have used it effectively to advance their argument for the termination of U.S. aid to Marcos. They believe that such a move would, by removing a traditional source of legitimacy, sharply erode his domestic political base. The efforts of the anti-Marcos forces have been supplemented by the home offices of missionaries concerned with human rights. Congressmen with substantial ethnic Filipino constituencies have naturally been especially sensitive to anti-Marcos pressures and hence to human rights. One of them, Representative Yvonne Burke of Los Angeles (since retired), introduced the successful 1977 Philippine security aid reduction, and another, the late Leo Ryan of San Francisco, subsequently murdered in Guyana, did so again in 1978.

Quite in contrast, the Indonesians, starting as a more or less unknown quantity in the Congress, have been able to make a positive, albeit modest, lobbying effort on their own behalf, largely through the activity of the government-sponsored Center for International and Strategic Studies, which operates under the aegis of President Suharto's principal political strategist, General Ali Murtopo. In general, there has been little congressional concern about Indonesian human rights violations, and Fraser was almost alone in his dogged pursuit of the East Timor issue. The contrast in the congressional relations of the two countries was indicated by the behavior of the late Representative Ryan. At a May 1976 hearing he joined with Wayne Hays in a strong attack on the credentials of Carmel Budiardjo, head of the controversial TAPOL group, expressing the opinion that under the circumstances of 1966 the mass detentions in Indonesia were fully justified.[37] However, as noted above, Ryan consistently supported efforts to cut Philippine military aid, and in 1977 he proudly described himself as the quasi-representative of escaped Marcos opponents Eugenio Lopez, Jr. and Sergio Osmeña III, both resident, with many wealthy relatives, in his district.[38]

Americans have assumed, far too easily in my opinion, that we have much more leverage with the Filipinos than with the Indonesians, and should use it. The assumption is vintage special relationship, reflecting the greater degree of possessiveness and familiarity normal between members of the same family, but it also reflects a totally different image of the two countries. "Manila," redolent of hemp, cigars, and wartime memories, has a more familiar ring to us than any other Pacific place name save perhaps "Honolulu." "Jakarta" is something else again. With its tinkling gamelan orchestras, brooding volcanoes, and Balinese allure, Indonesia epitomizes the remote and unpredictable. Although virtually all Americans tend to take Filipino friendship for granted, the comparatively few who are aware of Indonesia know that she was at one time hostile to us, was a founder of the nonaligned movement, and has a tradition of revolution and volatile nationalism well personified by Sukarno. Indonesian authoritarianism, evoked by bloodbath and infinite cultural diversity, is sensed to be beyond the reach of the West. What can be done to influence a country whose President, in moments of deepest perplexity, consults not his Berkeley mafia or even the IMF but a Hindu-Buddhist seer in Central Java?

Such impressionistic considerations are not without weight even among foreign policy experts. They have been encouraged by the Indonesians, who are skilled at explicating their own unique political traditions, from decision-making by consensus (musjawara-mufakat) to the mysteries of pancasila, the five guiding principles of the State. Resulting attitudes complement American appreciation of Indonesia's population, size, strategic archipelago configuration and mineral resources—in short, her status as one of the world's "new influentials"[39]—to dictate caution and emphasis on quiet diplomacy. Above all, the result helps to explain why in general Americans (including the Congress) have not made authoritarianism per se an issue in Indonesia.

In the Philippines, Martial Law has been an issue despite formal U.S. protestations to the contrary. And since American opinion does play a significant role in domestic Philippine politics, U.S. human rights policy has impinged on the legitimacy and survival of the present regime. But the result has hardly confirmed the assumption of greater U.S. influence. President Marcos has reacted to the threat with the kind of virtuoso tactical maneuvering that has been the hallmark of Filipino politicians since the days of the late, great Manuel Quezon, probably the most skilled who ever lived. He has employed a combination of rhetorical agreement (he says he is every bit as much for human rights as we are), indignant denial, and counterattack, interweaving human rights with other U.S.-Philippine issues, particularly the base negotiations.

Consider the record of 1977–78. Timing suggests that President Marcos' decision to renew the stalled base negotiations in August 1977 was at least in part a tactical response to the heavy U.S. human rights initiative which had commenced in May over the case of detained squatter organizer Trinidad Herrera. The Philippine president probably did not envision a rapid base settlement (the negotiations subsequently bogged down again) but he undoubtedly hoped that by flashing his trump card he would hold U.S. human rights pressures to a minimum, and perhaps extract signs of favor in other areas. He was correct. President Carter received Mrs. Marcos in New York in October, an unprecedented encounter largely ignored by the U.S. press but heavily publicized in Manila.[40]

U.S. human rights policy henceforth became even more entangled in Philippine domestic politics. On August 22, 1977, before a controversial World Peace Through Law Conference in Manila, President Marcos announced his intention to hold parliamentary elections.[41] He subsequently claimed (and the claim was widely believed) that the United States pressured him to do so because the State Department assumed that even semicredible elections would facilitate U.S. congressional acceptance of a military aid compensation package linked to a new base agreement.[42] The election campaign allowed Marcos to indulge in such time-tested histrionics as charging that the CIA was aiding his principal opponent, the imprisoned Senator Aquino.[43] The elections themselves, marked by obvious manipulation and the detention of opposition candidates, resulted in a deluge of bad publicity in the American press. If anything they damaged the prospects for U.S. congressional acceptance of a new base agreement, stimulating a critical letter to Marcos from members of the House. This unfortunate if wholly foreseeable denouement led directly to the debate in Washington, mentioned earlier, over Vice President Mondale's trip, a dispute in which both parties assumed that the visit would signify U.S. approval of the elections and enhance the legitimacy of the Philippine government. With U.S.-Philippine relations in one of their periodic phases of high altercation, the Vice President arrived in Manila to be greeted by headlines, in a paper edited by the wife of a Marcos aide, reminding America of the many human rights violations which have occurred at the U.S. bases over the years. Subsequently Mondale announced $41 million in economic aid agreements, met with some opposition leaders (but not the imprisoned Aquino), and signed a noncommittal agreement in principle on the seemingly endless base negotiations.[44]

Two months later, whatever goodwill might have been

recouped by the Mondale visit was dissipated when, on one of her frequent trips to the United States, Mrs. Marcos visited Capitol Hill and tried to explain her government's position to the congressmen who had signed the letter criticizing the elections. They pelted her with rude questions, and she returned to Manila much distressed.[45] The next step could almost have been predicted by any old Philippines watcher. Within a few weeks the President's daughter Imee was leading an antibase campaign, and there were dark rumors of friendlier relations and security cooperation between Manila and Moscow.[46] While such tactics may seem transparent, they are frequent enough to alarm our military authorities, who are painfully aware of the potential vulnerability of the sprawling base facilities to Philippine hostility whether contrived or genuine.

The roller-coaster emotionalism and confusion of issues that marked this year-long period are broadly typical of U.S.-Philippine relations. Under the circumstances it is hardly surprising that neither the cause of human rights nor the evolution of a rational U.S.-Philippine security relationship has prospered by juxtaposition. The record suggests that Marcos genuinely perceives American human rights policy as shrouding active hostility to himself and his wife. His relative success in maintaining the fundamentals of the U.S.-Philippine relationship, without altering the character of Martial Law to any discernible degree, has demonstrated that (as is so often the case with small allies) his effective leverage may be greater than ours—particularly as long as the United States is unwilling to move toward a significant revision of our military presence.

Conclusion

The representative of an international human rights organization recently asked an experienced diplomat how, in his opinion, the foreign ministries of Southeast Asia view President Carter's human rights policy. They see it, he replied, as the latest in a long series of American enthusiasms:

these things have come at them over the years in infinite variety, from counter-insurgency to malaria control. In local eyes they have usually, in the past, added up to a bonanza of jeeps and type-writers. None have lasted very long.

Their reaction to human rights usually boils down to polite evasion. If we mean business we can have some impact on them, of course, mainly by *not* doing something they want us to do. They value our relationship very highly and there are certain things they very much want from us . . . ranging from small but reliable sup-plies of arms, to the infinitely more important matter of markets for their commodities.[47]

Critics of the policy have contended that the requisite min-gling of morality with expediency merely results in the "triv-ialization"[48] of human rights, and Stanley Hoffman has writ-ten of the hell of good intentions.[49] In April 1978 no less an authority than Congressman Fraser warned that:

in some respects the rhetoric [of human rights] has outrun the de-velopment of implementing policies. In other respects the rhetoric has an overly ambitious ring to it, as though the U.S., having aban-doned its role as world policemen, is substituting for the uniform of a policeman the robes of a judge—this time, a world judge.[50]

As noted earlier, recent events suggest that the Carter Administration's enthusiasm for human rights has already peaked and that counterreaction expressed through neglect is, at this writing, well under way. The defeat of Fraser (which apparently had nothing to do with his human rights position) may have pulled the keystone from the highly effec-tive congressional involvement of recent years. Specifically with regard to the Philippines, the death or retirement of sev-eral anti-Marcos legislators (including Representatives Leo Ryan and Yvonne Burke) will have some short-term impact. But in the longer run human rights will not go away. Viet-nam and the activism of recent years have sensitized Ameri-can liberal opinion to the issue, and a substantial human rights lobby, including church groups, is now a permanent part of the Washington scene. Legal and bureaucratic sanc-tions created in the last few years will remain, although some (such as State's Humanitarian Affairs Bureau) are vulnerable to neglect, sabotage or circumvention. The popularization of human rights and its proven political appeal insure that it will continue to be used and misused by individuals and interests aiming at other targets ranging from the international financial institutions to specific foreign regimes. Country lobbies such as the one which inspired congressional concern in the case of the Philippines will also remain with us. Under these circumstances the question cannot be whether to have a human rights policy, but how to make it effective and durable and protect it as much as possible from flagrant abuse. With this aim in mind, our experience in Indonesia and the Philippines suggests both pitfalls and useful precedents.

As a general proposition it seems undeniable that a human rights policy marked by massive hypocrisy and tokenism will in the long run alienate American public opinion and do more harm than good across the board. In other words the policy must function as a reasonably consistent aspect of our overall relationship with friendly authoritarian states. This objective is obviously not an easy one and in most cases it will be impossible to achieve absolutely, but in the newly relaxed region of the world where Indonesia and the Philippines are located there is no reason why we cannot reconcile the demands of morality and expediency more effectively than at present. The most obvious step would be the termination of military aid as a means of expressing "supportiveness," a step proposed earlier on more fundamental political grounds. It violates both consistency and credibility to advocate human rights while simultaneously providing the lethal equipment, on the basis of officially sanctioned arrangements, for the kind of internal conflict, involving no U.S. interest, which has been taking place in Mindanao and Timor. The basic contradiction between concessional military aid and human rights derives from the fact that authoritarian regimes will inevitably use force against domestic political opponents when their political survival is threatened. In an imperfect world, however, weapons sales on commercial terms may in some cases be defensible, because they can meet the security needs of our authoritarian friends without implying the same degree of U.S. involvement and approval as outright military aid, and because, in the old but irrefutable argument, if we do not sell, someone else will.

The frustrating result of our Philippine human rights effort to date suggests the wisdom of restricting policy emphasis to torture, arbitrary arrest, and other crimes against the person, and of excluding pressures to alter systems of government. There are many reasons why, in the special case of the Philippines, American criticism of Martial Law is likely to have negative effects. Even under the Carter Administration the main thrust of U.S. policy has in fact sanctioned Philippine authoritarianism. To express disapproval suggests either *ad hominem* hostility to President Marcos or a degree of insincerity which strongly implies that strictures against torture are equally insincere.

Attacks on Martial Law in official American critiques of the Philippine human rights situation reek of the old and questionable assumption that the Philippines has strayed from the path of democracy and needs another dose of tutelage to find the way. Such criticism overlooks the unpalatable fact that there is much in Philippine society to suggest that authoritarianism may be no more a passing phase than it is in Indonesia, Thailand, Malaysia, or Singapore. It is likely to provoke unhealthy and ambivalent cross-currents of reaction, pleasing those Filipinos, and there are many, who still believe that we can and should play *deus ex machina* in Philippine affairs, but also arousing nationalist resentment.

All this is subsidiary to the more fundamental point that in the Philippines or anywhere else—certainly anywhere else in Southeast Asia—no human rights policy is likely to get very far if it appears to pose a fundamental challenge to the existing political order, much less to suggest a foreign-sponsored formula for change. If the Filipinos, or others, move toward democracy on their own terms, whether revolutionary or evolutionary, we should applaud and make every effort to increase cooperation after the fact. But the day has past when we can profitably attempt to be involved in initiating the transition.

Human rights not only requires a balance of morality with expediency; it can pit one morality against another.

Next to military aid the most obvious problem is the potential conflict between our desire to isolate regimes which violate human rights and the degree of cooperation which may be required if we are to help people meet development needs. Thus far in the case of Indonesia and the Philippines, the conflict has been more latent than real. There has been acrimonious debate between the human rights and regional bureaus in the State Department over symbolic abstentions on international bank loans, but in no case thus far have human rights considerations had any specific negative impact on multilateral aid disbursements. This may not always be the case. The Harkin Amendment, which applied human rights criteria to U.S. votes in the World Bank and its regional counterparts, may be the harbinger of a more vigorous effort to impose a variety of political criteria on "indirect aid," an effort which may be launched by genuine idealists but will no doubt be supported by those who are hostile to the international institutions for other reasons.

If so, the current practice of resolving the human rights versus basic human needs debate by a typical Washington process of bureaucratic competition may need to be replaced, or at least supplemented, by something a little more cerebral. For a start, we could do a much better job of attempting to understand and strengthen the human rights impact of present and future aid and cultural exchange programs. Popular participation is one of many areas where questions still outnumber answers. To cite one example, traditional Indonesian village hierarchies may be (as elsewhere in Asia) even more politically conservative than their national counterparts. If such hierarchies are the principal vehicle for "popular participation," the result could be the opposite of that hoped for by many advocates. If, on the other hand, new development-oriented organizations attract the least advantaged, those who in theory are the primary targets of our aid effort, the eventual result is more likely to be liberalizing. The United States still has at its disposal a vast arsenal of expertise concerning the institutions of an open society, including business, unions, the legal profession, the press, and many more, which can be transmitted through multilateral and bilateral programs at many levels. Renewed efforts in this traditional area are probably still the best hope for the future.

Human rights policy requires a mix of would-be omniscience (playing judge to the world, in Fraser's phrase) and cultural relativism, or understanding mitigating circumstances, which is exceedingly difficult to keep in balance. In the case of Indonesia U.S. policy has perhaps been unbalanced toward cultural relativism; in the Philippines we have stumbled heavily into the pitfall of postcolonial callousness, blind to the fact that years of special relationship have created a web of mutual interests and above all a pathological, reactive dependency on the Philippine side, which should dictate more rather than less tact, understanding, and even humility on our part.

Our Indonesian experience suggests that where human rights are involved quiet diplomacy is still preferable, even though, as everyone is aware, it can also become an alibi for nonaction, as it did in the Kissinger years. Further internationalization of the human rights effort is also desirable. If the Indonesians are now making a substantial effort to respond, it is because they do not see the issue as wholly the result of American initiative, since in fact there has been well-dispersed expression of concern, especially significant in Holland and Great Britain, for many years. It is vastly easier to accommodate outside criticism under such circumstances than when it is perceived as emanating entirely from a former colonial power.

For the future, the United States should continue to cooperate with nongovernment organizations like Amnesty International. If and when the opportunity arises we should encourage regional human rights machinery similar to the increasingly significant western hemisphere effort (which is as old as its equivalent at the United Nations) represented by the Inter-American Commission, the American Convention, and the newly created Inter-American Court of Human Rights. Although similar regional attention to human rights is beginning to stir in Africa, there is as yet nothing of the kind evident in Asia, either within ASEAN or elsewhere. Although the heavy identification of the United States with human rights in the eyes of most Asians will do nothing to make a regional approach any easier, this inhibition will diminish in time, and there are many Southeast Asians who would welcome such a development. It is only through this kind of institutional growth that human rights policy may begin to achieve the durability and sustained attention it deserves.

Chapter Five

American Prosperity and the Island World: Investment, Trade, and the North-South Agenda

> The dominating fact about the islands is that,
> like Croesus and John D. Rockefeller, Jr., they
> are rich. They are the Big Loot of Asia.
> —From a chapter on Indonesia in
> John Gunther's *Inside Asia* (1939)

The ravages of war and anticolonial revolution, followed by three decades of struggle toward development, should have demolished the myth of island Southeast Asia as an area of easy wealth. Even in Gunther's day the Big Loot was for the Dutch, not the Indonesians, who in some ways are still paying the bill for colonial prosperity. Yet despite greatly altered circumstances, the economic significance of the region for external powers, particularly the United States and Japan, remains great. This chapter attempts to refine this assertion with regard to Indonesia and the Philippines by examining some aspects of the American economic stake in the two countries.

The discussion does not presume to confirm or refute the fundamental Marxist argument that economic interests are determining, which (at least in its more sophisticated forms) is based on global considerations and is therefore impossible to debate at a regional or country level. It begins on a more modest level by describing present levels of U.S. trade, investment, and private bank lending, in full awareness that the statistics, which in many cases are highly imperfect, can at best suggest the character of American involvement. In no other area is it more important to bear in mind that interests, like beauty, lie in the eye of the beholder. If Americans perceive Southeast Asia as a resource cornucopia, which to a lessening extent they still do, that in itself may well be more important than economic reality.

The discussion then moves on to consider the argument that regardless of our direct stake, we have a clear if secondary interest insofar as the region is vital to Japanese prosperity. Levels of Japanese trade and investment are reviewed for both Indonesia and the Philippines and (since our concern for Japan is generally cast in regional terms) for the entire five-nation ASEAN grouping. The facts suggest that whereas the significance of Southeast Asia to the American and Japanese economies may be debatable, the importance of the economic superpowers to Southeast Asia is without question a matter of mortal concern to all the countries in the region, including Indonesia and the Philippines.

What are the implications of this unbalanced relationship? It is partly the inevitable consequence of disparity in size: small countries (and small economies) will always be dependent to some degree on big ones. Yet there is general agreement that the present imbalance is not healthy, and that failure to correct it will have adverse long-range consequences, both political and economic, for the United States. The question of development assistance is reserved for a later essay. This one examines several of the other issues on the north-south agenda, including commodity marketing, trade in manufactured goods, and the problem of debt management, as they affect Indonesia and the Philippines.

The chapter concludes by emphasizing the enormous and complex problem posed by the growing relative importance of U.S. economic behavior in our relations with Third World countries generally. The private sector is already the single most potent agent of American involvement with Indonesia and the Philippines. But the United States government, whipsawed by the contradictory forces generated by our domestic experience with private capital, is ill organized to interact creatively with this massive phenomenon, whether in terms of analysis, regulation, or encouragement.

U.S. Investment in the Philippines

The first Governor-General of our new island possession, William Howard Taft, dreamed of Philippine development stimulated by an unrestricted flow of American capital and entrepreneurship. But antiretentionist forces in the United States—those people who for ideological, economic, or racist reasons did not want closer association with the Philippines—achieved legislation which effectively limited American investment. With the establishment of mutual free trade in 1909, U.S. exporters had unrestricted access to the Philippine market, and there was little incentive for either American or Filipino investors to engage in local manufacturing. Aside from tariff policy, American overlordship brought little in the way of dramatic economic restructuring, serving rather to strengthen the position of the existing agrocommercial elite. Direct American investment, while highly visible, remained limited. It was estimated at about $160 million in the mid-1930s, and was concentrated in public utilities, sugar milling, and mining.[1]

The parity provisions of the 1946 Philippine Trade Act, which treated American citizens as nationals in the areas of resource exploitation and public utilities, were a deliberate effort to encourage U.S. investment. However, Philippine nationalism was able to diminish if not eliminate the intended effect of this measure during the fifties, in part through a policy of import substitution. Applying import and exchange controls, the Philippine government engineered a shift in incentives away from the export sector toward manufacturing for the domestic market, greatly favoring those Filipino entrepreneurs who were fortunate enough to obtain foreign exchange at windfall exchange rates. While the import substitution system limited the ability of American investors to repatriate their profits, it also encouraged them to reinvest in commerce and manufacture, accounting for an overall increase in American direct investment to a level of $415 million by 1963.[2] But during the same period there was net American disinvestment in the very sectors which had been the intended targets of the parity provisions, natural resources and public utilities.

In 1962 President Macapagal dismantled the exchange controls, signaling the end of the import substitution era. The more extreme apostles of Philippine economic nationalism have remained bitterly critical of this move, which they regard as a betrayal of indigenous entrepreneurship,[3] and indeed it was in some ways a more significant economic watershed than the declaration of Martial Law ten years later. But a more convincing case can be made that Filipinization continued to dominate economic policymaking. Through both legislation and regulation, the government clamped down on many aspects of American investment, especially in banking and utilities. The Philippine courts upheld new restrictions on foreign ownership of land. The so-called Investment Incentives Act of 1967 reserved many areas for Philippine investors and obligated the non-Filipino to meet the constitutional provision requiring 60 percent Filipino equity ownership within twenty years.

More important, political circumstances began to alter the foreign investment climate. The Laurel-Langley Agreement which had succeeded the Philippine Trade Act of 1946 was due to expire in 1974, and it seemed unlikely that it would be replaced by a legal framework equally favorable to the American investor. By the early seventies, Philippine nationalism was entering a radical phase. Professedly Marxist demonstrations against the U.S. Embassy may, in some cases, have been encouraged by Filipino capitalists who wished to acquire American holdings at fire sale prices. But this did not in the least diminish the unnerving effect of growing turmoil on the expatriate business community. Professor Frank Golay has estimated that no less than $290 million in direct U.S. investment was divested from 1962 to 1974, and while some new investment continued, the overall level stagnated.[4]

Golay notes that during the fifteen-year period ending in 1974 the ratio of U.S. direct investment in the Philippines to all U.S. direct investment dropped from 1.25 percent to 0.6 percent.[5]

With the declaration of Martial Law in September 1972, the amber-to-red light previously flashed to foreign investors changed to bright, unambiguous green, or so it seemed at the time. A reporter for the *Far Eastern Economic Review* supplied this assessment in 1974:

> For investors, the enforcement of a more stable climate has been a key factor in the rush to the Philippines over the past eighteen months. Out went the squabbling politicians, the lawless society, the uncertain investment regulations, the economic nationalism and oligarchical self-interest, to be replaced by a powerful regime opening its arms to foreign investment and determined to keep the lid on any opposition.[6]

Although the change of climate was more important than anything else, the Martial Law regime also took some specific steps to encourage foreign investment, such as opening the banking sector to non-Filipinos for the first time, and signaling clearly to the U.S. government that the expiration of Laurel-Langley would not injure U.S. interests, most of which had already prepared for transition by adjusting to the nonpreferential legal status applicable to other foreigners.[7] But despite Marcos' efforts, the increase in risk-capital inflow was only moderate, neither as much as the government desired nor as substantial as that received by other countries in the region. According to a 1971 government survey, total foreign investment outstanding at the end of 1970 was $650 million, of which 79 percent, or about $514 million, was American.[8] This figure compares with $724 million in new foreign investment recorded by the Philippine Central Bank between February 1970 and June 1977. The U.S. share during this period dropped to 45 percent.[9] U.S. investment continued to drop steadily in relation to total U.S. foreign investment and to U.S. investment in all less-developed Asian countries, recovering only slightly after 1975.

U.S. Investment in Indonesia

American investment in the Dutch East Indies was restricted to oil, rubber, and some minor miscellany, including a General Motors assembly plant on the Batavia (now Jakarta) harbor front. Goodyear and Uniroyal rubber plantations in northern Sumatra were among the largest in the world. The oil companies included Stanvac and Caltex Pacific, which together with Royal Dutch Shell were the prewar "Big Three" of the petroleum industry. Shortly after World War II Caltex began to exploit the fabulous Minas field in central Sumatra. It was soon producing the majority of Indonesia's oil, and together with neighboring Caltex fields has continued to do so down to the present day. But in general U.S. investment in Indonesia was, until recently, relatively insignificant.

The advent of Indonesia's "New Order" in 1966–67 brought a much more profound shift in economic policy than was the case in the Philippines under Martial Law. The communist-dominated closing years of the Sukarno era had been unremittingly hostile to foreign capitalism. In 1963, after tense negotiations in Tokyo, Sukarno approved new twenty-year "contracts of work" with the oil companies. Although they lost ownership rights to concession areas (all oil exploitation was henceforth in theory reserved for state corporations), they retained full management control of operations.[10] In Sumatra, one major rubber plantation operator, Goodyear, hung on by a thread. The other, Uniroyal, closed down. New U.S. or other foreign investment was, under the circumstances, out of the question.

The initial response of foreign investors to the "open door" policy announced by the Suharto government in January 1967 was dramatic. By the end of the year the Indonesian foreign investment board had approved the huge sum of $6.6 billion exclusive of the oil sector. It was concentrated mainly in manufacture ($3.7 billion, or 56 percent), mining ($1.5 billion, or 23 percent), and forestry ($0.6 billion, or 8.6 percent).[11] American firms pledged only 8.6 percent of the total compared to 37.4 percent for the front-runner, Japan. Such "approval" figures are often misleading, and in the case of Indonesia estimates of actual or realized investment range from 43 percent to only 30 percent.[12] In recent years, foreign investment generally and U.S. investment in particular has slowed. Only one U.S. project, worth $15 million, was approved in 1977.[13]

Because of its vital importance to the Indonesian economy, the petroleum sector, as in the Sukarno era, has been isolated from many of the constraints that affect other sectors, and the great majority of U.S. investment has been in oil. According to one report, foreign oil companies have spent an estimated $7 billion in Indonesia since 1967, of which about $6 billion, or 85 percent, has been by American companies.[14] The U.S. Embassy estimates that "total cumulative capital spending by U.S. companies in the petroleum sector probably approaches a level of $4 billion through mid-1977."[15] (Not all of this is reflected in the Commerce Department's "book value" investment figures but, as noted below, this omission is not unique to the oil sector.) In the last decade, more than thirty U.S. companies have signed production-sharing contracts with the Indonesian state oil company, Pertamina. The production-sharing formula, pioneered by Pertamina in 1967, differs from the 1963 "contracts of work" (still held by Caltex and Stanvac) on two points: first, Pertamina, not the foreign company, possesses overall management control; second, as distinct from profit sharing, the crude oil itself is divided between the state company and the contracting company.[16]

While production sharing proved acceptable to the oil industry (and has been adopted by many other Third World countries), reckless international borrowing by Pertamina led to its financial collapse in 1975. As a result, the Indonesian government found itself in dire need of revenues and initiated new contracts to provide Pertamina with a greater share of the product. Furthermore, in mid-1976, the U.S. Internal Revenue Service changed its accounting system and effectively disallowed further tax credits for oil delivered by U.S. companies to Pertamina under production-sharing requirements. A two-year period of uncertainty ensued while the Indonesian government and the IRS worked out a new formula.[17]

These developments, combined with the recession-related global slump in demand for oil, caused a considerable drop in exploration and investment. Nevertheless, it is certain that large sums of money will continue to be invested in Indonesian oil. As of 1978 at least $4 billion in natural gas, refining, petrochemical, and storage projects were pending or under discussion,[18] and while much of the capital will be Japanese, it is a sure thing that much will be American.

The Islands and Overall Investment

What can be concluded about the relative importance of these two countries in the overall pattern of American global investment? The tables below (5.1 and 5.2) are based on Commerce Department book value figures. Cumulative in nature, they reflect neither depreciation nor appreciated replacement value resulting from inflation. A more serious drawback in an increasingly globalized economy is that book value data reflect only outflows from the U.S. parent company, or other expenditures which affect the U.S. balance of payments account. They do not show capital raised locally or on international eurodollar markets that lend hard currencies held outside their country of origin. Nevertheless, for all their drawbacks, the book value figures are still the best comparative tool available for measuring trends in U.S. investment.[19]

On the basis of book value, the Philippine share of U.S. worldwide, direct investment fell from 0.94 percent in 1966 to 0.59 percent in 1975, rising slightly to 0.61 percent in 1977. Over the same period, the Indonesian share rose from 0.20 percent to 1.3 percent in 1975, recently falling back to 0.76 percent (see table 5.1).

Within a narrower framework, the Philippine share of U.S. investment in the developing countries of Asia fell from 37.2 to 14.6 percent between 1966 and 1977, while the Indonesian share rose from 8.1 to 18.2 percent. As a historical

Table 5.1 U.S. Direct Investment in Indonesia and the Philippines Cumulative Year-End Position, 1966–77 (Millions $)

Year	Indonesia				Philippines			
	Total	A	B	C	Total	A	B	C
1966	106	.20%	.76%	8.1%	486	.94%	3.5%	37.2%
1967	107	.19%	.72%	7.1%	550	.97%	3.7%	36.3%
1968	106	.17%	.64%	6.2%	592	.96%	3.6%	34.8%
1969	122	.18%	.69%	6.2%	672	.99%	3.8%	34.1%
1970	218	.29%	1.1%	9.6%	640	.85%	3.3%	28.3%
1971	399	.48%	1.9%	14.4%	663	.80%	3.2%	23.9%
1972	563	.63%	2.5%	17.5%	644	.72%	2.9%	20.0%
1973	797	.79%	3.5%	20.9%	656	.65%	2.9%	17.2%
1974	706	.64%	3.6%	15.6%	718	.65%	3.6%	15.9%
1975	1,587	1.30%	6.1%	27.6%	738	.59%	2.8%	12.8%
1976	1,475	1.10%	5.1%	24.9%	831	.61%	2.9%	14.0%
1977	1,138	.76%	3.4%	18.2%	913	.61%	2.7%	14.6%

Notes:
  A = % of total U.S. global direct investment.
  B = % of total U.S. direct investment in developing countries.
  C = % of total U.S. direct investment in Asian developing countries (i.e., all of Asia except Japan, Australia, and New Zealand)
All figures represent the book value of investments

SOURCE: U.S. Department of Commerce, raw data.

Table 5.2 U.S. Direct Investment by Sector (Millions $)

Sector	Indonesia			Philippines		
	1966	1971	1976	1966	1971	1976
Manufacturing	0	17	100	166	284	352
Petroleum	97	271	1,167	(A)	187	192(C)
Mining/Smelting	0	(A)	(A)	(A)	(A)	(A)
Trade	(B)	2	3	29	(A)	21
Finance/Insurance	2	(A)	7	9	20	84
Utilities/Transport	0	(A)	(A)	29	(A)	21
Others	7	(A)	(A)	34	(A)	(A)
All sectors	106	399	1,475	408	663	831

Notes:
  (A) = Data were suppressed to avoid disclosure of data of individual corporations.
  (B) = An amount between −$500 thousand and +$500 thousand.
  (C) = "Petroleum" investment in the Philippines is confined largely to marketing and refining facilities.

SOURCE: U.S. Department of Commerce, raw data.

portrait, the figures portray divergent trends on the part of the American overseas investor: a fairly steady decline from a colonial plateau in the Philippines; a dramatic increase in Indonesia, but for the most part limited to the petroleum sector. In the medium-term future, the trends should converge as the oil bonanza recedes in Indonesia and as the Philippine strategy of manufacturing exports develops further. Overall the figures reflect the impressionistic conclusion on the part of many investors that neither the Philippines nor Indonesia rates as a prime target for American venture capital.

Trade

The total turnover of U.S. trade with the Philippines in 1978 was $2.2 billion (see table 5.3). From 1973 to 1978, U.S.-Philippine trade grew at an average annual rate of 17.3 percent, just under the 18.5 percent annual rate at which U.S. global trade expanded over the same six-year period.[20] Since 1973 the growth of U.S. imports from the Philippines has slightly outpaced the growth of U.S. exports to the Philip-

Table 5.3 U.S. Trade with the Philippines (Millions $)

	1967	1973	1974	1975	1976	1977	1978
Exports							
Foodstuffs	76.5	80.3	128.8	117.8	134.8	145.9	136.3
Raw materials/Fuels	31.7	53.9	78.0	81.1	57.1	71.6	119.9
Industrial & Chemical							
Products	306.4	341.3	514.6	595.5	587.2	587.9	739.5
Others	3.1	9.4	10.0	15.2	9.8	9.7	13.3
Total Exports	417.7	484.9	731.4	809.6	788.8	815.1	1009.0
Imports							
Foodstuffs	180.3	330.4	585.8	297.1	317.7	396.1	293.5
Raw Materials/Fuels	123.7	177.7	323.0	236.6	235.1	303.5	325.7
Industrial & Chemical							
Products	73.9	150.6	175.0	221.4	323.1	397.0	576.4
Others	2.5	4.0	7.3	11.4	11.5	6.9	10.4
Total Imports	380.4	662.7	1,091.1	756.5	887.4	1,103.5	1206.8
Surplus/Deficit	+37.3	−177.8	−359.7	+53.1	−98.6	−288.4	−197.8

SOURCE: U.S. Department of Commerce, raw data.

Table 5.4 U.S. Trade with Indonesia (Millions $)

	1967	1973	1974	1975	1976	1977	1978
Exports							
Foodstuffs	16.4	139.2	41.0	63.9	168.5	148.0	211.7
Raw Materials/Fuels	12.6	56.4	71.3	65.5	75.5	107.7	127.5
Industrial & Chemical							
Products	38.6	235.7	405.3	666.1	776.7	493.8	373.1
Others	1.0	3.8	5.3	7.3	4.8	5.1	7.4
Total Exports	68.6	435.1	552.9	802.8	1,025.5	754.6	719.7
Imports							
Foodstuffs	60.5	77.2	109.4	82.2	160.6	310.7	247.1
Raw Materials/Fuels	109.8	394.4	1,532.2	2,095.1	2,787.5	3,101.3	3,225.0
Industrial & Chemical							
Products	2.8	24.7	84.3	43.3	56.1	85.1	129.6
Others	8.6	2.6	1.0	1.3	2.9	3.1	4.7
Total Imports	181.7	498.7	1,717.9	2,221.9	3,007.1	3,491.2	3,606.9
Surplus/Deficit	−113.1	−63.6	−1,195.0	−1,419.1	−1,181.6	−2,736.6	−2,887.2

SOURCE: U.S. Department of Commerce, raw data.

pines, leading to modest American deficits in each of the last six years save one.

The composition of U.S.-Philippine commerce has changed markedly over the last decade. For example, the share of manufactures in U.S. imports from the Philippines rose from 19 percent in 1967 to 48 percent in 1978. Although the definition of "manufactures" is liberal, including handicrafts and processed primary products, this statistic also reflects successful Philippine efforts to develop exports of garments and electronic components.[21] In 1975 sugar and coconut oil were the chief U.S. imports from the Philiipines, accounting for 26 percent and 21 percent, respectively, of total imports. In 1978 the leaders were coconut oil (still 21 percent), garments (16.5 percent), sugar (down to 13 percent, thanks in part to a depressed world market), and electronic components (10.7 percent).

United States trade with Indonesia was worth $4.3 billion in 1978 (see table 5.4). Mostly as a result of OPEC price hikes, the total value of U.S.-Indonesian trade has increased nearly three times as fast as American global trade since 1973. Although U.S. exports to Indonesia have grown at a respectable rate, they have not nearly kept pace with U.S. imports. Oil continues to dominate the latter, accounting for about four-fifths of the total in 1976. Other major imports include natural rubber, coffee, spices, teas, seafood, and fruit. U.S. exports are predominantly manufactures. In 1977, when the downturn in Indonesian oil exploration caused American exports of machinery to fall, the United States incurred a deficit of $2.7 billion in its bilateral trade account with Indonesia.

Overall, American dependence on the legendary natural wealth of the archipelago is rather minor. In reality, most raw materials from Indonesia and the Philippines go to industries in Japan and other Asian countries. Only for three major commodities—tin, natural rubber, and perhaps crude oil— can U.S. imports be construed as critically important. In 1977 the United States obtained 10.3 percent of its tin imports and 47.6 percent of its natural rubber imports from Indonesia.[22] From the Philippines, the United States purchased 25.8 percent of its sugar, 100 percent of its copra, and 98.3 percent of its coconut oil. The Philippines is also a major source of chromium, which is otherwise found only in Zimbabwe, South Africa, and the USSR.[23]

Because of its low sulfur content, Indonesian crude oil is in high demand by pollution-conscious industries in the United States and Japan (see table 5.5). In September 1973, before the oil crisis, Indonesia ranked fifth among our foreign oil suppliers. In 1976 it provided one-tenth of U.S. imports, rising to third on the list before falling to sixth in 1977 as Alaskan North Slope oil began to compete with Indonesian oil on the West Coast. Similarly, global recession has contributed to the decline in Japanese importation of Indonesian oil since 1973. Regardless of these recent developments, Indonesia's "sweet crude" should remain an important component of American and Japanese medium-term energy mixes. Over the long haul, the cardinal uncertainty about Indonesian oil exports will be supply, not demand. Indonesian officials have warned that if alternate energy sources are not developed, growing domestic requirement will totally con-

Table 5.5 (I.) U.S. and Japanese Imports of Indonesian
Crude Oil (%)

	1973	1974	1975	1976	1977
Percent U.S. Imports[a]	7.2	8.2	9.2	10.1	7.6
Percent Indonesian Exports[b]	22.0	27.0	36.0	41.0	
Percent Japanese Imports[a]	18.1	14.0	11.4	12.0	18.6
Percent Indonesian Exports[b]	71.0	62.0	49.0	43.0	

[a] September 1973 (precrisis level). Central Intelligence Agency, *International Energy Statistical Review*, Jan. 11–Apr. 19, 1978.
[b] *Bulletin of Indonesian Economic Studies* (Nov. 1977), 13:41.

(II.) Six Leading Foreign Suppliers of U.S. Crude Oil
Imports (%)

September 1973		1978	
(1) Canada	28.8	Saudi Arabia	18.2
(2) Saudi Arabia	17.3	Nigeria	14.4
(3) Nigeria	11.8	Libya	10.0
(4) Venezuela	11.7	Algeria	9.9
(5) INDONESIA	7.2	Iran	8.7
(6) Iran	5.9	INDONESIA	7.8

SOURCE: U.S. Department of Energy, raw data.

Table 5.6 U.S. Trade with the Philippines and Indonesia
(Millions $)

	Philippines				Indonesia			
Year	Total	A	B	C	Total	A	B	C
1967	746	1.4%	4.6%	14.4%	239	0.4%	1.4%	4.5%
1973	1205	0.8%	2.8%	9.1%	976	0.7%	2.3%	7.4%
1974	1916	0.9%	2.6%	9.4%	2,344	1.1%	3.1%	11.5%
1975	1666	0.8%	2.0%	7.7%	3,257	1.5%	4.0%	15.1%
1976	1813	0.7%	1.9%	6.8%	4,313	1.8%	4.4%	16.3%
1977	2106	0.8%	1.8%	6.9%	4,509	1.6%	3.9%	14.9%

Note: Discrepancies with U.S. Department of Commerce figures used in tables 3 and 4 are due to different accounting procedures.

A = % of total U.S. global trade.

B = % of total U.S. trade with developing countries.

C = % of total U.S. trade with Asian developing countries (all of Asia except Japan, Australia, and New Zealand).

SOURCE: International Monetary Fund, *Direction of Trade*, Annuals 1966–70 and 1970–76; June 1977.

sume Indonesian oil production within fifteen years or sooner.[24]

Assessed solely in terms of value, Philippine and Indonesian trade make up only a small part of the U.S. global total (see table 5.6). As with investment, trade figures reflect the relative rise of Indonesia and the relative decline of the Philippines as commercial partners of the United States.

Private Bank Lending

American international banking has grown enormously in scope and profitability in the last decade. The expansion of offshore banking and syndicated lending in cooperation with Japanese and European banks has made it increasingly difficult to separate the strands of specifically U.S. interests from those of the north in general. However, one need only observe the burgeoning international divisions of U.S. banks, which now employ more officers than the entire U.S. diplomatic service, to conclude that our stake is considerable. As recently as 1960 only eight American banks had overseas branches, with total assets of $3.5 billion. By 1972, the number stood at 108, with assets of $90 billion.[25] In 1976 foreign operations accounted for nearly one-half of the total earnings of thirteen large U.S. banks. From 1972 to 1976, over 95 percent of the increase in total earnings for these thirteen banks was derived from their activities abroad.[26]

Initially, this expansion was prompted by the financial needs of newly established foreign subsidiaries of U.S. corporations. However, during the early seventies, when corporate demand for investment financing dropped off, the multinational banks became interested in lending to capital-hungry countries with ambitious development programs.[27] After the 1973 oil price hike, balance-of-payments lending by private banks became the norm rather than the exception. As the Arab OPEC countries placed the bulk of their surpluses in the industrialized countries, commercial banks took on the role of recycling petrodollars to deficit-plagued developing as well as developed countries. As a result, the estimated cumulative foreign loans of major multinational banks, including Japanese and Western European banks, doubled from 1973 to 1976, from $154 billion to $300 billion.[28] For American banks alone, the level of foreign loans stood at $195 billion at the end of 1977.[29] Of these American private bank loans, 32 percent went to the developing world (excluding such offshore banking centers as the Bahamas).

Both the Philippines and Indonesia have generously availed themselves of eurocurrency loans in recent years. Following the 1975 Pertamina crisis, Indonesia's borrowing from private sources increased substantially. Table 5.7 shows that loans from private banks, as a percentage of the total Indonesian public debt outstanding, have risen from a negligible share in 1970 to one-quarter of the Indonesian external debt in 1976, or roughly $3.7 billion. At the end of 1976, In-

Table 5.7 Philippine and Indonesian External Public Debt[a] by Category of Source (Billions $)

	1970	1971	1972	1973	1974	1975	1976	1977
Philippines								
Cumulative debt outstanding[b]	0.8	0.9	1.2	1.3	2.0	2.6	4.3	5.6
Percent private banks	38%	30%	24%	20%	22%	25%	31%	28%
Percent official lenders[c]	54%	64%	72%	78%	74%	70%	56%	58%
Others[d]	8%	6%	4%	2%	4%	5%	13%	14%
Indonesia								
Cumulative debt outstanding[b]	3.0	4.3	5.1	6.8	9.2	11.8	14.6	15.9
Percent private banks	negl.	negl.	2%	10%	8%	23%	25%	21%
Percent official lenders[c]	91%	90%	86%	80%	69%	61%	61%	68%
Others[d]	9%	10%	12%	10%	23%	16%	14%	11%

[a] Includes public debt and only private debt which is guaranteed by the government.
[b] Includes disbursed and undisbursed.
[c] Includes governments and international organizations (except IMF transactions).
[d] Includes mainly suppliers' credits.

SOURCE: World Bank, World Debt Tables, External Public Debt of Developing Countries, July 29, 1977 and Sept. 2 and 7, 1977.

donesia ranked fourth among less-developed customers of private multinational banks, preceded only by Mexico, Brazil, and Algeria.[30] In the Philippines, during the first few years following the proclamation of Martial Law, the total external public debt more than tripled, from $1.3 billion in 1973 to $4.3 billion in 1976 (see table 5.7). The rise in the share of cumulative loans from private banks—from 20 percent or $0.25 billion in 1973 to 31 percent or $1.3 billion in 1976—reflects an increasing eagerness on the part of the Philippine government to tap the eurocurrency market.[31] In 1976 the Philippines was the third largest non-oil, developing country borrower in private markets.[32]

According to a survey by the U.S. Federal Reserve Bank, the total value of U.S. private bank loans to the Philippines and Indonesia as of the end of 1977 was $2.0 billion and $2.2 billion, respectively.[33] In percentage terms, the Philippines received 3.3 percent and Indonesia 3.6 percent of American bank loans to the developing world (again, exluding the offshore banking centers).

The rapid growth of private bank lending initially raised numerous doubts and fears, foremost of which was concern that default by a major debtor country might endanger the entire international financial structure.

These fears were much diminished by 1977. At this writing the U.S. government regards the phenomenon as a useful means of recycling the oil profits of the Middle East. In the high priesthood of orthodox international development theory it is now dogma that as concessional aid levels continue to drop, only a further expansion of private lending can meet the growing capital requirement of the developing world.[34] In 1977 many countries, including Indonesia, were able to refinance earlier loans at the lower interest rates then prevailing.[35] The distressed reaction in the banking community was ample evidence that developing nations are by no means always the helpless victims of market forces.

The Japanese Rationale

Since the fall of Vietnam, U.S. officials have increasingly perceived the U.S.-Japanese alliance as one major rationale for a continued American presence in Southeast Asia. While the argument is primarily political, it has an obvious economic dimension. Whether or not Southeast Asia is essential to us—so goes the reasoning—it is certainly vital to the Japanese economy, and hence, to the extent that we are both mainstays of the international economic order, critical to our own material well-being.

The figures in table 5.8 give some idea of the comparative American and Japanese regional economic stake. In 1977 Japan's ASEAN trade amounted to about one-tenth of her worldwide total and roughly two-fifths of her trade with developing countries. Japanese exports took 23 percent of the ASEAN market in 1976.[36] Clearly, Japan is more dependent on ASEAN raw materials than is the United States. Over half of her regional import bill pays for Indonesian oil. In 1977 she obtained almost all her tin, 95 percent of her natural rub-

Table 5.8 Japanese and U.S. Economic Interests in ASEAN

I. Trade (1977)
(Billions $)

	Total	ASEAN/World	ASEAN/ Developing Countries	Average Annual Growth Rate (1973–77)
Japan	$15.9 (Exports $6.9, imports $9.0)	10.4%	21.1%	21.3% (Exports 18.7%, imports 24.3%)
U.S.	$11.6 (Exports $3.9, imports $7.7)	4.2%	10.0%	29.7% (Exports 18.7%, imports 38.1%)

II. Direct Investment (1976)[a]
(Billions $)

	World	ASEAN	ASEAN/World	Average Annual Growth Rate (1971–76)
Japan	$19.4	$3.9	20.3%	44%
U.S.	$137.2	$3.4	2.5%	20%

[a] Japanese figure represents those overseas investments approved by the Bank of Japan. U.S. figure represents book value of investments. Thus, it should be noted that the two sets of data are not directly comparable.

SOURCES: International Monetary Fund, Direction of Trade, June 1978; Japanese investment figures from Ministry of Finance and Bank of Japan documents obtained from Japanese Embassy, Washington, D.C.; U.S. Department of Commerce.

ber, about a third of her nickel and copper ore, and substantial amounts of bauxite, tungsten, and titanium from ASEAN sources. Her wood industries are the major consumer of tropical hardwood logs from island Southeast Asia, a fact with serious environmental implications discussed in chapter seven. Although figures available are not strictly comparable, Japanese investment in the area is of much greater relative importance to her total foreign investment than its American equivalent, and growing at a much faster rate.

The ASEAN countries have exerted heavy pressure on the Japanese to recognize a special dimension to their relationship by extending preferential trade arrangements and guarantees of stable export earnings (the so-called "stabex" proposal). While the Japanese have recently concentrated almost half their foreign aid in the region,[37] they have been reluctant to endanger global interests by yielding substantially to these pressures, a stance generally shared and encouraged by the United States. The "Fukuda Doctrine" announced by Japanese Prime Minister Fukuda on his appearance at the ASEAN Kuala Lumpur summit meeting in 1977 included a pledge of one billion dollars to five proposed ASEAN regional industrial projects, contingent on feasibility.[38] However, although Fukuda listened with sympathy to ASEAN demands for greater access to Japanese markets and other requests, it was not immediately apparent whether his doctrine represented much more than a cosmetic gloss on Japan's natural economic primacy as the nearest if not the best beloved of the major industrial powers.

A decade ago most American traders and investors in Southeast Asia regarded Japanese economic expansion as a dangerous source of competition. More recently, while rivalry has remained a factor, there has been a general shift in perception toward awareness of the complementary character of American and Japanese activities. It has been obvious for some time that as overall levels of trade and investment in Southeast Asia rise, everyone benefits and that (uncomfortable as the idea of rich-nation fraternity may be) the United States and Japan share the same range of concerns and problems vis-à-vis the entire Third World. In natural resource projects Japanese finance sometimes creates added demand for U.S. goods and services. The executive of a major American construction firm noted in an interview that his firm "keeps a close eye on Japanese investment as a source of potential projects."[39] At the regional level, American businessmen are still periodically upset by sharp Japanese business practices and the difficulties of competing with a highly integrated political and commercial system which, unlike our own, is fundamentally export oriented. But to senior corporation executives in New York, whatever adverse results may flow from Japanese activities in Southeast Asia are simply not very significant compared to the huge profits (and equally monumental friction) generated by U.S.-Japanese bilateral trade.[40]

In fact, the majority of U.S. investment in Southeast Asia, concentrated in extractive industries, is to some degree dependent on the Japanese market. The logs felled by Weyerhaeuser in Kalimantan, the copper ore mined by Freeport Sulphur in West Irian, and (until recently) most of the oil pumped by Caltex in Sumatra all go to Japan. The interlocking application of big American and Japanese capital and technology is perhaps best illustrated by the ongoing development of liquified natural gas (LNG). In 1973 two American energy corporations—Mobil and Huffco—signed production-sharing contracts with Pertamina to tap two Indonesian gas fields. Shortly afterwards, the Indonesians secured agreements with American and Japanese utility companies for guaranteed supplies of LNG for a period of twenty years, commencing in 1978. The bulk of the financing for the on-site facilities was provided by Japanese consortiums in loans to Indonesia of over $1.5 billion. Upon completion, the two LNG projects, including the cost of tankers and regasification facilities in Japan and California, will total over $4 billion for all parties involved. When both fields come on stream, Indonesia may be the largest producer and exporter of LNG in the world. Total foreign exchange revenue from future LNG exports is projected to be $20 billion over the next twenty years. In this case Japanese finance and American companies are working in tandem to develop raw materials for a global market, including not only Japan but the United States (assuming that regulatory delays regarding American imports can be resolved) and Western Europe as well.[41]

North-South Issues

The year was 1965, a time of momentous change and bloodshed in Southeast Asia. Every evening an American graduate student doing research in provincial Borneo would treat himself to a beer and tune in the official news broadcast from the distant national capital. And every evening, without fail, regardless of what cataclysms might have occurred elsewhere, the program would end with a seemingly pedestrian statistic, the amount of tin sold from the American government stockpile during the previous twenty-four hours.

Up to now we have been considering the weight of American economic interests in Southeast Asia. The discussion has been confined to the more obvious trade and investment indicators. The facts suggest that while these factors are important to us and even more so to our Japanese allies, they cannot be considered vital. But while we are not economically dependent on Southeast Asians, they are assuredly to a great degree dependent on us. To rephrase it, for those who feel that "dependence" is a pejorative term, the existing interdependence is unbalanced in our favor. Most educated Southeast Asians are painfully aware of this situation, sometimes to the point of paranoia. The anecdote above pertains to Malaysia, whose government has for years been obsessed with the sword-of-Damocles threat to markets for two key commodities, tin and rubber, posed by U.S. stockpiles. But there are similar fears everywhere, and for good reason. The ability of Southeast Asians to influence global economic trends which impinge directly on their own welfare and perhaps survival is often minimal.

Table 5.9 illustrates the extent to which the Philippines and Indonesia rely on the industrialized West and Japan as trading partners. Similar patterns of imbalance are evident with regard to investment, government aid both bilateral and

Table 5.9 The Share of ASEAN Trade with the "North"[a]

	U.S.		Japan		EEC[b]	
	Exports	Imports	Exports	Imports	Exports	Imports
1970						
INDONESIA	13.0%	17.8%	40.8%	29.4%	14.9%	21.6%
Malaysia	13.0%	8.6%	18.3%	17.5%	19.3%	23.3%
PHILIPPINES	41.6%	29.4%	40.1%	30.6%	7.3%	15.4%
Singapore	11.1%	10.8%	7.6%	19.4%	15.6%	15.6%
Thailand	13.4%	14.8%	25.5%	37.4%	18.3%	22.6%
Total ASEAN	*17.4%*	*15.1%*	*24.2%*	*25.4%*	*15.4%*	*19.0%*

Total Share with "North"[a]
Exports—57.0%   Imports—59.5%

1976						
INDONESIA	28.7%	17.4%	41.7%	26.2%	7.2%	21.2%
Malaysia	15.6%	12.3%	21.1%	20.5%	20.9%	16.7%
PHILIPPINES	36.0%	22.2%	24.3%	27.1%	18.8%	12.1%
Singapore	14.6%	13.2%	10.2%	16.0%	14.3%	10.8%
Thailand	9.6%	13.0%	25.7%	32.5%	21.1%	13.2%
Total ASEAN	*21.0%*	*15.3%*	*26.0%*	*22.8%*	*14.5%*	*14.5%*

Total Share with "North"[a]
Exports—61.5%   Imports—52.6%

[a] In this context, "North" does not include other industrial market economies outside the United States, Japan, and the European Economic Community (EEC).

[b] Includes those countries which joined the EEC in 1973.

SOURCE: International Monetary Fund, *Direction of Trade*, Annuals, 1966–70 and 1970–76.

multilateral, and private bank credit. Infinitely more important is the fact that both markets and flows of credit and investment are the creatures of international economic conditions determined by events in the First World. It is generally acknowledged, for example, that the slump in U.S. investment in Southeast Asia since 1976 has been as much the result of global recession as of any other single factor. The sense of vulnerability resulting from this situation has motivated ASEAN to be an active proponent of the southern position in the north-south debate. At the same time the relative prosperity of the ASEAN countries compared to many developing nations, combined with sharply divergent levels of development within the regional grouping, has up to now inclined ASEAN to regard with disinterest the more radical Third World demands for complete restructuring of the international economic order.[42]

What do Indonesia and the Philippines stand to gain from equitable resolution of north-south issues, and what stake does the United States have in helping them toward the goal? The first part of the question can be briefly answered by examining three critical categories: trade in commodities, trade in manufactures, and debt.

Manufactures

Since the first U.N. Conference on Trade and Development (UNCTAD) in 1964, developing nations have stressed trade rather than aid as a means of increasing their collective share of the world's wealth. Typically, the tariff barriers which they face in the industrialized world resemble a pyramid: zero or very low tariffs on traditional exports of primary commodities, moderate tariffs on semiprocessed goods such as vegetable oil or timber, and high tariffs on nontraditional labor-intensive manufactures (textiles, electronics, etc). To increase their share of value added (i.e., processing of raw material inputs) the LDCs proposed that the developed countries grant preferential treatment to manufactured exports originating from the Third World. After protracted negotiations throughout the sixties, a Generalized System of Preferences (GSP) was established by certain industrialized nations in 1971.[43] Since the developed countries could not work out an agreement encompassing all markets and all manufactured products, each individual industrialized nation constructed its own GSP. The U.S. preferential tariff scheme, the last of those in major countries, became operational in January 1976.

The United States is the only major industrialized country to base eligibility for its GSP on political as well as economic criteria. The 1974 Trade Act which activated the GSP stipulated inter alia that OPEC countries were to be excluded from the system. Accordingly, Indonesia, as an OPEC member nation, was ineligible. On the other hand, under the GSP $77 million of Philippine goods entered the U.S. market duty free in 1977.[44] Insofar as the interest of the Philippine government in establishing pioneer export-oriented industries remains high, the Philippines will continue to benefit in the future. Although the ASEAN countries would like the United States to raise the current dollar ceilings on the program in order to allow more of their goods duty-free entry, the ceilings, in another sense, shield the ASEAN countries, whose volume of manufactured exports (except in the case of Singapore) is still small, from the more competitive exports of Third World "newcomers" such as Brazil, Taiwan, South Korea, and Hong Kong.

Commodity Price Stabilization

Indonesia and the Philippines export a number of the eighteen primary products which are included in UNCTAD's Integrated Program of Commodities (IPC; see table 5.10). In order to sustain development and service their already hefty debt burdens, the two countries must improve both the volume and the reliability of annual export earnings lest they fall deeper in debt or, even worse, default on their existing loans.

In no other area of the north-south dialogue are experts of both hemispheres more agreed on the mutual benefit which in theory should result from cooperation.[45] Stabilization of commodity markets would eliminate one major source of inflation, since thanks to a "ratchet" effect the impact of violent price surges on consumers is rarely undone by subsequent price slumps. Stabilization would help to guarantee reasonable and dependable income to producer countries, whose planners, as things stand, face bewildering uncertainties in attempting to foresee future resource levels. The elimination of short-lived price escalations, such as those which affected many commodities in 1974, would also discourage the development of synthetic alternatives. Rubber and sugar are among the major Indonesian and Philippine products

Table 5.10 Price Series for Philippine and Indonesian IPC[a]
Commodities (Index 1972 = 100)

Commodity (% of total exports) Philippines	1970	1971	1972	1973	1974	1975	1976
Sugar (17%) ($/mt)	153	159	172	186	478	597	297
Index	89	92	100	108	278	288	173
Coconut Oil (12%) ($/mt)	283	259	181	354	916	375	346
Index	156	143	100	195	506	207	191
Copper (11%) ($/mt)	293	227	232	360	473	265	282
Index	126	98	100	155	204	114	121
Logs (5%) ($/mt)	59	60	54	92	108	86	137
Index	109	111	100	170	200	159	254
Lumber (3%) ($/mt)	140	164	136	194	250	253	326
Index	103	120	100	143	184	186	240
Total (48%)							
Indonesia[b]							
Lumber (7%) (1000 ¥/m³)	20	22	30	31	35	45	45
Index	67	73	100	103	117	150	150
Rubber (5%) ($ c/lb)	18	16	28	43	29	37	38
Index	64	57	100	153	103	132	135
Tin (2%) (£/ton)	1,484	1,505	1,732	3,435	3,060	3,620	4,435
Index	86	87	100	198	177	209	258
Palm Oil (2%) ($/ton)	278	217	265	620	510	371	435
Index	105	82	100	233	192	140	164
Coffee (2%) (Str. $/pikul)	116	85	90	168	113	211	300
Index	129	94	100	187	126	234	333
Tea (1%) (£/kg)	.33	.36	.38	.50	.58	.58	.76
Index	87	95	100	131	153	153	200
Total (19%)							

[a] Integrated Program of Commodities (UNCTAD)—18 Key Commodities.
[b] Indonesian Fiscal Year (April–March; September–August starting 76–77).
SOURCES: Central Bank of the Philippines; Bank Indonesia.

which are not, in the final analysis, "vital" to anyone except perhaps the producers, since modern industry is quite capable of making substitutes at prices which are already competitive under many circumstances.

At the first ministerial-level U.S.-ASEAN meeting, held in Washington in August 1978, Secretary of State Vance openly pledged American support for the creation of a common fund to help finance buffer stocks for all critical commodities, a mechanism which has long been central to the southern agenda.[46] This development, combined with commendable progress toward the attainment of individual commodity agreements, particularly for rubber and sugar, was gratifying to the ASEAN states. Unfortunately, the U.S. Congress does not yet share the perception of the experts that additional commodity agreements will be good for everyone. Instead it tends to regard them both as threats to various single-interest constituencies (e.g., Idaho sugar beet growers, represented by the chairman of the Senate Foreign Relations Committee) and as attempts to raise prices at the expense of the American housewife. It is therefore by no means clear that the United States will be able to cooperate as wholeheartedly in this critical area as the rhetoric of the ASEAN-U.S. dialogue would suggest.

External Debt

It was noted earlier that both Indonesia and the Philippines are major customers of northern hemisphere bankers. Like most debtors, neither country finds this status altogether comfortable. As illustrated by table 5.11, both are on the edge of the 20 percent debt service ratio (interest payments over export earnings) which is generally regarded as the borderline between respectable credit consumption and potential insolvency. Beyond this there is little that is similar about the two cases. True to its capitalistic tradition, the Philippines has played the international borrowing game with enthusiasm and finesse, although as of mid-1979 the extent of the Philippine debt burden was again causing concern. Continuing growth of the Philippine export sector, particularly in nontraditional manufactures, may be the key to long-term viability.[47] In Indonesia's case, chronic balance of payments problems were apparently solved by the OPEC price hike in late 1973, then to some extent undone by the financial collapse of Pertamina, considered at greater length below. Indonesia's future solvency is by no means assured, especially if food import bills remain at the high levels of recent years. Her painful experience with foreign lenders stimulated latent nationalist fears and resentments even among those technocrats who, in the eyes of critics, were responsible for leading Indonesia into the "debt trap" in the first place. As a result, and despite her recent ability to re-schedule some debt at lower interest rates, Indonesia could be expected to look with no small degree of sympathy on rad-ical proposals for the reform of international lending proce-dures.

American interest in resolving north-south issues is of course partly political in character, and nowhere is this more

Table 5.11 Projected Debt Service: Export Ratio[a]

	1976	1977	1978 [b]	1979 [b]	1980 [b]
Indonesia	13.0	16.6	18.6	19.5	17.0
Philippines	15.0	15.0	18.0	20(?)	(?)

[a]Debt service: export ratio = debt service payments (including principal and interest)/export earnings.
[b]Estimated.

Note: There is considerable uncertainty about the Philippine debt service ratio. Philippine law prohibits more than a 20 percent ratio, and the government uses a formula to compute it which differs considerably from IMF and other international practice and is widely believed to yield a lower figure.

SOURCES: *Far Eastern Economic Review, Asia 1978 Yearbook*, pp. 201, 295, sup-plemented by interviews.

clearly the case than with regard to ASEAN. Until the end of the Vietnam conflict U.S. policy toward the five-nation grouping stressed caution and aloofness, partly out of fear that an overly eager embrace would, in the eyes of potentially hostile neighbors such as Vietnam, needlessly summon the specter of SEATO. Events since the fall of Saigon have di-minished the relevance of this concern, and the Carter Ad-ministration has abandoned former inhibitions about seeking closer U.S.-ASEAN relations. While geopolitical consider-ations still play a considerable role, the mix of motives be-hind U.S. policy differs considerably from what it would have been a decade ago. Today ASEAN is seen less as an in-cipient alliance than as an influential subsector of the Third World, composed of relatively advantaged countries with mixed economies, a like-minded coalition with which the United States should be able to cooperate in its dealings with a sometimes hostile south. Officials are fully aware that if "moderates" such as Indonesia and the Philippines become sufficiently alienated, the result would be to stimulate economic radicalism on a global scale. The greatest cloud over the evolving relationship is the questionable U.S. ability to make innovative policy on trade, commodity, and other north-south economic issues in the face of domestic political constraints.

Leaving aside the political dimension, future northern prosperity may be at stake to a much greater degree than is suggested by current statistics on trade and investment. Some authorities argue that the south may in time become an indispensable "engine of growth" for the north. The argument assumes that economic growth rates of industrial countries will continue to stagnate under the influence of unemployment and recession, and that the more dynamic middle-income southern states (such as the ASEAN five) are the only visible source of long-term stimulus.[48] But those who believe in this formula for more genuine interdependence would be the first to admit that, for the moment, progress hinges on enlightened trade, aid, and private lending policies in the north.

American Business and the Third World's ASEAN Subsector

Regardless of whether long-term interdependence is likely, it is hardly debatable that the American private sector is already the most potent agent of U.S. influence in island Southeast Asia. More is involved than the mere weight of the U.S. economy. The Southeast Asians know that the American genius lies largely in trade and business. Besides admiring the product of our capitalism they see it as less formidable in adversary dealings than the Japanese brand. They are therefore anxious for U.S. commerce to maintain a vigorous presence. It is pertinent that in its first specific policy initiative to Washington, ASEAN urged retention of the threatened U.S. tax deferral system to encourage American investment abroad.[49] Yet, while there is no denying mutual eagerness for trade and investment, there are constraints on both sides which are rarely acknowledged in public statements. The Indonesian reaction suggests the extent to which ASEAN societies fear as well as desire greater economic involvement with the north. For its part, the United States government, accurately reflecting a never-ending domestic debate, is divided against itself in this area as in few others. The balance of this chapter will attempt to illustrate by example the diversity, complexity and persistence of the specific problems involved.

Pertamina

The most resounding event in the economic history of Indonesia since 1966 was the financial collapse of the state oil company, Pertamina, in January 1975. While the full story of the Pertamina affair may never be known, its general outlines, and the implications for northern policymakers, are sufficiently clear. General Ibnu Sutowo, the founder of Pertamina, was a former army medical doctor with unusual entrepreneurial skills. He personally created the famous production-sharing formula, a framework for international cooperation that made possible a rapid expansion of Indonesian oil exploration and production. In political terms Pertamina was a Janus-like institution, at once an expression of the old statist ethos, with its overtones of xenophobia, and a mainstay of the outward-oriented New Order. General Sutowo courted and supported the more traditional Javanese figures among his military colleagues, and scorned the systematism and caution preached by the Western-trained technocrats and their foreign advisers in the planning and finance ministries.[50]

The major flaw in the Pertamina formula may have been that, for a time, it worked too well. Operating from the confines of his seemingly impregnable state-within-a-state, General Sutowo expanded with reckless haste into a bewildering array of oil and nonoil activities, including petrochemical plants, a steel mill, a new seaport, an airline, a mechanized rice estate, resort hotels, lavish staff facilities, and a generous sprinkling of village mosques throughout Indonesia. Subsequent events have made it clear that his reach greatly exceeded his grasp. The state oil company turned out to be shot through with inefficiency and corruption on a monumental scale. Well before the collapse, it was apparent to economists in Jakarta (both Indonesians and foreigners) that the Pertamina non-system, shrouded though it was in mystery, might prove costly in the long run. But many influential foreign observers remained convinced that Sutowo's assets as a man of action outweighed his liabilities. Americans found it easy to equate him with John D. Rockefeller, althogh Jay Gould might have been a more apt comparison. Above all, American and other international banks fell over themselves in unseemly haste to lend him eurodollars for his constantly expanding empire. They apparently did so in full knowledge that Sutowo was exploiting Pertamina's ambiguous, quasi-official status to ignore a ceiling on government debt imposed by the IMF and the technocrats. In the case of one $200 million credit, syndicated by First National City Bank in 1973, circumstances suggest that the foreign lenders conspired in a calculated evasion of Indonesian government regulations.[51]

The bankers were gambling that, if the bubble did burst, the Indonesian government would feel compelled to stand behind Pertamina, as indeed it did. The most careful study of the episode suggests discreetly that they also counted on American and Japanese interest in strategic Indonesia as the ultimate guarantee factor.[52] Because of the risk involved in these calculations, Pertamina was obliged to pay substantially more than market rates for its escalating loans.

The Pertamina affair may have been a salutory lesson for Indonesia, but it was a costly one. General Sutowo was retired, Pertamina's nonoil projects were curtailed, and the government brought its errant stepchild under control. The immediate impact on development programs was cushioned by the decision of concerned Western nations and Japan to maintain high levels of aid. However, the revelation of state oil company debts amounting to $5 to $10 billion (the exact figure is still uncertain) suddenly confronted the technocrats with the unpleasant prospect of debt service requirements two and a half to four times greater than had been calculated in 1973.[53] By 1977, interest payments would soak up the equivalent of half Indonesia's oil earnings. If present predictions of waning oil export capacity turn out to be correct, Indonesia may have squandered a substantial portion of her petroleum heritage. In the view of one expert, the episode resulted in the greatest peacetime financial loss ever suffered by one country relative to national income.[54]

Assuming that the United States wants to see a strong and prosperous Indonesia, American interests were seriously damaged. Well before the collapse American officials were aware that the bankers were embarked on a dangerous course, but within the prevailing framework of government-corporate relations they could do little more than offer warnings if asked.[55] On balance the episode did more than anything since the end of the Sukarno era to encourage criticism of Indonesia's tentative commitment to foreign investment and an open market economy, for it suggested a dangerously irresponsible attitude on the part of the international banking community.

The Pertamina affair illuminates one corner of a vast topic. While few would deny the financial benefits conferred by foreign economic activity in Indonesia, there are lists of unanswered questions about its effect on employment and political culture. For partly political reasons, in the early New Order period, foreign investment received an undiscriminating welcome. One result, which everyone now agrees was unfortunate, was the wholesale elimination of small-scale, labor-intensive soft-drink, textile, and cigarette manufactures.[56] Protesting Indonesian students seized on this issue in 1973 when a traditional textile center in West Java, Majalaya, was hard-hit by new Japanese-financed competition. Their slogan was "a thousand yen are invested and a thousand Majalayas die." The multiplier effect of foreign investment in such situations may or may not be sufficient to offset the "negative multiplier" resulting from the elimination of services for replaced, "inefficient" industries. The problem is complicated by the fact that even what appear to be "appropriate" intermediate technologies by international standards may be highly mechanized in the Indonesian context.[57] On Java, as explained in chapter six, the introduction of hand-powered sickles to replace finger knives in rice harvesting has been sufficiently radical to have a serious impact on the rural labor force.

Additional social and political costs have resulted from the post-1966 pattern of development. Inevitably, foreign investment has served to bolster the already dominant economic status of the overseas Chinese, who in many cases are the best qualified joint-venture partners. The increasingly profitable official-military patronage of Chinese financiers has generated repeated scandal and protest, to which the government has responded with a formal policy of economic incentives for *pribumi* ("natives"), as opposed to ethnic Chinese regardless of citizenship. The forces at work, however, are far too strong to be checked by the implementing efforts made thus far, and to students and other critics the pro-"native" policy seems a hypocritical charade. Resulting resentment has nourished the statist ethos and, as the government is aware, could in time generate another pendulum swing in Indonesian politics which might effectively negate the genuine economic progress that has occurred since 1966. The net result is doubly unfortunate: it encourages both corruption and official ambivalence about foreign investment (often reflected in bureaucratic inefficiency). These factors confuse and discourage would-be investors, especially those who regarded Indonesia with unrealistic euphoria only a few years ago.

The Philippine Nuclear Reactor

In the Philippines, for historical and cultural reasons mentioned earlier, private investment does not risk as much labor displacement, social distortion, and potential political destabilization as it does in Indonesia. Our economic relationship nonetheless involves an equally difficult range of challenges. One case pertains to the broader issue of whether U.S. legal and environmental standards should be applied to foreign transactions. Beginning in 1971 the U.S. government promoted the sale of a Westinghouse nuclear power plant at an estimated cost which by 1978 exceeded $1.1 billion. In 1974 the Export-Import Bank initially approved financing for the plant, to be located at Bagac on the Bataan Peninsula near Manila. The Philippine government was anxious for the nuclear plant as one element in an aggressive energy diversification scheme which, it hoped, would reduce dependence on Middle Eastern oil, regarded as potentially vulnerable to Arab boycott in response to the never-ending Muslim rebellion in Mindanao. The Nixon-Ford Administration saw the transaction as a lucrative export to a country where, because of military alliance, risk of nuclear proliferation would be acceptable.[58]

The advent of the Carter Administration brought new emphasis on regulation of nuclear exports. In 1977 the U.S. Nuclear Regulatory Commission (NRC) reviewed an earlier site inspection report which it had conducted at the request of the Philippine government. The NRC review found various deficiencies, including earthquake hazard and an absence of salt formations suitable for underground waste storage. Further site inspection by the International Atomic Energy Association (IAEA) confirmed risk of earthquakes powerful enough to damage the strongest structure. Not long after the NRC review, the American press publicized alleged illegal payments by Westinghouse to one of President Marcos' most favored associates, Herminio Disini, in connection with the reactor sale. The Three Mile Island nuclear accident of April 1979 further aggravated concern on both sides of the Pacific. In June, President Marcos responded by suspending construction at the site and announcing the formation of a special commission to review the entire project, while in Washington the State Department continued to defer approval of the reactor export license.

Two separate issues are involved. The Westinghouse payoff, if it occurred, may have violated SEC regulations. If it took place today such behavior would be illegal under the

Foreign Corrupt Practices Act passed in March 1977. The second issue involves the export of hazardous, in this case nuclear, technology. Partly as a result of the Philippine controversy the Natural Resources Defense Council sued the Ex-Im Bank for failure to endorce provisions of the (U.S.) National Environment Protection Act (NEPA) which, it argued, required an environmental impact assessment for all major government-funded foreign transactions (although not for private sales or investments). In January 1979 President Carter issued an executive order mandating the impact assessments, and the suit was dropped.[59] The environmentalist position does not dispute the sole right of the Philippine government to determine whether or not the Philippines should opt for nuclear technology. But it believes the U.S. government has an equally clear obligation to move beyond export promotion (as it did not in this case until 1977) and acquaint the purchasing government with the full range of hazards and alternative technologies.

Needless to say, the business community does not agree with this kind of judgment. Would-be exporters and investors are convinced that attempts to apply American standards to foreign transactions are one major aspect of a growing network of self-imposed disincentives which merely put the United States at a comparative disadvantage vis-à-vis Japanese and European rivals in doing business with the Third World. Besides corporate corruption and environmental measures, other alleged disincentives include efforts to increase taxes on foreign operations, and the application of human rights conditions both to Overseas Private Investment Corporation (OPIC) insurance and to Ex-Im loans. Businessmen naturally stress the developing countries' need for capital as well as the importance of the United States' maintaining a strong export position. As the Philippine nuclear imbroglio suggests, the result is an extension of the traditional internal American debate over government regulation of free enterprise. Indeed, as indicated by the often aggressively anti-multinational stance of American labor, the same ideological and material interests and sentiments are still manning the same ramparts. As a result, major foreign relations issues are settled (or not settled) by the same process that governs the present relationship of business to government in the United States.

The increasingly cumbersome nature of our decision-making process is understandably aggravating to foreign governments. Approval of Indonesian liquified natural gas exports to the Pacific Coast was tied up for over five years in a morass of regulatory red tape. Originally the problem was not wholly procedural; the Indonesians wanted to link LNG pricing to OPEC oil prices, while the U.S. Department of Energy demurred on the grounds that cartel-set pricing is undesirable, and that there is no more connection between oil and gas prices than (say) between oil and coal. Lurking in the background was the future possibility of massive gas imports from Mexico, a non-OPEC country. After agreement was reached on a pricing formula, environmental controversy over the regassification site in California continued to postpone implementation. Most observers believe that the Indonesians are justified in blaming the endless delays less on disagreement in substance than (to quote Minister of Mining Subroto) on "the peculiar American machinery that apparently causes delays in decision-making." A recent *Wall Street Journal* commentary observed that in the LNG matter, "U.S. bureaucrats have demonstrated convincingly that when it comes to producing red tape, they can hold their own with counterparts who reputedly paralyze the administration of developing countries." [60]

The LNG case is a spectacular and specialized trade problem involving gigantic American and Japanese corporations. The behavior of such actors will be of great significance to Southeast Asia for some time, whether or not, as some accounts claim, the heyday of the multinational corporation is already over even as the accompanying debate reaches maximum decibel level. [61] In the long run, however, more mundane trade issues involving U.S. willingness to receive the products of newly established industries will be of greater importance to Indonesia (which has not yet developed a significant manufacturing export capacity), as they already are to the Philippines. Across the board, American behavior at home increasingly will have more impact on the welfare of Southeast Asians than American foreign policy narrowly defined.

As in the case of human rights, U.S. policy regarding private-sector relations with the Third World continues to suffer from the prevalance of decision-making by bureaucratic conflict. There is little evidence of effective effort to evaluate the apparent contradictions posed by competing interests, perhaps to determine that some are illusory. Caught in a maze of unanswered questions and competing ideologies, U.S. officials abroad (to the extent that they have any freedom of action at all) often fall back on questionable assumptions, such as the view that since robber-baron entrepreneurship served American development well, it is a benign phenomenon in developing countries today.

Given the vagaries of the American political system, the ability of our official establishment to regulate private economic involvement overseas without doing more harm than good is assuredly slight. But it seems equally clear that there is an acute need to educate would-be investors about some of the more obvious constraints and opportunities, relating to broader American interests, which apply to problems of trade and investment in countries like Indonesia. Multinational managers should, for example, be fully acquainted with the labor problem as it relates to national development.[62] The question of who can perform such essentially educative tasks is difficult to answer. In the long run it is probable that the only solution, aside from whatever tutelage may be provided by the Indonesians themselves, must come in the form of corporate self-enlightenment: more investment in understanding alien societies, based eventually on long-term commitment and willingness to accept lower rates of immediate gain. Unorthodox, noninvestment, advisory relationships, with state as well as private enterprise, may be desirable in many cases. Such concepts are not exactly popular in corporate boardrooms and they are not encouraged by the widespread perception of countries like Indonesia as hazardous territory where only fast profits can justify political risk. In other words, irresponsible or at best unimaginative capitalism and unstable authoritarianism tend to interact in a vicious circle. Under these circumstances it seems clear enough that U.S. policy should follow a dual approach, encouraging American investors toward unorthodox relationships and at the same time doing whatever may be done to bolster the ability of governments and societies to deal with the multinationals on more equal terms. The Overseas Private Investment Corporation (OPIC), which insures U.S. investors against political risk in the developing countries, is one obvious vehicle for the first half of the strategy. Already OPIC has extended its coverage well beyond equity investment, to include goods and services provided under contractual, licensing, and technical assistance agreements, and even joint ventures with state enterprises in socialist countries.[63] The second and far more difficult task can only be accomplished by improving the reservoir of human skills necessary for both effective regulation and partnership with the multinationals. Aid programs should be able to play at least a marginal role in this enormous undertaking. There is less conflict between the two halves of the strategy, one aimed at encouraging investment and other forms of foreign economic involvement, the other at facilitating regulation, than might be supposed. The example of "successful" developing countries from Singapore to Brazil demonstrates that improvement in the investment climate tends to be proportional to the competence and self-confidence of host governments—that while the game is anything but friction-free, neither is it zero sum.

Chapter Six

Malthus in Eden:
The Land-Labor-Food Crisis
of Inner Indonesia

The island of Java is the political and economic key-stone of Indonesia, the largest country in Southeast Asia and the fifth largest in the world. It is the site of what by any yardstick is the gravest development problem in the region, and one of the most difficult anywhere. It is a classic problem of too many people and not enough land, compounded by acute communal cleavages which make the likely conse-quences of failure to cope particularly unattractive. The prob-lem of Java is also, perhaps, a classic example of the poten-tials and limitations of external assistance. The debate over what, if anything, foreigners can do to help the Indonesians in their quest for a solution illustrates about as well as possi-ble the nature of the choices that the United States faces in the field of foreign aid generally.

This chapter assumes that most Americans share in the desire to help 300 million Southeast Asians, including the Javanese, improve their own welfare, if only because they in-habit a substantial portion of the same planet that we do. The discussion is limited to a description of the problem, plus a summary of the debate that goes on around it; it does not presume to offer solutions. Too often, debate over aid strategies implies an unhealthy assumption that the foreign role can somehow be determining. In fact no sensible person would dispute the truism that in the final analysis only the Indonesians can help themselves, or its logical corollary—that excessive aid, disbursed without sufficient under-standing, perhaps for political motives, can do more harm than good. In the case of Java, it is clear that far from having arrived at any clear answers, development strategists (both

Indonesians and foreigners) are only beginning to understand what they are up against.

Inner Indonesia includes Java plus two smaller nearby islands, Bali and Madura, where demography and soil conditions are roughly similar. These islands stand in stark contrast to the more typical Southeast Asian pattern of relatively generous land-population ratios, a pattern which prevails in Outer Indonesia.[1] Java, about the size of New York state, has less than 7 percent of Indonesia's total land area, but 85 million, roughly 63 percent, of her 135 million people. That the island remains one of the most beautiful places on earth contributes in a small way to the problem. Visitors, hypnotized by the verdant landscape and intrigued by the depth and density of Javanese culture, often find it hard to accept the magnitude of Javanese poverty. The Javanese themselves are understandably reluctant to live anywhere else.

As is so often the case in Southeast Asia, however, appearances are deceptive. The poverty of Inner Indonesia is, in fact, comparable in scale to that of Bangladesh. Populations, areas, and land-population ratios of the two are about the same. Both are regions with heavy food deficits and have imported about 10 percent of annual grain requirements in recent years. By coincidence, each consumed approximately $220 million in U.S.-provided PL 480 food supplies in 1976 and 1977 (assuming that only a relatively small percentage of food aid to Indonesia went outside Java), making them major customers of the U.S. farmer.[2] On balance, Javanese are undoubtedly better off than Bengalis. Since World War II starvation has not been a major factor on Java, as it has been in Bangladesh; even before the famines and floods of recent years no one would ever have portrayed East Bengal as an Eden. To some extent Java is being saved from worse extremes of poverty by resource transfers from Outer Indonesia, which thanks to finite oil and mineral assets generates the majority of Indonesia's foreign exchange. By the same token, the poverty of Java is the single most serious restraint on Indonesian national development.

Inner Indonesia is a tragedy born of phenomenal success. Under the Dutch, Java was the centerpiece of what may have been the most profitable colony in history. The island is a 600-mile-long series of volcanoes, and thanks to constant showers of ash, Javanese soil is exceptionally fertile. A thousand years before the Dutch arrived, Javanese agriculture produced the surplus food necessary to sustain a brilliant Hindu-Buddhist civilization, leaving monuments, like the Borobodur temple, which are the equal of any in Asia.

One of the most significant features of colonial rule on Java was the Dutch discovery that cash crops, most notably sugar, could be rotated with rice in the same irrigated fields. The result was a subtle but eventually devastating form of exploitation. Europeans were not allowed to own land; instead, peasants were compelled to grow sugar and then to provide the labor for the sugar mills after the harvest. With "one foot in the rice terrace, the other in the mill,"[3] Javanese farmers manned and provisioned the booming export sector, yet remained isolated from its modernizing influences.

As Dutch capital extended the irrigation systems, sugar, rice, and population growth advanced inexorably together. The elastic rice-sugar ecosystem seemed capable of absorbing endless increments of increasingly refined hand labor and irrigation technology without inducing significant social change, always responding with more sugar production and just enough more rice to support a growing population at static or only slightly declining levels of welfare. To describe the resulting stagnation—economic, technological, and social—anthropologist Clifford Geertz coined the phrase "agricultural involution." By the 1920s, Java was the world's largest sugar producer next to Cuba. Population grew from 6 million in 1830 to 41 million in 1930.[4]

Two-thirds of the sugar mills on Java failed during the Great Depression. The anti-Dutch independence struggle of 1945–49 and two subsequent decades of economic chaos under Sukarno destroyed or heavily damaged much of the remaining sugar-rice infrastructure. But as mills were burned and irrigation canals silted up, population continued to grow. Increasingly, land was pressed into full-time rice culture, and Java became a sugar-deficit area. In a brilliant exegesis which has deeply influenced subsequent scholarship on Indonesia, Geertz described how the Javanese peasantry responded to declining welfare levels by communal burden-sharing, or "shared poverty."[5] No matter how small the pie or how many the consumers, custom dictated that everyone in the village should get a slice. As population pressures increased, land was divided and subdivided to the point where one-third of Javanese farms are now less than one-quarter hectare in size,[6] and in some areas much smaller ones are common. Although large-scale landlordism in the conventional sense is rare, many part-owners of Lilliputian land-parcels are also part-time tenants on the miniplots of others.[7]

In 1963 Geertz noted that Java was not exactly a problem of haves and have-nots, but of "just enoughs" and "not quite enoughs."[8] But today there are growing numbers of have-nots; absolute landlessness has been on the increase for some time, and the landless now comprise from one-third to one-half of Java's total rural population.[9] Java is distended with people. Population densities in some areas are so high (up to 4,000 per square kilometer) that the distinction between "urban" and "rural" has lost much of its validity. Well before government family planning efforts began in 1969, Inner Indonesia's growth rate had dropped to around 2 percent, considerably lower than that of Outer Indonesia. Population was already crowding against the Malthusian restraints of poverty, infant mortality, and poor nutrition. Demographic pressure has forced farmers and firewood gatherers into upland areas, resulting in widespread deforestation and massive soil erosion. Yet despite an unusually successful population program, Inner Indonesia may have to support twice as many people in forty years.[10]

Javanese poverty has kept Indonesia high in the ranks of the world's major aid-receiving nations, despite the relative wealth of her oil and other mineral resources, and (exclusive of Java-Bali-Madura) a lack of serious land pressure. Indonesia is today one of the world's largest recipients of multilateral aid (unlike India, she gets loans from both the World Bank and the Asian Development Bank) and in absolute terms (as opposed to per capita) the largest recipient of U.S. bilateral economic aid in Asia.[11] Of U.S. project aid, which has increased dramatically in recent years, approximately 70 percent is devoted to rural development, with considerable debate now under way as to whether and how this effort should be focused on the food and manpower problems of Inner Indonesia.

The End of "Shared Poverty"

In the mid-1960s "miracle rice" strains were introduced, along with government programs to increase farmers' access to credit, fertilizer, and other "inputs." By the early seventies it had become painfully apparent that the "miracle" had its dark side, as farmers began to abandon some aspects of their traditional, labor intensive technology. For example:

—Traditionally, landlords allowed their neighbors to participate in the harvest, permitting each to take a small share of the rice in payment. Formerly about 400 to 450 people per hectare (mostly women) might appear to take part in this activity. By 1970 population pressures and rural poverty had increased to the point where the number was in excess of 1000, often amounting to an uncontrollable crowd which damaged the grain. Caught between proliferating mobs on the one hand, and growing economic opportunity on the other, landowners began to sell their ripening rice in the field to middlemen who harvest the grain with hired labor from distant areas. The neighbors are left out. This method of harvest now prevails in an estimated one-quarter of Java.[12]

—Until recently the Javanese harvested rice one stalk at a time with a small hand knife known as an *ani-ani*, the most labor-intensive and grain-conserving method possible. It was felt that the rice goddess, Dewi Sri, would be offended by any other method. But the new, shorter-stemmed "miracle" varieties are unsuitable for *ani-ani* and there has been a widespread switch to sickles. It is assumed that since the new varieties are "foreign," the rice goddess, who is Javanese, won't object.[13]

—Until the sixties, most rice was hulled by village women using hand pounders. Now, however, mechanical rice mills have spread to half the villages on Java, eliminating millions of part-time seasonal jobs and labor earnings estimated at $50 million.[14]

—Recently some farmers have been encouraged by misguided government credit policy, plus an artificially low exchange rate, to purchase imported tractors and mechanized hand tillers.[15] (The currency devaluation of November 1978 should ease this problem.)

—As an added complication, in coastal areas where hundreds of thousands of Javanese families depend on the sea, village fishermen using primitive technology are being displaced by motorized trawlers and purse seiners based in large ports. While the result has been profitable for highly capitalized, city-based operators, resulting in a twentyfold increase in fish and shrimp exports since 1968, it is also creating further unemployment in the rural areas.[16] In September 1974 angry fishermen at Muncar, East Java, reacted by destroying seven motorized fishing boats and gear worth $241,000.[17]

In theory, the high-yielding rice varieties should have generated more employment, because they permit double and even triple cropping, require more weeding, spraying, fertilizing, and cultivating, and prosper when irrigation systems (which require much laborious maintenance) are in top condition. It is possible that labor displacement might have resulted from population pressure and the increasing capitalization of the Javanese rural economy, regardless of the "green revolution." However, the majority of scholars who have studied the problem, admittedly on the base of limited evidence, believe that the new technology catalyzed the institutional changes described above, which, in their entirety, may have eliminated as many as 3.5 million jobs on Java in the last ten years.[18] Meanwhile, the Javanese labor force continues to grow at a rate of perhaps two-thirds of a million annually.[19]

Whether rural labor displacement on Java has contributed to an overall decline in the welfare of the poor majority, nationwide, is open to debate. In his national day address of August 17, 1977, President Suharto claimed that between 1967 and 1976 the number of Indonesians living below the poverty line had decreased from nine out of ten to only three out of ten.[20] This assertion, which was widely challenged, has tended to politicize an already heated debate over employment, absolute welfare trends, and the even more sensitive subject of income distribution. In general, foreign observers who confine themselves to short visits and concentrate on admittedly inadequate national statistics are more likely to come up with relatively optimistic conclusions. However, among researchers with long experience at the village level in Inner Indonesia, there is a fairly high degree of consensus that real wages for rural labor have continued to decline and that, for the rural poor majority, welfare trends have been downward since about 1970.[21]

One may argue that in the West, human suffering caused by the enclosure movement, or the early stages of the Industrial Revolution, was a cost worth paying as the price of evolution toward more productive economic systems. Unfortunately this cannot be said of Java, at least not yet. The displacement of labor, landlessness, and (perhaps) declining welfare of the poorest which has accompanied—if not been caused by—the green revolution has not been balanced by a much-hoped-for end to the country's food problems. Only a few years ago this was a real hope. In 1972 both Indonesians and foreign advisers were confidently talking of rice self-sufficiency within two years. Instead, Indonesian food deficits have continued to grow at an alarming rate. In 1977–78 Indonesia imported 2.6 million tons of rice—about one-third of the total amount on the world market—plus a million tons of wheat. The 1978–79 rice crop was much better (estimated 17.6 million tons) but Indonesia's total cereal deficit was still in the vicinity of 2.5 million tons.[22] A recurrence of poor harvests could cause annual rice imports to climb as high as 4 million tons. Indonesia is already something of a "price maker" in the international rice market, meaning that her own domestic shortfall has a direct impact on the amount that she must pay. At the moment, thanks to oil, Indonesia has the foreign exchange to finance massive imports, but if a future crisis coincides with international shortage, as occurred in 1972, the result would be vastly more expensive. Moreover, it is possible that, barring dramatic new discoveries, which are not expected, and thanks to growing domestic energy consumption, Indonesia could become an oil-deficit nation within the next decade.

The social and political implications of the land-food-population problem are equally alarming. Some scholars now believe that Geertz's evocation of "shared poverty" and communal burden-sharing may have been somewhat overdrawn, and are willing to project current detraditionalizing trends well back into the Dutch period.[23] But there is more general agreement that such trends are accelerating, and that continuing capitalization and labor displacement could destroy the social fabric of the Javanese rural world, long a system under stress.

The eventual result could be a gradual process of anomie and atrophy, or it could be mass violence of the same variety that claimed up to half a million lives on Java and Bali in the wake of the communist coup and countercoup of October 1965. The 1965 killings are often regarded as solely the result of army-supported vendettas against communist peasants. In fact, the Javanese disturbances reflected the deep cleavage between devout Muslims and nominal (or syncretic) Muslims which has already been mentioned as a fundamental political determinant in Indonesia. Islam was in some areas identified with landowning and wealth, while the syncretic peasantry provided the main constituency for the massive communist party and its farmers' affiliate. For many months before the violence peaked, the communists had been mobilizing their "not quite enough" clientele in "unilateral actions" (aksi sepihak) directed against small and medium landlords, and aimed at implementing the 1959 land reform law. These rural razzias resulted in a build-up of religious tension which later found an outlet in the killings.[24] Although the Indonesian Communist Party no longer exists, the underlying division

between devout and syncretic Muslim is as deep as ever, and
(as is the case with any kind of communal cleavage) is likely
to become more profound and sensitive in times of growing
poverty.

What Went Wrong

The food picture is by no means all bleak. Overall, Indonesian rice production has roughly quadrupled since the
1950s. It stagnated in the 1960s, then rose by almost 50 percent in the first five years of Suharto's New Order, thanks
largely to "green revolution" factors. Per hectare yields, already high, are now (at 1.9 tons per hectare) the highest of
any country in Southeast Asia, although still far from those
attained in Japan and Taiwan. But the increase has not been
enough to outstrip the continued growth in population, and
during a recent five-year period (1973–77) production did not
improve significantly. Consumption of fertilizer, perhaps the
most critical "input" for the new varieties, also leveled off in
1973 because of inadequate distribution mechanisms, despite
government subsidies and the fact that Indonesia (fortunate
to be amply endowed with the natural gas required as a raw
material for nitrogenous fertilizer) has reached self-sufficiency and is beginning to export this commodity. The
problem is in part the result of success, in the sense that the
relatively more affluent urban and rural middle classes have
been eating more rice, increasing total per capita consumption by 25 percent from 1967 to 1975.[25]

Other causes add up to a combination of exaggerated expectations—the term "miracle rice" was unfortunate, everyone would now agree—weak and often corrupt administration, a pricing policy aimed more at consumers than
producers, bad weather, and pests. Most of this story is familiar in the annals of other rice-producing countries. The initial
surge of production after the introduction of new varieties
resulted from the fact that relatively wealthy farmers, the first
to adopt them, had the money and expertise to provide the
requisite tender loving care. It is always a far more difficult

matter to sustain this trend among the less fortunate. Beginning in 1965, Indonesia launched the first of a series of government programs to equip rice farmers with the necessary package of "inputs" and credit. Like similar efforts in other countries, this one has experienced many problems, but it has also demonstrated in the eyes of most observers fairly steady improvement. More controversial is a program of government-sponsored, village-level quasi-cooperatives (Village Work Units or BUUDs). Although many foreign observers would agree that Java badly needs a system of strong farmers' organizations, the only authority which has ever rallied the rural Javanese masses into organizations with teeth was the Communist Party. This experience, combined with a Dutch heritage of centralized administration and a strongly authoritarian cultural bias, has disinclined the government to experiment with giving the Javanese farmer a voice in his own destiny. The Village Work Units have accordingly developed an evil reputation for excess paternalism, as well as inefficiency and outright corruption. They got off to a bad start during the rice shortage of 1972, when they were used to compel farmers to sell rice at a government-approved floor price which under the prevailing circumstances was confiscatory.[26]

The 1977–78 crop year was marked by severe drought, the second in a row, and an alarming upsurge of pest infestation. By 1978–79 the government extension service had developed seeds resistant to the *wereng* or brown leaf hopper, principal pest of the previous season, and the weather improved, resulting in a record crop. However, disaster could strike again from some unexpected direction. Because the growth cycle of the new varieties is compressed into a relatively short time span, they are more sensitive to problems of practically all kinds, including weeds, vermin, pestilence, flooding, and drought. Moreover, the triple cropping made possible by the new varieties, plus their genetic uniformity, insures that once an explosion of pests occurs, there is a never-failing homogeneous supply of host plants to feed on. It remains to be seen whether research scientists and extension workers will be able to keep up with the vagaries of weather and the natural evolution of new biotypes of insects and diseases.

Government and Donor Reaction

Until recently the Indonesian government did not share the sense of impending Malthusian nightmare which afflicts many foreigners when they ponder the food and population problems of Inner Indonesia. In the early years of the New Order, overburdened technocrats and planners were preoccupied with restoring international confidence in Indonesia and other macroeconomic concerns, including repair of the once clockwork-like physical infrastructure of the Dutch East Indies. Persistent food deficits have probably done as much as anything to refocus official concern on the rural countryside. As in many Asian countries, rice is a highly political subject, and the prospect of serious shortage, or severe price rise, can rapidly undermine political legitimacy. Accordingly, the government's primary concern has been to solve the rice supply problem. But because the Indonesian Army remains aware of the revolutionary potential of the Javanese countryside, there has been a growing sense of urgency about the manpower side of the equation. In addition to family planning, the government has launched a series of labor-intensive public works programs at the local level known collectively by the acronynm INPRES (for "presidential instruction"). Expenditure for this purpose has quadrupled since 1974, and INPRES now provides the equivalent of three days' work per year for each member of the labor force on Java. But it is not clear whether INPRES has resulted in any permanent job creation.[27]

As the bogey of active communist insurgency recedes, there have been a few tentative signs that the government's historic suspicion of decentralized initiatives in the rural areas may be lessening. For the first time local governments at province and subprovince levels are being allowed some staff and money of their own. In one district of Central Java, a new semiofficial "Social and Economic Committee," organized at local initiative, has been permitted to negotiate directly with foreign and domestic welfare agencies such as Oxfam.[28] Whether this trend will continue, and how deep it will go, is very much open to question. It can also be argued that the increasing resources available to the Indonesian bureaucracy, plus continued, apparently growing reliance on military officers to staff key jobs, has on balance accentuated the traditional pattern of top-down, "command" style administration, which tends to stifle popular participation.[29] As a recent AID report points out, "currently, independent organizations to promote the interests of the rural poor do not exist."[30] Perhaps the most optimistic observation warranted at this time would be to note that Indonesians themselves, and hopefully an increasing number of the military, are aware that rural development short of revolution may ultimately depend on resolving what the authorities perceive as the contradiction between participation and stability.

Stimulated partly by American congressional emphasis on helping the "poorest of the poor," a significant shift has taken place in the attitudes and policies of many foreign aid donors. Assistance to the agriculture sector is, of course, hardly a new phenomenon. From its inception in 1948 the American bilateral aid program placed continuing emphasis on agriculture. In addition to the surplus food program (discussed below), a team from the University of Kentucky worked for several years training the staff of the primary Indonesian agriculture faculty at Bogor under an AID contract.[31] From 1951 to 1958 alone about 350 Indonesian agricultural specialists went to the United States at a cost of $1.8 million for additional training.[32] It is generally agreed that the current situation, uneven as it is, would be worse had it not been for these programs.

After the resumption of foreign aid to Indonesia in 1966 initial emphasis reflected (and probably encouraged) the government's concern with infrastructure—roads, ports, major dams and irrigation works, and the rehabilitation of export crop estates and supporting machinery. Most activities of the multilateral lenders, particularly the World Bank, were "bankable" and emphasized "hardware" to a degree which was sometimes callous.

For example, in 1973 both the World Bank and the Asian Development Bank approved loans for the rehabilitation of sugar mills on Java. The justification was purely macroeconomic; Indonesia had become a sugar-deficit country, imports were costing foreign exchange, and old factories were there waiting to be repaired. The unfortunate aspect of the situation lay in the fact that the practice so eloquently described by Geertz, whereby peasants were compelled to grow sugar cane (a sixteen-month crop) in their rice paddies, had never been eliminated. By 1973 the mills were government owned, and a military-dominated local administration made sure that suitable blocks of land were organized and leased to them when needed. Research already available in 1973 showed that under this arrangement, in effect the old "culture system" dressed in modern olive drab, farmers made only about half the amount of money they would have earned had they been able to keep their land in rice.[33] Bank officials were not impressed with this evidence at the time and went ahead with the projects, which (at least in some cases) have hurt the interests of the local farmers.[34]

There is less chance that such blatant insensitivity to the little man would recur today. Both the World Bank and the U.S. bilateral program are now obsessed, perhaps to the point of overreaction, with desire to help the "poor majority" as directly and demonstrably as possible. "Hardware" is out; "software" is in, and aid bureaucrats are manfully struggling with the intractable problems involved in helping people, as opposed to financing things. (This generalization does not include the Japanese, now the largest bilateral donors, who have been content by and large to stick with infrastructure and resource transfers, and whose legislature does not attempt to make aid policy.) Not surprisingly, Inner Indonesia is increasingly recognized as the greatest challenge of all to the new "basic human needs" aid philosophy. Like its volcanoes, viewed across the brilliant green of new rice, Java conveys a sense of ominous calm, surface tranquillity masking unpredictable energy, and no small amount of hypnotic appeal. Among foreign observers there is debate about whether and to what extent external assistance should be focused on "the Java problem." Discussion tends to revolve around a number of issues including the role of food aid, the merits of a food production versus a labor absorption strategy, and, last but not least, the effectiveness of a program (historically much favored by the Indonesian government) whereby Javanese peasants are resettled in the Outer Islands. Each of these is discussed briefly below.

Rice vs. Labor

The most perplexing issues involve an apparent contradiction between growing more food and employing more people. Further increases in production may be linked inexorably to further capitalization of the peasant economy with attendant labor displacement. Switching emphasis to nonrice crops, such as corn and cassava, which virtually everyone agrees is desirable, will not necessarily eliminate the dilemma. It could be argued, on rather solid historical grounds, that the least painful way out of a detraditionalization process is to push it along as fast as possible. According to this theory, the relatively wealthy farmers who are most productive will inevitably displace the less efficient sooner or later. The way to take care of the latter is through dispersed rural industry, plus whatever palliatives do not interfere with production. Advocates of progress should not be distracted by idyllic visions of communal burden-sharing, which (if it ever truly flourished) is gone forever. It is futile, according to this argument, to think that peasant society on Java can be revitalized. Humpty Dumpty is well and truly off the wall.

Of course, practical politics will prevent adoption of the sort of "kulak" strategy which such thoughts might suggest. However, it seems equally likely that in one sense the argument is correct—that labor displacement will continue, come what may. Hence practical necessity will also force continuing attention to nonagricultural employment generation. The rural works program (INPRES) is fine as far as it goes. Rural electrification, which is becoming a major focus of the American aid program, may stimulate small-town industry, as it has to some extent in the Philippines. Development of major, labor intensive, export-oriented industry, feeble to date, is unlikely to pick up (despite the 1978 currency devaluation) unless the government takes far more effective steps to stimulate private investment. While such a strategy appears logical to foreign economists, Indonesian policymakers will inevitably be deterred by the inescapable corollary of lopsided benefit to the ethnic Chinese who dominate domestic capitalism. In general there is little reason to expect dramatic breakthroughs in employment generation given the obvious administrative and political bottlenecks and the conservative nature of Javanese officialdom.

Alternatively both nonofficial experts and the government have recently, for the first time since the beginning of the New Order, suggested the possibility of implementing "land reform." What most of them mean is *stabilization* of land holdings at present levels, not redistribution in the classic sense. As we have seen, average holdings in Inner Indonesia are already less than one-half hectare in size, and the basic problem is one of insufficiency. Redistribution would necessarily be limited to the relatively small amount (less than 5 percent) of Java's arable land still in tea, teak, and rubber estates (mostly upland and mainly government owned) or to the communal village lands (*bengkok*) traditionally allocated to local officials for lifetime use in lieu of salary. Individual *bengkok* plots are sometimes up to ten hectares in size, a relatively enormous amount, but eliminating them would have a revolutionary impact on the structure of existing rural elites, and for that reason alone is not likely to be seriously considered. The existing land reform law, passed in 1959 but never implemented, is generally acknowledged to be irrelevant, since it mandates an absurdly generous maximum family holding of five hectares and a utopian minimum of two hectares, at least four times the present average holding.[35]

Advocates of land tenure stabilization would not agree

that social revitalization is out of the question for Java. Armed with findings based on village-level research, they believe that the current growth in concentration of land holdings, often involving nonownership mechanisms such as the *gadai* or pawning technique, may be far more widespread than official statistics suggest. Rising land values, stimulated by green revolution possibilities and foreign-funded irrigation projects, have coincided with ballooning population, further encouraging those who inherit tiny, fragmented holdings to sell or lease them. The new middle classes in the cities are eager to buy a hectare or two here and there. The result is an apparent if ill-documented shift from near to absolute landlessness, and the exodus of many of the victims from the agricultural labor force. Even where nonfarm employment is available, the poor (especially women) may be suffering serious welfare losses as a result of this process, since they can no longer take advantage of relatively remunerative part-time opportunities once they lose the minimum land base required to meet basic food needs.[36]

Those who are appalled by this phenomenon argue (in my view convincingly) that labor absorption rather than food production should be the first priority on Java, and that the food effort should eventually be concentrated in the Outer Islands. They believe that the social and political costs of "development" in the rural areas have thus far outweighed the benefits, so far as the poor majority is concerned. They would favor, as a first step, a strenuous effort to comprehend the gothic network of owner-lessee-laborer relations on Java. They tend to be highly critical of major foreign aid efforts, especially those of the World Bank, for failure to calculate the often deleterious impact of projects on rural institutions which, although patently in danger of destruction, are as yet ill understood.

The possibility of social upheaval is sufficiently appreciated in official circles to have provoked the recent references to land reform and stabilization of holdings, although most observers do not believe that any firm action will result. The government has also tolerated a growing academic debate on rural development issues. Indonesia's most prestigious newspaper, the Catholic-oriented daily *Kompas,* recently summarized the work of Indonesian social scientists who believe more emphasis must be placed on "simple" village-level projects and self-help organizations. One of them argued that all development efforts based on "modern economic concepts" should be suspended for a decade while such efforts are under way, or the result will merely increase the widening gap between poor and poorest.[37] (Regardless of their logic, there is in such arguments both overtones of xenophobia and a somewhat disturbing echo of "dualistic" Dutch colonial theory, which approvingly emphasized the isolation of an innocent peasantry from modernity.)

Beyond official circles, proponents of a more radical alternative see political revolution as a necessary first step, followed by a policy of economic self-reliance, heavy emphasis on the rural sector, abolition of private landownership, and the systematic mobilization of labor in lieu of capital. While such a solution is not advocated publicly in Indonesia, for obvious reasons, it retains considerable appeal for many students and intellectuals, including noncommunists who despair of genuine progress under the current system. No one can say with confidence how the Javanese peasant would react to a radical strategy, or whether (assuming the emergence of highly motivated and talented revolutionary leadership) it could be made to work on Java. All the usual caveats on the feasibility of implementing the "Chinese model" beyond China apply, and its recent compromise in China itself may cause some proponents to wonder about the long-term practicality of radical self-reliance.

Inner vs. Outer Indonesia

At present a good deal of Indonesia's external assistance, including about 40 percent of total U.S. bilateral aid, is going to the Outer Islands. Moreover, a preponderance of private foreign investment is concentrated beyond Java. Advocates of a "Java first" strategy (virtually all of them foreigners) believe that since Java is the greatest potential source of crisis, it should absorb most of the aid effort—at least in terms of thought, if not money. Foreign assistance to the Outer Islands should, it may be argued, be restricted to infrastructure efforts which would stimulate a spontaneous process of private-sector development.

The most obvious objection is largely political but nonetheless compelling. If Java, Bali, and Madura suddenly disappeared, Sumatra, Sulawesi, Borneo, and the rest of Outer Indonesia would still constitute the most populous country in Southeast Asia. By its very political and demographic weight, Java demands and usually gets preponderant attention from Jakarta. Areas of Sumatra and Sulawesi which have local cultures with strong entrepreneurial traditions have, in the past, been stifled by centralized and largely Javanese-manned local administration, and national economic policies have frequently displayed a rather blatant Javanese bias. (One typical example: in 1972 new coconut oil factories on Sulawesi were prohibited from exporting their product to Java to protect older and less efficient Javanese manufacturers, thereby contributing to the continuing stagnation of what was once one of the world's major copra-producing areas.)[38] Although regional rebellion has not recurred on a serious scale since the ill-fated uprisings of 1958, the underlying causes have never been fully eliminated. The Indonesians, keenly aware of this, would be most unlikely to risk provoking Outer Island unrest by concentrating foreign aid (highly visible and carrying considerable symbolic impact) on Java. For the same reason, the first two five-year plans placed major rhetorical emphasis on Outer Island development.

As usual, there is a polar opposite to the "Java first" argument. It involves hope that rapid growth of commercial and industrial centers in the Outer Islands might exert an economic "pull" on Java itself, attracting migrants (both farmers and laborers) and stimulating the entire Indonesian economy. The argument is not new, and nothing of the sort has happened so far. The mineral, oil, and other economic activities in the Outer Islands are major sources of foreign exchange, but to a disturbing extent they have remained enclaves, with limited employment or developmental impact on local societies and (thus far) little significant role as stimulators of diversified regional development. Outer Indonesia's failure to pace national development is partly a result of Javacentric administrative bias, and it is still possible that with a healthy injection of laissez-fairism an "Outer Island" strategy might pay handsomely. But even assuming that laissez-fairism is feasible, which isn't likely given the heavily statist economic culture of Indonesia, it seems probable that much more would be required. For all its potential, Outer Indonesia is many ways deprived compared to Java, and it has some very special problems of its own, such as poor soils. In addition to its infrastructure needs, its development will require a much greater allocation of educated human talent—the scarcest resource of all—than it is currently getting. In this area the competition between Inner and Outer Indonesia is genuine and not subject to easy solution.

Public Law 480

Since World War II the United States has provided Indonesia with more than a billion dollars in PL 480 food aid. Until recently there were two basic programs. The Title I program, consisting of government-to-government sales on highly concessional credit terms, has been much more important in the case of Indonesia than the more purely humanitarian Title II program involving donated food usually channeled through private agencies such as CARE. The complex motivation behind Title I PL 480 food aid is, of course, by no means entirely charitable, a point that was underscored in 1977 when fourteen U.S. senators from food-producing states instantly protested the temporary suspension (on human rights grounds) of food aid shipments to Indonesia (see chapter four). Critics of food aid claim that it has generally undermined, rather than stimulated, agricultural development, by enabling governments to maintain artificially low prices to producers. The real purpose, they maintain, has often been to prop up governments by providing assured food supplies for key urban constituencies, usually the military, the civil service, and the middle classes.[39] This argument has been most fully developed in the case of Bangladesh, where it seems clear that until recently PL 480 was not reaching the rural poor.[40]

It is less clear to what extent this critique applies to Indonesia. PL 480 has never constituted more than a fraction of Indonesian imports—about one-quarter and one-fifth of rice and wheat imports, respectively, in 1977 (see table 6.1). An overvalued rupiah has also been a major component of food import strategy in recent years. Thanks to oil, the Indonesians have never lacked sufficient foreign exchange to buy rice when necessary, if concessional food aid were not available. There is little doubt, given the political importance of rice, that they would have done so in the past, and will continue to do so in the future.

The welfare implications of Title I PL 480 are similarly shrouded in controversy. Granting for the sake of argument that U.S. surplus food has contributed to a disincentive pattern for producers, the same low-price, import-reliant strategy has probably benefited not only city dwellers at all income levels (from generals to pedicab drivers) but also the majority of the rural poor who are net consumers of food. William Collier of the Agro Economic Survey in Bogor, an American who is among the most experienced of foreign observers of rural Java, notes that:

Low rice prices. . . . benefit most of the rural villages even in the major rice producing regions. Only the small proportion of the rice farmers who have perhaps one half and more hectare can produce enough rice for their families and still have a surplus and able to sell rice and benefit from higher rice prices.[41]

It is difficult to ignore this argument without advocating a "kulak" strategy—realistic in one sense, perhaps, but inconceivable on political or humanitarian grounds.

Leaving aside the question of who may have suffered or benefited, there is no doubt that PL 480 food aid has often been used to articulate U.S. political support for the Indonesian government. It is relevant that most Indonesian rice is consumed in the area where it is grown. Thus the mobile

Table 6.1 U.S. Food Aid (Title I PL 480) to Indonesia

Year[a]	67/68	68/69	69/70	70/71	71/72	72/73	73/74	74/75	75/76	76/77	77/78	78/79[f]
Domestic milled rice production (000 tons)	10,402	11,666	12,249	13,140	13,724	13,183	14,607	15,276	15,185	15,845	15,876	17,598
Rice imports[b]	354	628	806	773	524	1,234	1,225	1,148	670	1,526	2,500	1,845
Rice imports/ Rice consumption	3%	5%	6%	6%	4%	8%	8%	7%	4%	9%	14%	10%
PL 480 rice imports	95	148	327	351	323	346	105	—	—	10	541	161
PL 480 rice imports/[b] Total rice imports	27%	24%	41%	45%	62%	28%	9%	—	—	1%	22%[e]	9%
Wheat imports	170	335	685	455	487	711	1,156	769	834	1,025	1,064	1,154
PL 480 wheat imports	—	55	278	272	442	183	420	—	—	41	334	153
PL 480 wheat imports/[c] Total wheat imports	—	16%	41%	60%	91%	26%	36%	—	—	4%	26%[e]	13%
Urea fertilizer[d] consumption	—	—	—	—	—	480	668	603	670	665	850	

[a] All figures calculated according to Indonesian FY (Apr.–Mar.), unless noted otherwise.

[b] PL 480 figures calculated according to U.S. FY (July–June until 1976, thereafter Oct.–Sept.; July 1976–Sept. 1976—TQ or transitional quarter). Total import figures calculated according to Indonesian FY. Hence, this ratio is only an approximate figure. PL 480 figures used include Title I shipments only.

[c] Same as note b, except from FY 68–69 to FY 71–72 the calculation reflects a direct time comparison (i.e., in these years the total wheat import figures were available according to the U.S. FY).

[d] In thousands of metric tons. Recent data from U.S. Agricultural Attaché Jakarta shows a figure of 1345 (estimated) for calendar year 1978, not directly comparable with figures above, but suggesting further improvement.

[e] For PL 480 figure, transitional quarter amounts included in FY 77–78.

[f] 1978–79 figures are preliminary.

SOURCE: U.S. Department of Agriculture, Foreign Agriculture Service, raw data.

stocks available to the state logistics agency (BULOG) in times of crisis are derived mainly from imports.[42] These are used for market interventions to maintain price stability. But BULOG is also charged with insuring that adequate supplies are available to the military (250,000 of them) and the civil service. Although in recent years U.S. surplus stocks have usually constituted no more than a fraction of annual imports, their overall impact, as a result of timing, the political prestige of the source, and the fact that their sale generates revenue, has undoubtedly been disproportionate.[43] How much so must remain a matter for conjecture, since despite the great size and long duration of the program, there has never been a serious research effort, by either the U.S. government or outside scholars, to evaluate the economic and political impact of PL 480 in Indonesia.

Stung by criticism that concessional food aid was contributing to production disincentive patterns, the United States, at congressional behest, has started to experiment with curatives. Until 1966 the United States placed few conditions on Title I credits. Beginning in that year host governments were required to provide "self help" reports to prove that efforts were under way to stimulate food production.[44] This was, in general, little more than ritual. More recently, in 1977, Congress authorized a new "Food for Development" provision, Title III, that offers host governments the option of using proceeds from PL 480 sales for development projects conceived in cooperation with U.S. AID officials, in which case repayment of the PL 480 loan is waived.[45] For the first time the new law allows us to make long-term commitments of food aid (up to five years, if commodities are available), thereby eliminating some of the year-to-year uncertainty that has plagued the Title I program.

"Food for Development" advocates in the Carter Administration, buoyed by strong congressional support, hoped that the proviso would be a vehicle for stimulating governments to adopt innovative policies to solve food deficits and other problems. PL 480 would, for the first time, become an integral part of a sophisticated development strategy rather than (as the critics charged) a thinly disguised means of dumping American agricultural exports in the underdeveloped world. Indonesia was seen as a natural field for Title III. It was envisioned, for example, that the program might be used to encourage the government to experiment further with such activities as food production and employment projects designed and staffed at the local level with help from provincial Javanese universities.

Unfortunately Food for Development has encountered heavy resistance both from the multi-agency U.S. bureaucracy that presides over food aid and from intended recipients, including Indonesia. Officials of the U.S. Department of Agriculture have little reason to favor Title III. Mindful primarily of the interests of American (not Javanese) farmers, they want to maximize food exports, not tie them up in red tape. State Department crisis managers have traditionally viewed PL 480 as a source of "quick fix" balance-of-payments relief and political support for friendly countries. In this scheme of things Title III can only be a complicating factor. Planners at the Office of Management and Budget (OMB) do not care for the five-year forward commitment proviso, which violates "ordinary" (i.e., one year only) budgetary practice. They have therefore argued that Title III is justified only in cases where recipient governments have made an equally "extraordinary" commitment to fundamental reform in agricultural or developmental policy.

Such conditions may easily appear offensive, if not downright neocolonial, to a strongly nationalist government. Under the regular Title I program (which is supplemented, not replaced, by Title III) there is no restriction whatever on the money generated by PL 480 food sales. Repayment, over forty years at less than 3 percent interest, is hardly a major concern in an age of chronic double-digit inflation. Under Title III, at a minimum, the same PL 480 revenues must be used for joint projects which are subject to all the burdensome planning, administrative, and auditing requirements of any bilateral U.S. aid project. Hence it came as no great surprise when, during the course of negotiations in 1978, the Indonesians concluded that the old Title I way was preferable, and rejected, at least for the time being, a Food for Development program. Questions raised earlier about the long-term impact of American food aid remain unanswered.

Transmigration

More than seventy years ago the Dutch began to resettle Javanese peasants in Sumatra and other islands. The policy has been continued by all successive regimes. Motives have varied over the years. The original colonists were intended to supply labor in the pepper-producing Lampung region of southern Sumatra, and later to grow rice. Gradually, however, the primary purpose of the program became the relief of population pressure on Java. Most recently overpopulation has been largely displaced as a motive, at least in the formal prose of planning documents, by "development" and the need to fill up "empty lands." By 1940 transmigration, as this activity came to be known, was running at the rate of about 10,000 families a year. From 1950 to date, approximately 150,000 Javanese have been settled with government assistance.[46]

The Suharto government is continuing to place major emphasis on transmigration. The original target for the Second Five Year Plan (1974–78) was 250,000 families, later revised downward to 87,000 because of administrative difficulties. It was hoped that these would attract another 200,000 "spontaneous" transmigrants, i.e., colonists who would pay their own way to the resettlement areas. An even more ambitious goal of 500,000 families has been set for the Third Five Year Plan (1979–83).[47] Such a program, if successfully implemented (an enormous if), would represent a five-fold increase over current transmigration rates and more than cancel out Inner Indonesia's annual growth rate of 1.5 million people per year. In support, the World Bank in 1977 apparently promised the relatively vast sum of $1 billion over the five-year period.

The technical and administrative difficulties involved in transmigration are enormous. Settlers, who usually receive two hectares of land per family, face obstacles ranging from malaria to lack of irrigation facilities. Outer Island environments are typically both hostile and fragile, which is precisely why they have remained underpopulated. "Improving" them requires capital and technology as well as persistence. In recent years most transmigrants have been located either in deltaic, peat swamp areas (there are vast expanses of such land in eastern Sumatra and southern Borneo) or in upland regions made accessible by recent road construction. Farming the soil of such areas is fraught with technical challenges which are, as yet, little understood even by the scientific community. In southern Sumatra, past transmigration resulted in reckless deforestation when pioneers without irrigable land were compelled to practice slash-and-burn agriculture. Relocating Javanese peasants to culturally alien areas certainly poses as great an administrative challenge as, say, persuading unemployed Baltimore slum dwellers to work in the labor-short apple-producing regions of the Shenandoah Valley, a task which apparently exceeds the capacity of American government. Unfortunately, the Indonesian bureaucracy in charge of transmigration, until recently divided between two ministries, is by no means the strongest in the country.

Despite seventy years of effort, the results of transmigration are debatable. Although perhaps two million people have been relocated[48] (including spontaneous followers-on) the program has failed to make a significant impact on the population of Java, and may have merely stimulated fertility surges in the transmigrants' original homes. In the past, transmigrant communities frequently hindered rather than helped Outer Indonesian development by creating "basket case" communities which absorbed the attention of already overtaxed local governments. The oldest transmigration areas, such as Lampung, have tended to evolve into rather dismal replications of Java, complete with overpopulation.

The most serious criticism of transmigration may be that it distracts the government from more realistic programs. The appeal of transmigration to the Indonesian leadership is somewhat mysterious, but it owes something to the continuing force of Dutch precedent, visible in many aspects of bureaucratic thought and practice. Anyone contemplating the dilemma of Java is understandably tempted to look for external solutions, as opposed to concentrating on the excruciating realities at the source of the problem. Big programs with heavy foreign participation have an especially appealing "modern" quality. Several years ago, for example, there was much talk of mechanized rice estates in Sumatra as a means of eliminating food deficits. One such estate was to be established by the state oil company, Pertamina, and another by Caltex. Pertamina's collapse in 1975, plus dawning awareness of the costs involved, have dampened earlier eagerness. In the case of transmigration, World Bank support may be encouraging the Indonesians in a massive illusion which could result in a tragic waste of resources. It is difficult to judge, even in those instances where transmigration succeeds, whether it is cost effective compared to other development programs. The estimated average cost per transmigrant family is about $5–6,000[49] including a small house, free food for eight months, and infrastructure costs (but not, in cases of failure, the expense of maintaining or relocating dependent communities). Beyond its money costs, the program is already absorbing a high proportion of Indonesia's limited bureaucratic capacity.

In the past, the Javanese have been reluctant pioneers. But whether this involves an immutable cultural attitude remains very much in doubt. Today, proponents of transmigration point out, there are surplus applicants in Javanese villages for every transmigration opportunity. Although the pioneer settlements tend to appear appalling, especially in their earliest years, inhabitants are usually better off than they were in their home villages. Improvement in interisland communications, presently inefficient and erratic, might reduce reluctance to move by, in effect, bringing Inner and Outer Indonesia closer together. It seems likely that the supposed cultural immobility of the Javanese could dissolve rather rapidly, especially if Outer Indonesia develops at a rapid rate. However, the result might not please everyone. It could be something like a repetition of what has happened in the southern Philippines, where the U.S. government, commencing in 1913, sponsored a land settlement program inspired by the homestead ethos. The Philippine program succeeded altogether too well; the result was an influx of Christians who now far outnumber original Muslim and tribal inhabitants, a major cause of the continuing Muslim insurrection. Similar irritations could easily arise in the Outer Islands, whose inhabitants have traditionally been restive under Javanese political dominance, and are unlikely to welcome demographic envelopment as well.

The World Bank's $1 billion commitment, never officially acknowledged, generated controversy and apprehension among other aid donors and within the Bank itself. It was apparently made on the basis of personal contact between Bank President McNamara and Indonesian leaders, including President Suharto. From the Bank's point of view, transmigration is attractive because it is a poverty-oriented program and will absorb large sums of money. Critics see the program as a manifestation of McNamara's unfortunate propensity for large, mechanistic solutions—perhaps unfairly, they recall the famous electronic barrier across the Vietnamese DMZ—and an illustration of the Bank's tendency to plunge ahead without adequate consideration of social and political constraints.[50]

The Indonesian government has clouded the issue by suggesting (and then denying) that former political prisoners might in future be "voluntarily" relocated to transmigration sites.[51] While the more recent denials are apparently sincere, lingering suspicion is natural in view of the fact that until a few years ago the government routinely "transmigrated" slum dwellers who, for cosmetic purposes, had been evicted from Jakarta and other cities. In 1977 the government successfully approached the U.S. Export-Import Bank to obtain loans for the purchase of Lockheed C-130 aircraft to move transmigrants.[52] The fact that such a scheme could be considered was deeply discouraging to those who believe that Indonesia should concentrate her limited resources on labor- rather than capital-intensive programs.

In light of continuing controversy and the World Bank's own acknowledgment that transmigration would have little impact on the manpower problem in Java,[53] Bank officials have recently backed away somewhat, suggesting that the $1 billion commitment was cast in general terms and could apply to a range of related projects, such as estate development, with only a tenuous connection to the core "people-moving" effort. As of late 1978 only one, $30 million Bank transmigration project loan had been signed, although a second was about to be formally launched and at least three more were in various stages of development. Although the Bank is unlikely publicly to acknowledge any change in policy, it is now more probable that its support for transmigration will proceed at a pace determined by the attendant administrative problems rather than by five-year-plan rhetoric, which is to say, not very fast.

That would probably be a happy ending. Transmigration should not be condemned out of hand, as some of its more emotional critics are inclined to do. But given its complexities and uncertainties it seems equally obvious that such an activity is particularly unsuited for the a priori commitment of large sums of foreign aid. At the very least, more field research should precede major spending. Unfortunately, it is not easily obtained, since Indonesia's limited research capacity is already overburdened with similar tasks, and the government is reluctant to allow foreigners to do such work. The key to successful transmigration will lie in establishing core communities which become self reliant as soon as possible and, in the process, begin to attract the voluntary movement of relatives and fellow villagers from Java. This suggests not only research but experimentation on a small scale, possibly for years, until the dynamics of success, as well as the possible political hazards, are better understood.

Conclusion

Despite certain unusually exotic components—rich soil, dense culture, multiethnic politics—it would be rash to assume that Javanese poverty is any more complex than Bengali or American poverty. Certainly, however, it is no better understood. In each of the areas discussed above there are fundamental information gaps, a few of which may be less than wholly accidental. It is possible, for example, that the U.S. government has never made a serious effort to evaluate the overall impact of surplus food programs out of concern that the results might support allegations of conflict between the interests of Javanese and American farmers, assumed in the past to be equally well served by PL 480. In most cases the information shortfall results from a lack of statistics and research capability on the Indonesian side. On Java, for example, there has been only one project in recent years which systematically attempted to gather time-series data on farm wages.[54] As a result of such deficiencies few major generalities can be stated with certainty. No one is totally certain about the impact of new rice varieties on Javanese labor, or the extent of rural welfare shifts, or the width of the gap (stationary? widening?) between rich and poor. There is an even more serious absence of understanding of the factors that motivate people to work harder, save money, or transmigrate. The prevailing lack of information encourages a blind polemic between pollyannas and prophets of doom that, by shedding more heat than light, compounds uncertainty.

Nevertheless some things are sufficiently clear about the nature of the Inner Indonesian land-food-population problem. First, it is an old problem. Second, it is going to be a problem for many years to come. It might be logical to conclude that the issues at stake should be approached in expectation of sustained involvement over decades. Yet political pressures and budgeting practices constrain both donor and recipient to evaluate aid by volume of money spent and immediate, visible impact. If real progress is to be made, the problem may demand a reorientation away from immediacy toward a pace more in keeping with the deliberate nuance and indirection of Javanese culture itself.

Conventional aid strategies are particularly ill-suited to Inner Indonesia for a number of reasons. The availability of foreign exchange, for example, may not be a very critical factor one way or another. Regardless of what one may think of "Chinese models," it is undeniable that mobilizing and managing Java's labor resources will be a much more crucial component of any solution than resource transfers (financial or other) from abroad. Java may well be a case where many small, experimental projects, dispersed into the countryside, are likely to be more valuable in the long run than big projects—a frustrating situation for aid officials who are under pressure to spend large sums of money with small numbers of supervisory personnel. Small projects cost less money (a distinct bureaucratic liability) and they tend to be management as well as labor intensive.

It is equally apparent that foreign understanding (no matter how technically expert or culturally attuned) can never substitute sufficiently for Indonesian understanding without recreating a streamlined version of colonialism. This is unacceptable, as the Indonesians have made clear if only by insisting that most project-related research efforts be conducted by Indonesians. The most effective contribution that foreigners can make is to train Indonesians to the level where they can train themselves. Of course, donors have been attempting to do this for many years, and in the process have achieved some major results, the most famous of which was the Ford Foundation's education of Professor Widjojo and the other economists who have dominated Indonesian planning since 1966. Unfortunately, the more recent preoccupation with direct aid to the poor majority has distracted attention from the less fashionable category of "institution building," including training, and research bottlenecks have been perpetuated which could perhaps be eliminated with effort. In Indonesia, for example, lack of English-language capability has long made it difficult for some of the best students to qualify for training abroad. It would be far wiser if aid donors concentrated on identifying the best potential trainees and then provided whatever language training may be required to do the job. In the final analysis Indonesia's need for skilled human resources is practically infinite. The fact that only small sums of money can be absorbed in this area should not be allowed to obscure its fundamental importance.

On the other hand, large amounts of aid, dispensed without sufficient understanding, can easily do more harm than good in a complex, largely traditional society like that of Indonesia. The external origin of aid arouses both cargo cult hopes and scapegoat resentments which may move the country away from rather than toward either self-reliance or sufficient self-examination. At worst, aid can foster corruption and cynicism in the thin layer of officials and scholars who deal with foreigners, encouraging them to neglect non-aid-related responsibilities, distorting bureaucratic organization by favoring some segments over others, and warping the priorities of the recipients to accommodate the concerns of the donors. A more subtle but often more serious drawback results from the proven capacity of Indonesians to use foreign advisers in a variety of unhealthy ways—as bureaucratic mediators among isolated, vertically organized bureaucracies, as bearers of bad tidings, as proxies in interministerial wars, or even as convenient lightning rods for the political tensions which inevitably accompany change. These are not arguments against foreign assistance, but they do suggest the need for caution and a step-by-step approach, all the more so when dealing with the vastly complex problems involved in a direct assault on poverty.[55]

In the past, the U.S. government has often regarded economic aid as support for friendly governments, as well as a prophylactic against social upheaval. For reasons advanced in chapter two, attempting to use aid as a source of political support or leverage is no longer desirable under Southeast Asian circumstances, if it ever was. The desirability of avoiding social upheaval is a motive less easily dismissed. Current conditions on Java could lead to massive violence in the future, as they did in 1965–66. While the United States should not assume an antirevolutionary, pro–status quo stance, no one can blink away the likelihood that such upheaval would be terribly costly in human and perhaps political terms. As noted earlier, to the extent that violence developed anti-Chinese overtones, it could well spread across international boundaries, particularly into Malaysia, and severely shake if not destroy the prevailing trend toward regional harmony.

But such considerations are not a clear rationalization for aid. It is a truism that the process of development, on Java as elsewhere, may be more socially disruptive and destabilizing than a prolonged drift into economic and social stagnation. Indeed, the fact that certain types of aid may in the long run prove revolutionary (hopefully in the most genteel, non-violent sense, but perhaps not) is one of the more appealing arguments in favor of continuing or increasing the present modest level of effort.

As noted in the previous chapter, some recent studies argue that the United States may in future be economically dependent to an increasing extent on the development of the southern hemisphere and resulting trade. If the argument can be sustained, it will certainly provide a degree of "hard nosed" rationale for aid, but it seems more likely that the only undeniable basis for our interest will remain ethical, as deceptively soft and ultimately realistic as the humanitarian instinct itself.

In the final analysis, our interest in Inner Indonesia is inseparable from our interest in the entire country, the region, and the less-developed world generally. U.S. aid officials are fond of pointing out that given our noninvolvement in China, slight recent involvement in South Asia, and minimal poverty programs in Latin America, Indonesia contains about one-third of that rather small proportion of the world's poor about whom Americans are attempting to do anything. According to this line of reasoning, Java is part of our chosen field of endeavor, a proving ground for a much wider concern. Our limited knowledge of the case suggests that what counts is the quality, not the quantity, of the effort.

A Philippine Postscript

I will end with a brief comparison of the Philippine and Indonesian development situations, in full awareness that to do this adequately would be a book-length project in itself. While there is nothing in the Philippines to match the scope and drama of the Inner Indonesian food and employment crisis, the range of problems is hardly less complex. Furthermore, of course, our involvement with Manila has been more considerable. In per capita terms bilateral U.S. economic aid to the Philippines is substantially more than to any other country in Southeast Asia ($1.28 in fiscal year 1978 vs. $1.15 for Indonesia).[56] As noted earlier, the Philippine program has traditionally been conducted in a manner which projected Americans into local decision-making on terms of somewhat paranoid familiarity typical of the entire postcolonial relationship.

The difference in levels of development between the two countries is obvious. Philippine per capita GNP is almost double of that of Indonesia ($450 vs. $240), although the Philippines is not a significant oil producer. Despite the Philippines' deserved reputation for social stratification, income is more evenly distributed than is the case in Indonesia. The respective ratios of doctors to population (1 doctor to every 16.9 thousand people in Indonesia, 1 to 2.7 thousand in the Philippines) are probably a fair reflection of the Philippines' comparative advantage in human skills and the development of a middle class.[57]

The Philippines should be on the verge of graduation from underdevelopment to the intermdiate status of countries like Taiwan and Korea. The country is imbued with the physical resources and (much more important) the human resources to make the transition. Failure to make more rapid progress is, far more clearly than in most cases, a function of insufficient mobilization and development of internal assets. While Philippine rural poverty is as bad as any in Asia, and malnutrition among the worst in the world, the Philippines exports skilled manpower of all kinds. While the government energetically taps international capital markets, domestic financial resources are often misused. The construction in Manila of fourteen luxury hotels in 1976 at a cost of $400 million, almost all of it raised internally from government trust funds, is a good illustration. Factors holding the country back assuredly include the usual consequences of endemic rural poverty, but they also reflect unwise or questionable political leadership. The sagacity of the Philippine technocrats is often canceled out by capricious economic decisions made primarily to benefit individuals with connections to the palace.

Why, then, does the United States continue to allocate such relatively high levels of aid to the Philippines (see table 6.2), and what is the ultimate effect? One cause is habit; a traditional pattern of involvement with an ex-colony and ally. Another is the fact that the Philippines, with its relative wealth of skills, is an easy place to design viable assistance projects and to find competent, like-minded counterparts, all of whom incidentally speak English. Finally, of

Table 6.2 U.S. and Multilateral Aid to Indonesia and Philippines (Million $)

Indonesia	FY 78 (actual)	79 (estimated)	80 (proposed)
AID			
Loans	19.7	101.9	77.8
Grants	1.8	15.2	21.9
Total AID	21.5	117.0	99.8
PL 480			
Title I	135.7	104.3	101.3
Title II	7.1	6.6	6.1
Total PL 480	142.8	110.9	107.4
Total AID and PL 480	164.4	228.0	207.2
Asian Development Bank	205.2		
World Bank/IDA	490.1		
Philippines			
AID			
Loans	32.1	58.8	39.0
Grants	4.9	14.8	10.2
Total AID	37.0	73.6	49.2
PL 480			
Title I	8.8	10.0	—
Title II	12.8	12.3	17.4
Total PL 480	21.7	22.3	66.3
Total AID and PL 480	58.8	95.9	66.3
Asian Development Bank	136.5		
World Bank/IDA	526.1		

Note: Figures represent resource flows or disbursements, not obligations.

SOURCE: Agency for International Development, *Congressional Presentation, Fiscal Year 1980* (Washington, 1979) Annex II (Asia).

course, there is the factor of our military bases, for which the entire U.S. aid program is in some degree a tacit form of compensation.

A relatively high proportion of the American assistance program is channeled directly to the rural poor—for instance, a massive Title II (grant) PL 480 program administered largely by CARE and Catholic Relief Services which provides nutritional supplement to school children and nursing mothers throughout the Philippines. Additional aid goes into projects such as family planning which are related to vital American interests—in this case the prevention of Malthusian disaster on a global scale. No one would dispute the direct, immediate humanitarian benefit of such programs. Nevertheless, it seems clear that in the unique political and psychological context of U.S.-Philippine relations, continued bilateral American aid *at current high levels* acts as a subtle deterrent to more effective self-help efforts against such problems as rural poverty, malnutrition, underemployment, and an education system which, although once the finest in the region, is showing increasing signs of stagnation and neglect.

If this is correct, the contrast between the Philippines and its southern neighbor is explicit and warrants a different strategy on our part. Aid policy to Indonesia should, as its primary goal, attempt to help the Indonesians develop the institutional capacity to understand and solve their own problems. At least for the short-term future, there should also be a continuing element of resource transfers. In the Philippines our policy should be one of explicit, phased reduction in aid levels, particularly in the category of development assistance, with the aim of encouraging this talented and relatively advantaged people to use the self-help capacity which they already possess. To minimize the harmful consequences of postcolonialism we should, in the case of the Philippines, rely on multilateral aid channels to the maximum possible extent. Filipinos with a sophisticated knowledge of our relationship already regard our bilateral aid as a tawdry, anachronistic substitute for the more enlightened trade policies which would convey vastly greater benefit to the Philippine economy without perpetuating dependency. It will be an unfortunate paradox indeed if our military bases motivate us to maintain aid at harmfully high levels and thereby contribute to the erosion of our long-term interest in seeing the Philippines achieve self-reliant prosperity.

Chapter Seven
Environmental Problems and Opportunities

> Some biologists (informed scientists—not merely case-hardened econuts) would go so far as to assert that, through rainforest destruction, man has permanently diverted the course of evolution.
>
> —S. D. Richardson
> "Foresters and the Faustian Bargain"
> (May 1978)[1]

Island Southeast Asia is an environmental as well as an ethnographic mosaic. The variety of the terrain is often demonstrated in the last few minutes before an airplane lands at any major town. Passengers will probably see most, if not all, of the following: virgin tropical rainforest, an active volcano, evidence of shifting cultivation, and perhaps coral islands if the approach is from the sea. In the final minutes before touching down the plane will pass over irrigated rice fields, a variety of garden agriculture, a silt-clogged river, and finally the rooftops of varied urban humanity from slum dwellers to oligarchs. Human beings in nearly every stage of social evolution are juxtaposed in close proximity. From the Presidential Palace in Jakarta to the primitive Badui tribal villages of West Java is only fifty miles as the hornbill flies, and loincloth-wearing Mangyans in the mountains of Mindoro can, at night, see the yellow glare of Manila lights reflected in the sky.

Precolonial Southeast Asian kingdoms were relatively small islands of civilization in oceans of jungle. Until the nineteenth century, far greater areas were occupied by seminomadic societies based on shifting cultivation than by the practitioners of settled, "civilized" agriculture. The nineteenth century brought enormous population growth and accelerating change, but large segments of the social evolutionary spectrum are still visible. Each societal type has made a different kind of impact on the landscape, and in some areas the land has not been affected at all, or so it seems.

The appearance of a rather static world, with many traditional elements still in place, is of course deceptive. What is most remarkable about Southeast Asia is not the occasional proximity of deep forest to city lights but the rate at which the forest is receding. The variety of social and geographic settings is real enough. What may be less obvious is the ease with which enormous, often harmful change can take place as a result of only moderate population pressure. For many people the word "jungle" is associated with the tropics and suggests an environment ultimately resistant to human endeavor. But the reverse is true. Tropical settings, and particularly tropical forests, are far more easily subjected to permanent damage at the hands of man than their temperate counterparts. Despite the environmental furor of recent years, the potential consequences of this fragility are not widely appreciated, least of all by Third World rulers, who all too often see their natural surroundings only as a source of fast profit. Western political leaders are rarely much better informed. During debate over the Panama Canal, for example, it might have astonished most members of Congress to learn that the controversial waterway will be a worthless mud-filled ditch by the year 2000, regardless of who controls it, unless erosion caused by the rapid deforestation of the surroundng uplands is stopped.[2] The tropical environment is loaded with similar sleeper issues, most of which are all too likely to be appreciated too little and too late.

That Southeast Asia might be suffering from environmental problems first became apparent to Western readers when defoliation in Vietnam and its residual effects became a *cause célèbre* in the antiwar movement. Later there were reports (probably exaggerated) of Indochinese forests whose trees were so impregnated with steel shards that a potential timber industry had been ruined. Unfortunately, problems of a less dramatic but more persistent nature are prevalent and growing elsewhere in the region.

Failure to reverse environmental deterioration in Southeast Asia could, in some cases, affect global welfare within a few decades. But the picture is not entirely bleak. Despite the severe problems that already exist, Southeast Asians have more time to regain equilibrium with their surroundings than do the inhabitants of some more crowded regions. Moreover, in addition to hazards there are numerous opportunities for sustained, rational use of tropical resources, especially in the plant world. The most obvious constraints to intelligent utilization are human and institutional, but there is also a critical need for more research and experimentation. For although the tropical environment is more diverse and complicated than the temperate environment, it has received only a fraction of the scientific attention devoted to the latter. The opportunity to conduct such research diminishes with every passing day.

This chapter will briefly examine a few topics extracted from that ultimately elastic concept, "the environment." It will attempt to suggest the persistence, complexity, and fundamental importance of issues like forestry, the destruction of coral reefs, goethermal power, and the social constraints on more effective human adaptation to tropical surroundings.

The Population Factor

In the tropics as elsewhere, most environmental problems are the result of population pressures. Where shifting cultivation is the norm and soils are poor, even low levels of human settlement may outstrip resources and result in permanent damage to the land. In other areas better soils and irrigation may permit much higher population densities, but, as the case of Java so well illustrates, there is always an outer limit. The primacy of population policy is today acknowledged in both Indonesia and the Philippines. Family planning has been a major focus of foreign aid in both countries for some years. The results are at best a beginning.

Government-supported population programs began in Indonesia in 1969. Earlier, President Sukarno had argued that a billion Indonesians would not be too many, and spurned family planning as immoral. Initial efforts were restricted to Inner Indonesia (Java and Bali). The Outer Islands, which would by themselves constitute the second most populous country in Southeast Asia, were without any government program until 1974. The Indonesian effort has made great progress. It is "a success story probably unrivalled in family planning history," according to one recent study. Total fertility in Inner Indonesia has been reduced by more than one-third, and the national birthrate has declined from 2.2 to 1.7 percent since 1969. The government is hoping to reduce the Java-Bali rate to 1.2 percent by 1985—an accomplishment which would compare favorably in scope to the achievement reported from Communist China.[3]

The story of Indonesian family planning is so dramatic that a tone of euphoria pervades much recent commentary. Some experts are worried by this because they feel that the easy part of the job has been done, and that achieving further reduction in fertility may encounter complex social and psychological barriers. They are concerned because part of the decline in Indonesia's birthrate apparently resulted from little understood factors which had nothing to do with government efforts, including later marriage age, as evidenced by the fact that the decline has taken place even in areas of the Outer Islands where there was no program. They note that there has recently been a decline in absolute numbers of practitioners of contraception, and that as the program grows it has started to encounter bureaucratic problems. Progress to date has been influenced by cultural factors to an extraordinary degree. The program has been most successful among the Hindu peasantry of Bali, acutely sensitive to land shortage and receptive to innovation. East Java has also responded well, thanks partly to a tradition of strong local government dating to Dutch days. Family planning has made less headway among the socially conservative inhabitants of Central Java, and has encountered most resistance from the devoutly Muslim Sundanese of West Java, who were originally repelled by stories of male doctors inserting IUDs into the genitals of women. In Outer Indonesia the program is too new to have yielded significant results, but it appears to be off to a promising if equally variegated beginning.

Philippine family planning began in about 1970, somewhat later than in Indonesia. Comparatively rapid progress might have been expected in view of the higher average income levels and greater prevalence of middle-class mores. However, there were also formidable obstacles. The Philippines began with one of the highest birthrates in Asia, and the lack of a strong, centralized system of local administration impedes any program which must operate at the village level.

As is frequently the case in the Philippines, resounding official endorsement of family planning at the national level has not been matched by consistent implementation. Population, health, and nutrition programs have, since the declaration of Martial Law in 1972, been the special preserve of Mrs. Imelda Marcos, whose enormous energy is often negated by failure to provide staffing and long-term support for her innumerable projects. Partly as a result, family planning in the Philippines has been impeded by a muddle of overlapping jurisdictions, uncertain leadership, and bureaucratic rivalry.[4] Roman Catholicism, professed by 85 percent of the population, posed another major obstacle. The Church found it unnecessary to confront directly the stated objective of lowering population growth in the name of development. Instead, opposition to methods other than Church-approved ones has been skillfully articulated through conservative lay Catholic groups. The hierarchy has confined itself to opposing abortion, sterilization, and official pressure in support of family planning, which it claims violates citizens' freedom to follow the dictates of conscience. On broader political questions the Church leadership is deeply divided between a conservative majority and a small band of "liberals" who are frequently critical of the Martial Law regime. It seems likely that the family planning issue, linked with abortion in the minds of many Catholics, has been welcome to the hierarchy precisely because it is one of the few questions on which both "liberal" and "conservative" clerics agree.

Venturing into this hazardous terrain, foreign aid donors

(with the United States in the lead) tried to move too fast. In 1976 the U.S. aid program promoted a controversial advertising campaign for commercial sale of condoms which would have generated a hue and cry in the West, much less in a socially conservative, Catholic country. More recently, AID endorsed an ambitious "outreach" program which, with the help of $36 million in promised grant assistance, would for the first time extend family planning services to the barrio (village) level. Unfortunately, the provincial governors, who are eventually supposed to assume the cost of the program, were apparently not fully aware of their obligation, resulting in delay and confusion.

In sum, overzealous assistance tactics provided the Church with an easy target and compounded vexatious rivalries within the Philippine population bureaucracy. Nevertheless, whether because of government programming or because of the continuing diffusion of middle-class attitudes, population increase has started to level off in the Philippines. The national growth rate declined from 3 percent (1960–70) to 2.8 percent (1970–75) while contraceptive use increased from near zero to 24 percent. However, the rate of new "acceptors"—i.e., new practitioners of birth control—has, to the dismay of many observers, changed little since 1974.[5]

While continuing decline in population growth rates could have a major impact on rural development and food problems in both Indonesia and the Philippines, it is not likely to reduce human pressure on natural resources during the next few decades. Meanwhile, development, with its likely corollary of increasing consumption, may accentuate certain threats to the environment—for example, by stimulating the exploitation and settlement of remaining frontier areas.

High-Density Deforestation: Erosion on Java and Other Problems

The environmental ramifications of overpopulation are nowhere more obvious than on Java, whose food and labor problems were discussed in chapter six. The primary problem—at least the only one widely recognized to date—is erosion. Malthusian pressures have already forced people to cultivate increasingly steep slopes, and the quest for firewood (a major source of fuel here as elsewhere in the Third World) has resulted in additional denudation of high ground. Two-thirds of Java's forests—four million hectares according to government figures—are estimated to have disappeared since 1940, and 5 percent of Java's once arable land has been abandoned because of erosion.[6] There has been a dangerous surge in river siltation, already heavy under normal conditions thanks to the unstable, recent volcanic nature of most Javanese soils. One major river, the Citarum, exhibited a sevenfold increase in silt load in the space of three years.[7] Siltation is particularly serious on Java because it accelerates clogging of irrigation canals upon which the already inadequate food production system is dependent. On the island of Madura, off Java's northeast coast, wholesale deforestation has already resulted in partial "desertification," in the form of intensified dry-season drought, accelerated runoff, and increased erosion. Madura well may be a vision of Java's future.

In response to the obvious and growing problem of erosion the Indonesian government launched a massive "greening" (penghijauan) project in 1974. Although the program is sometimes termed "reforestation," the goal is not reforestation in the conventional sense but controlled land use in erosion-prone upland areas, with emphasis on tree crops. By most accounts the greening program has not been a success thus far, mainly because the government attempted to expand it from a pilot basis too fast. At the very least, however, it testifies to a commendable sense of urgency about a problem that was almost totally unrecognized five years ago.[8]

Java is a prime example of what might be termed high-density deforestation resulting from direct, massive population pressure, as opposed to the low-density variety, resulting from a combination of commercial logging and shifting cultivation, found in Outer Indonesia and Malaysian Borneo. Although the Java case is extreme, similar processes are at work in many areas of the Philippines, wherever high ground is adjacent to densely settled, rice-growing areas, such as the northern rim of the central Luzon plain. In that area deforestation-induced erosion has been compounded by the destructive impact of millions of tons of mine tailings dumped into rivers, which deposit them on once-fertile irrigated land.

Many other types of high-density environmental problems are becoming more serious in both Indonesia and the Philippines. Near Manila, for example, Laguna de Bay Lake, upon which the capital city may someday depend for its water supply, is being damaged by a combination of pollution, excessive commercial fish-raising, and eutrophication (oxygen depletion) caused by fertilizer-laden runoff from surrounding rice-growing areas.[9] Urban pollution problems in both countries are, despite the absence of major industrialization, as bad as any in the world, and growing. Jakarta, a city of more than five million, lacks the rudiments of a sewer system. Dutch-built canals which were noisome enough forty years ago, when the city was one-tenth its present size, are now hopelessly clogged with waste.[10] Manila's air is choked with particle pollution emanating from the maladjusted engines of ancient "smoke belchers"—buses and "jeepneys" whose owners are deterred, by an unrealistically low fare structure, from maintaining them. Such conditions impact more immediately on the urban poor, whose numbers are legion and growing. Manila's population is about one-third squatters, and the figure for Jakarta is comparable or greater. Nor is the situation confined to capital cities. The familiar Third World landscape of slums filled with displaced rural labor is found in nearly every provincial center as well.[11] In Cebu, trade and communications hub of the central Philippines, a large community of squatters has lived for some years on "land fill" which in fact consists largely of recent garbage. For such people the nadir of environmental deterioration has already been reached.

Low-Density Deforestation: Logs, Generals, and Vanishing Wilderness

The province of East Kalimantan, on the island of Borneo, is at the opposite end of the Indonesian demographic scale from Java. Half again as large, it has only one-sixtieth of Java's population density. While Java's forests are mostly gone, East Kalimantan remains one of the world's great sources of hardwood timber, for the moment. Approximately half the provincial area of 20.2 million hectares, including virtually all the commercially valuable forest, has been allocated to timber concessions. Several major multinationals operate joint ventures with Indonesian partners. They include two American firms, Weyerhaeuser (with a concession area of 601,000 hectares) and Georgia Pacific (350,000 hectares), at least two Japanese firms, Misubishi and Sumitomo, and the Kayan River Timber Company, until recently a venture of the Philippine-domiciled, U.S. citizen Soriano family. However, U.S. and Japanese forestry investment is far outweighed by Philippine, Korean, Hong Kong, and Malaysian investment, and relatively small operators from these Asian countries hold the majority of concessions.[12]

Timber has become very big business in Indonesia only in the last decade. In the Philippines some large-scale logging of tropical hardwoods began before World War II, primarily for the American market. The Malaysian Borneo state of Sabah was the next area to develop, producing a crop of ethnic-Chinese timber millionaires in the 1950s. During the Sukarno years, Japanese interests made a feeble effort to cooperate with the Indonesian state timber enterprise (Perhutani) but the prevailing economic chaos, and the fact that the Japanese market had not yet really taken off, effectively protected Indonesia's forests for the time being. Heavy exploitation began after the change of regimes in 1965–66. From 1968 to 1974, Indonesian export of logs rose from 1.5 to 18 million cubic meters, making her the world's largest source of raw hardwood, followed by Malaysia (12.2 million cubic meters in 1974), the Philippines (4.7), and the Ivory Coast (3.9).[13] Indonesia's foreign exchange earnings from timber rose from U.S. $12 million (1968) to more than $900 million in 1976.[14] For some years timber has been the largest source of Indonesian foreign exchange next to oil.

The development of Indonesian logging is contributing to a global problem, the rapid destruction of the world's tropical rainforests. There are about 8.35 million square kilometers of such forests in the world, of which the biggest single portions (4 million) are in Latin America, mainly in the Amazon basin. Of the rest, 2.5 million square kilometers are in Southeast Asia (the majority in Indonesia, Malaysia, and the Philippines) and 1.8 million in Africa. According to the best current estimates, up to 40 percent of this enormous resource will be consumed by the end of the century or shortly thereafter. Most of the balance is either inaccessible or consists of lands that may (with luck) be preserved in parks and nature preserves. Nowhere is the pace of destruction faster or subject to less control than in Indonesia, where accessible timber will probably be gone within two decades. In remote swampy or upland areas the damage may be delayed, but it is precisely the more vulnerable lowland rainforest that is ecologically richest as well as commercially most valuable. Moreover, new technology is constantly extending the profitable range of logging to new, hitherto "worthless" or inaccessible habitats.[15]

There is, of course, nothing new about deforestation. Americans recklessly destroyed most of the hardwood forests which once covered the eastern and midwestern United States, without being lectured or regulated by anyone and apparently without doing what most citizens of this country would regard as major or irreparable ecological damage.

Unfortunately, there is strong scientific evidence that this relatively benign experience is unlikely to be repeated in the tropics. It is a critical but little appreciated fact that rainforests, much more fragile than their temperate counterparts, are, under present political and administrative circumstances, a nonrenewable resource. These complex aggregations of trees, animals, and insects are the world's oldest and most diversified biological communities. They have evolved under exceptionally stable conditions, without experiencing the kind of constant climatic variation that characterizes temperate areas. They are therefore peculiarly sensitive to change of the variety that results from logging. Species occur in tremendous profusion—fifty times or more the average number per hectare found in temperate areas—but many are restricted to a limited geographic range, hence vulnerable to extermination. A single small Philippine nature preserve, Mount Makiling near Manila, has more varieties of trees and shrubs than the entire United States. Destroying the habitat of one plant or insect may set off chain reactions with harmful results across entire communities.[16]

Tropical forest soils are paradoxically poor to sterile, because under conditions of constant heat and rainfall nutrients are rapidly dissolved out of the soil. Decay takes place with great speed, in as little as six weeks compared to a year for a similar process in a temperate pine forest. Shallow but complex root systems accomplish the almost instant recycling of plant foods, leaving virtually none in the ground. "Ecologically the [tropical] forest is a desert covered with trees," one authority has written.[17] Normally the felling and burning of the forest deposits enough fertilizing ash to grow one or two crops, but in some areas of Kalimantan soils are so excessively poor that although in an undisturbed state they support a population of great trees, they will not produce even one rice harvest.[18] To say that deforestation "destroys" soil fertility is thus unfortunately to understate the problem, since fertility is lacking in the first place.

When the forest canopy is broken a number of harmful consequences may result. Despite their poverty, tropical soils are often very deep. Once exposed to the force of tropical rain they can be washed away with spectacular speed—in one area the recorded rate of soil removal went from 3 pounds per hectare per year (forested) to 34 tons per year (deforested).[19] Over long periods of time some soils may compact into laterite, a water-resistant clay which hardens on contact with air and was employed to build Angkor Wat and other temples in ancient Southeast Asia. It is virtually useless for agriculture. If damage is sufficiently severe, permanent stands of tough grass (Imperata cylindrica, also known as alang-alang) may result. Even when tree species do regenerate, it may be centuries, if ever, before the original stand is duplicated. In Cambodia areas which were cleared by the ancient Khmers more than six hundred years ago are still distinguishable from the surrounding climax forest.[20]

So Who Cares?

The most alarming consequence of tropical deforestation could be alteration of climate. At the local level, as on Madura, removal of trees definitely results in higher temperatures, often sufficient to retard the regeneration of shade-loving species. The forest acts as a sponge, retaining moisture and releasing it gradually. Removing it results in flooding in the rainy season and empty stream beds in the dry season. On a worldwide scale, tropical forests generate oxygen. Through photosynthesis they absorb some of the CO_2 generated by man's ever-increasing combustion of fossil fuels, acting as a storage bank for some 55 percent of the world's carbon, according to one estimate. Scientists now fear that tropical forest destruction could seriously upset the balance of atmospheric CO_2 and modify climate on a global scale.[21]

Another problem involves the destruction of wildlife habitat and the livelihood of nomadic hunting and gathering peoples whose folkways are as yet unstudied and who are never consulted about logging in their areas. Leaving aside the difficult moral issues involved, it is possible that study of such endangered societies could yield much practical information about the forest. These nonfarming peoples should not be confused with the more widespread shifting cultivators whose role in deforestation is discussed below.[22] Similarly, there has apparently been no systematic survey of the impact of logging on the habitat of endangered animals, like the orangutan, although it may be assumed that over time it will be considerable. For example, there are four species of primates which are found only on the minor Indonesian island of Siberut off the coast of western Sumatra, which is now almost wholly parceled out in logging concessions.[23]

Many of those who are most concerned about deforestation rail against an approach which takes into account only the potential economic loss involved. Apostles of growth limitation (virtually all in the West) prefer to stress aesthetic and humanitarian values, and argue that it is precisely man's exploitative attitude toward nature which created the problem in the first place. But eventually the aesthetic, moral, and economic considerations converge, and are mutually supporting. As things are proceeding, tropical deforestation is going to exterminate great numbers of species, and with them the genetic material that is the source library of evolution, before they can be discovered and catalogued, much less studied, appreciated, or exploited.

At least two-thirds of the world's species are in the tropics, but about 90 percent of the scientific research to date has been conducted in the temperate zones. About five-sixths of the estimated tropical species have not even been named. Island Southeast Asia is particularly rich. Although it has only about one-quarter the forested area of the Amazon basin, it has almost as great a diversity of plants, animals, and insects. Localization is particularly acute, thanks to archipelago geography. Many remote, heavily forested islands in Indonesia are, like Siberut, currently the scene of heavy logging activity. No one knows how many species have been lost by the destruction of geographically restricted ecosystems, but it is likely that lowland areas in heavily exploited countries, such as the Philippines, or where population pressure is a factor, as on Java, have already been hard hit. Plants are the least publicized but probably the most critical part of the problem. Worldwide, one out of ten flowering plant species is extinct or endangered and 20,000 (about 10 percent of the total) are in need of protection.[24]

In the future, development of the soil-poor tropics may hinge around the discovery of practical applications for materials drawn from this largely unexplored natural storehouse—if it is not utterly ravaged first. One of the great success stories of tropical agriculture, rubber, resulted from the nineteenth-century discovery and utilization of one tree, *Hevea brasiliensis*, in the Amazon jungle. Coffee, tea, and even rice culture all derived from similar discoveries at earlier periods. Fifteen hundred years ago Chinese traders were drawn to Southeast Asia by its forest resins, which became a mainstay of the traditional Chinese pharmacopoeia. Today about a quarter of the drug prescriptions sold in the United States contain, as a principal or sole active ingredient, an agent derived from a natural plant. Of the 76 major plant-derived compounds used in pharmacy, only 4 can be synthesized economically. Curare, from Latin America, and rauwolfia, from Southeast Asia (used in heart surgery), are among the best-known jungle products upon which modern medicine relies. Yet only about 5 percent of the total tropical inventory has been investigated for pharmaceutical or other applications. According to one authority,

Despite limited knowledge about genetic reservoirs, it seems a statistical certainty that tropical forests contain source materials for many pesticides, medicines, contraceptives and abortifacient agents, potential foods, beverages, and industrial products. Of particular value for human purposes are the specialized genetic characteristics of many localized species—yet these attributes are associated in many instances with restricted range, precisely the factor that makes them vulnerable.[25]

Forestry Policy

Indonesia, Malaysia, and the Philippines all profess a formal policy of selective logging in which natural regeneration is supposed to restore the forest to its original condition. The details of policy differ from place to place. In Malaysia only trees that have been individually marked by forestry staff can be cut. Permissible minimum tree diameters vary—54 centimeters in Malaysia, 55 in the Philippines, 50 in Indonesia—as does the length of assumed regeneration cycles.[26] But there are few fields where the gap between rhetoric and reality is more glaring. Throughout the region the normal end product of ever-accelerating logging is devastation. The obstacles in the way of more enlightened practice appear virtually insurmountable. The mere act of building logging roads and using heavy machinery often damages remaining immature trees and compacts the soil in a way which may prevent regeneration. There are only a few documented cases on record in which a logged forest of dipterocarp trees—the class of more than 500 species which predominates in island Southeast Asia, and which produces nearly all the commercially valuable hardwoods known collectively as "Philippine mahogany"—has revived to a healthy state. Tropical botanists believe that regeneration is possible under carefully controlled conditions and the supervision of trained forestry staff.[27] But in Southeast Asia (and especially in Indonesia) forestry staff is notoriously inadequate. Government foresters, who are rarely paid as well as the skilled machine operators employed by timber companies, can hardly be expected to resist bribes or even to leave their offices, especially when their numbers are altogether insufficient to cover the vast areas involved.

Local populations of shifting cultivators are widely regarded as a major cause of forest destruction. The accusation is (so far as Southeast Asia is concerned) only partly justified. Anthropological research has repeatedly demonstrated that slash-and-burn farming does not permanently damage the forest if there is a sufficiently long cycle between crops.[28] Since areas felled by farmers are not large, forest will usually regenerate inwards from the edges of the plot. Many hill tribes are meticulously careful to preserve watershed areas, to the point where motivation has become a matter of religion. The Ilongot of northern Luzon have developed a method of shifting cultivation which involves felling only the smaller trees in the field. The larger ones are pollarded, an elaborate branch-trimming technique which allows light to penetrate but often does not kill the tree.[29] Unfortunately, many of today's shifting cultivators consist not of indigenous tribal peoples but of "civilized" lowlanders who have been driven, by population pressure, beyond areas where irrigation, and hence more settled farming, is possible. Such people are not subject to the kind of elaborate cultural constraints which often regulate the behavior of "natives."

There is, moreover, an often fatal link between shifting cultivation and logging. Until recently shifting cultivators were usually unable to penetrate large areas of forest. Felling the enormous trees of a primary forest is no small job, and in most cases farmers preferred, with reason, to hang on the fringes, returning frequently to areas of secondary growth.[30] In many areas, including Borneo, access was usually limited by rivers, which were the only means of transportation. Logging has changed all that, because the first thing that a logger does is to build a road—rough, to be sure, but still a road—to extract his product. Logging roads have, throughout Southeast Asia, opened irresistible new frontiers for land-hungry populations of shifting cultivators.

In many areas a three-stage deforestation process is now apparent. The first stage is the large, commercial logger, perhaps a multinational corporation. The foreign operator may want to abide by sustained yield regulations. As a foreigner he is generally anxious to stay on the right side of the law, and if his concession area is large enough he may have some interest in regeneration. But in many cases he is followed by small, illegal operators, often in cahoots with local authorities, who extract remaining trees with commercial value regardless of girth. The shifting cultivator, his work made easier by the absence of big timber, then completes the destruction.

Everywhere there is conflict between differing, uncoordinated land use policies. In Lampung, southern Sumatra, Javanese transmigrants were initially forced to practice shifting cultivation because there were no irrigation facilities. They subsequently destroyed an estimated two million hectares of valuable dipterocarp forest, including areas where tree cover was required for erosion-free catchment areas necessary for the future provision of irrigation. A foreign expert who visited Jakarta in 1973, armed with satellite photographs, demonstrated to surprised Forestry Service officials that someone was logging in what was supposed to be a nature preserve. It turned out that a previous provincial governor had indeed granted a concession there to the Indonesian Navy, while in a nearby region, supposedly reserved for watershed protection, an Indonesian-Chinese company was extracting timber.[31] In the Philippines deforestation has reduced the lifespan of the important Ambuklao Dam by half and severely endangered the prospects for several other hydroelectric facilities. It is a major cause of increased flooding, including the disastrous central Luzon flood of 1972.[32]

Conservationists argue that, given the range of habitats

involved, at least 20 percent of the world's tropical moist forests should be preserved, if only to insure an adequate reservoir of species. Some Southeast Asian countries, including Indonesia, have established commendable conservation targets—in Indonesia's case, 5 percent of the entire area of the country is supposed to be destined for wildlife or nature preserves of various kinds (not all of which prohibit logging).[33] However "paper parks" are a familiar phenomenon throughout the region. Illegal logging is hard to prevent and preserve boundaries are often changed to accommodate the appetites of powerful would-be concessionaires. It is altogether too easy to announce, at an international conference, that an ambitious list of nature preserves has been established, and then do absolutely nothing about it. In the Philippines (where the international biosphere reserve at Puerto Galera is only one of numerous paper preserves) the problem is compounded by the fact that parks are under the jurisdiction of the exploitation-oriented Department of Natural Resources, also in charge of developing forestry.

The gravest barriers to more rational forestry practices are political. The rapid development of forestry has produced a flood of foreign exchange for governments, and bonanzas for others throughout national and local power structures. It was timber money generated by the enterprising Chinese of Sabah (Malaysia) which nurtured the political machine of Tun Mustapha in the 1950s.[34] Since then the same symbiotic pattern has been repeated on a grander scale in Indonesia. Although exact figures are lacking, it is likely that the great majority of Indonesia's 600-odd timber concessionnaires are ethnic Chinese, either foreign or domestic, with partners who are either military or local officials (and many local officials are military). Georgia Pacific's counterpart is a Chinese golfing partner of President Suharto, Bob Hasan. Weyerhaeuser's partner in the International Timber Corporation Indonesia (ITCI), with 35 percent ownership, is Tri Usaha Bhakti, a Department of Defense (HANKAM) holding company involved in at least fourteen timber concessions. Others are held by the Army's Strategic Reserve (KOSTRAD), by the Ministry of Interior, and by high-ranking Indonesian officials and their families.[35] In addition to the 35 percent share of profits channeled to Tri Usaha Bhakti, ITCI paid 29 percent of gross sales revenue, or more than $50 million, to the Indonesian government between 1971 and 1976, plus a variety of provincial taxes and levies. Erratic world demand for commodities, including timber, has resulted in wildly fluctuating earnings. The price of logs ranged from a low of $25 per cubic meter during the 1974–76 recession to a high of around $85 in 1977–78. The Indonesian government responded to this boom by suddenly doubling export taxes. Nevertheless, and although exact figures are lacking, Weyerhaeuser has probably earned a handsome profit on its original (1971) investment of $32 million in Indonesia.[36]

Western observers are quick to focus on the corruption inherent in business partnerships between foreigners or ethnic Chinese and generals. So are some Indonesians, especially students and others critical of the government.[37] But this puritanical outlook is not shared by everyone in Indonesia, where the military establishment has traditionally, from the early days of the 1945–49 revolution, depended on "extrabudgetary" income from business activities operated by units down to divisional level and below. Such funding currently meets up to 40 percent of the armed forces' expenses, and is officially deemed legitimate. The practice is often said to be fully justified by the dual function (dwi fungsi) doctrine, according to which the army has social, economic, and political, as well as merely military, responsibilities. Whatever the ethics, the system clearly motivates the ruling establishment of the country toward all-out exploitation of the timber resource. It bolsters a traditional mind-set which regards the forests of Kalimantan and Sumatra as inexhaustible. The fact that the Indonesian official or military partner rarely contributes any capital (the percentage division of the partnership is a polite euphemism representing profits delivered, not shares purchased) and usually remains wholly isolated from operation of the enterprise, does little to encourage development of either management or forestry skills, or any sense of responsibility for the resource involved.[38]

In view of the difficulties, many commercial foresters

have concluded that sustained yield-cutting and natural re-generation are, in the underdeveloped tropics, technically unfeasible, economically unsound, and politically quixotic. They argue that replanting with fast-growing softwood species is a more practical if less perfect solution,[39] a view shared by Weyerhaeuser, which has logged the only remaining natural forest within easy distance of its company town, Kenangan. This area, originally to be conserved for research purposes, has been converted to an experimental plantation instead. A recent company brochure notes:

> Tropical plantations on an industrial scale may provide an opportunity to grow many times more wood per hectare than is possible through natural regeneration. These plantations can confine growth potential to preferable species by eliminating weeds, vines and undesirable trees which compete with desirable species in the natural rain forest.
> Generally, ten to fifteen times more marketable wood can be grown on each hectare each year on plantations of pine and eucalyptus than grow in the selectively harvested forest.
> Thus plantations may offer the possibility of a higher sustained harvest from a substantially smaller land base. As a result the rotation of the virgin forest may be prolonged and more of the natural watershed may be allocated to other uses such as watershed and wildlife protection.[40]

However, Weyerhaeuser has thus far refused to commit itself to more than experimentation on some 2,500 hectares of land. In the meantime, the American firm is continuing to cut the natural forest in its huge concession area at maximum speed, and it will probably be exhausted by 1990 if not before.[41]

Tree plantations are without question preferable to deserts of *alang-alang* grass and will undoubtedly play a major role in any rational solution to the tropical forestry problem. However, it is equally clear that a monoculture stand of alien trees is a very different creature from an indigenous hardwood forest with its myriad species and complex gene pool. As the green revolution has demonstrated in the case of rice, genetically uniform monocultures tend to be dangerously susceptible to pests and diseases. Those few botanists with deep experience of the natural tropical forest angrily criticize commercial forestry experts for failing to appreciate the possible long-term advantages of developing the rich natural resources in situ, even though it might take a few more years of research. Sooner or later, they point out, plantations and natural forests are interdependent. The most successful softwood plantation tree in the Western hemisphere is the Monterrey pine (Pinus radiata), once on the edge of extinction in a localized area of California. It was discovered and cultivated only in the nick of time. "There are probably 30,000 local endemic trees like the Monterrey Pine, mostly in the tropics, any one of which could be forever lost in one afternoon's cutting by an FAO or AID sponsored 'development' project," notes professor Hugh Itlis of the University of Wisconsin herbarium.[42]

Another significant recent trend in forestry has been the development of pulp and wood chip technology applicable to entire tropical forests. Diverse natural stands can now be efficiently pulverized to produce a variety of products essential to modern supermarkets and housing developments. Stimulated by booming world demand for pulp, paper, and fiberboard, chipping supposedly eliminates the "waste" of nonmarketable species which are otherwise often left to rot. Skeptics argue that "omnispecific" wood chip harvesting is even more destructive of natural forests than is orthodox logging, and poses a new threat to previously unexploitable habitats such as mangrove swamp forests. There is little doubt that the new technology could find sufficient and less controversial application in areas of second growth, or where forests are being cleared in any case for settlement.

A recent discussion of the new log-chipping technology noted that like many forestry issues it poses a Faustian choice between short-term gain and long-term damnation.[43] At present there seems to be only one established example of a rational middle way. In the Philippines, where forestry practice is on the whole no more enlightened than in Indonesia, the rich and powerful Soriano family, in cooperation with the International Paper Company, has established a unique, multiproduct forestry complex at Bislig in eastern Mindanao, the Paper Industry Corporation of the Philippines (PICOP). On a 183,000 hectare concession PICOP practices sustained yield logging in those areas where (according to a company brochure) there is a "good virgin stand to begin with." As of December 1975, the PICOP concession already included 81,000 hectares of selectively logged dipterocarp forest "stocked with vigorous young trees fast gaining in volume for the next harvest cycle," which takes place after a thirty-five-year interval. Elsewhere, where the original stands are "poor," the company is practicing clear cutting and replanting with fast-growing pine and eucalyptus species. Already some 25,000 hectares have been converted in this manner to "industrial plantations" with an additional 45,000 hectares scheduled. Together these operations support lumber and plywood mills and the first pulp and paper factory in the world using tropical hardwood waste. The third phase of the operation is an agroforestry program, modeled on small-holder tree-farming operations in the American South, which encourages former shifting cultivators in the surrounding areas to grow trees for PICOP. An extension of this program is now being supported by a loan from the World Bank. To cap this vision of enlightened profit-making the Sorianos have installed pollution control equipment at the pulp and paper mill.[44]

Although PICOP is beginning to attract widespread attention, it apparently has not yet been subjected to detailed on-the-ground scrutiny by conservationists. Nevertheless, most would agree that PICOP's integrated approach, with its emphasis on permanent operation and intelligent attention to the problem posed by neighboring communities of slash-and-burn farmers, could be a model for the region if not for the entire tropical world. From an economic standpoint the manufacture of finished products is vastly preferable to the export of raw logs, which still predominates in Indonesia despite the government's continuing efforts to stimulate more construction of sawmills. In the Philippines, integrated operation is being encouraged by a partial ban on log exports imposed in 1977. Behind this is growing domestic demand, which now absorbs 40 percent of all wood production, processed and unprocessed, and forests which are already seriously depleted. Nevertheless, many of the most valuable logs are still exported.[45] Progress is greatly inhibited by the fact that the Japanese, who are the principal buyers, continue to levy tariffs on finished timber products while admitting logs duty free. It is also pertinent to note that the Sorianos made no effort to replicate PICOP on their own huge concession in East Kalimantan, which they recently sold to an Indonesian military-controlled firm. There they were in the same position as any other foreign corporation. In Indonesia everyone has had enough experience with the seamy side of the business, ranging from capricious taxation to log poachers to the less-than-pristine politics of concession granting, to be cautious. Such hazards and uncertainties, compounded by the roller-coaster market for logs and understandable doubts about the long-term climate for foreign investment, are enough to motivate the multinationals in the direction of maximum speed logging on existing concessions, plus a little cosmetic experimentation with plantations—often no more than enough to deflect criticism and demonstrate good intentions.

The Fuelwood Problem

Firewood is a major energy source throughout the Third World,[46] and its consumption a growing cause of deforestation. But since firewood trade takes place outside the modern sectors, reliable statistics are rarely available. Indonesia is a case in point. A recent article by a leading energy official noted that wood may contribute as much energy as the total "commercial" requirement met by oil, coal, and hydro, but he was unable to quantify this observation.[47] In 1978, Research Minister Sumitro asserted that fuelwood consumption in Indonesia amounts to one ton per capita per year, sufficient by itself to create a net drain on Indonesian forests.[48]

Much firewood is gathered by rural folk from nearby high ground, with consequences on Java already mentioned. But the problem is probably more complex and serious than this aspect alone would suggest. In Indonesia even major metropolitan areas are, for the most part, intensely compacted villages. City dwellers are dependent for cooking on either wood or wood-derived charcoal, as testified by the blue smog that hangs over Jakarta every morning. It seems likely that some of this fuel is being imported from the Outer Islands, often by traditional sailing craft,[49] and that demand for firewood may be contributing to deforestation beyond Java. Moreover, the link between wood consumption and development is poignantly clear. Wood is used as fuel in many types of traditional construction industries, such as tile factories and lime baking kilns, which are booming as a result of development. On the island of Bali, for example, lime for new tourist hotels was, until recently, produced by baking coral collected from nearby reefs with wood gathered from rapidly vanishing upland forests, a double ecological disaster. On Bali this practice was halted by local decree for fear that reef destruction would destroy the beaches, which are almost as important to the tourist industry as new hotels, but it continues elsewhere. The problem is also serious in the Philippines, where it is estimated that more than twice as much wood is cut for fuel as for other uses.[50]

The Maritime World

The Western world view which pervades a growing international political culture is obsessively land-centric. Not so the traditional world view of island Southeast Asians, manifested in the Indonesian concept of *tanah air*, or "homelandwater." The local view is a better reflection of reality. Southeast Asia has the highest ratio of coastline to land area in the world. Arguing for a maritime perspective on the region, Donald Emmerson has noted that its geographic heart lies under shallow waters on the Sunda Shelf. Long before the advent of offshore oil drilling these archipelagic seas were the scene of intense economic acivity, crisscrossed by traders, explorers, pirates, fishermen, and refugees. In Southeast Asia "peasants" are often ocean based, man-water ratios

already matter, and the day may not be far off when governments must worry about "sea tenure" and perhaps even "sea
reform."[51]

The more unitary Southeast Asian outlook has already
found significant expression in the ongoing international negotiations on the law of the sea. Both Indonesia and the Philippines have insisted on an "archipelago principle" which
recognizes the right of island states to interisland waters.
They have thus far rejected the claim of the great powers to
free transit (including submerged passage by submarines and
overflight rights) through straits which traditionally have
been used by international commerce, acknowledging only a
much more restricted right of "innocent passage" which does
not include subsurface navigation. As a major nickel producer Indonesia has a secondary interest in the negotiations,
which (if successful) will result in agreement on deep seabed
mining of nodules so rich in nickel that unless quotas are set
present land-based mining of this metal could become un-
economic.

In 1977 law of the sea negotiators produced an interim
negotiating text which recognizes the archipelago principle.
According to this document waters enclosed by baselines
joining the "outermost points of the outermost islands" are
defined as "archipelagic waters." The sovereignty of an island state extends to such waters "regardless of their depth
and distance from the coast."[52] The draft treaty also gives the
great powers the right to free transit through and over defined sea lanes, thus satisfying the principal interest of the
United States. Neither the United States nor the major island
powers have accepted this version of the archipelago concept, and at present the entire treaty is still endangered by
much more intense dispute over other provisions, mainly
those relating to exploitation of the deep seabed. Even if the
treaty is never enacted, however, the growing acceptance of
200-mile coastal economic zones will probably in time give
Indonesia and the Philippines a de facto equivalent—the
recognized right to manage, for better or worse, their far-
flung archipelagic ocean resources.

Marine Problems: One Example

In large areas of the Philippines and Indonesia, but especially the former, coral reef habitats are being rapidly destroyed, primarily by fishermen using dynamite and toxic chemicals. Either agent will kill fish of all sizes and eventually reduce a prolific reef to sterility. In the Philippines the problem is an old one, dating from the abandonment of huge quantities of explosives in rural areas by American forces after World War II. More recently, toxic pesticides and other chemicals have become widely available as a by-product of the green revolution. Using them requires no more than a plastic bag and a long wire. The fisherman lowers the bag into a school of fish, or over a teeming reef, and trips the wire. Some chemical agents will drift back and forth for hours, killing everything. In the Philippines, where coastal areas are often thickly populated, and where small but effective motorized "banca" craft are universally in use, these diabolical techniques have penetrated to all but the smallest and most remote islands, doing tremendous damage. A recent nationwide survey indicated that more than three-quarters of reefs have suffered heavy damage, defined as more than 50 percent destroyed.[53] Reefs are also being devastated by excess siltation resulting from deforestation and by the collection of shells and coral for export, which has become a major industry in the last decade. The biggest importer of coral is the United States, which protects its own Florida corals and regulates the exploitation of Hawaiian reefs. In Indonesia, thanks partly to less motorized technology and the nonseagoing mentality of some major cultural groups, such as the Balinese and Javanese, damage is as yet less widespread. It is only a matter of time. When the city of Jakarta reclaimed land for a housing project and an amusement park a few years ago, it obtained the fill material by mining coral from reefs around nearby islands which were, in theory, to be developed for tourism.[54]

Efforts to control dynamite fishing in the Philippines are a parable for the would-be Third World conservationist. The problem has been recognized at the highest levels of government. Shortly after the declaration of Martial Law in 1972 President Marcos decreed the death penalty for anyone found guilty of fishing with poison or explosives. The press has repeatedly publicized the fact that such methods permanently damage reefs, eventually destroying the fisherman's own source of livelihood. However, no one has been executed, and although thousands of arrests have been made, the practice has at best been slowed, not stopped. Local law enforcement officers are reluctant to get tough, partly because they frequently receive "shares" from the illegal fishermen, and perhaps more fundamentally because they do not understand or sympathize with the law and have no desire to arouse community hostility by overzealous enforcement. There is some evidence that the small-scale Philippine fisherman is being squeezed between the effects of his own dynamite fishing on accessible reef areas and the impact of large, motorized operators in offshore areas, where in any event the little man's primitive technology puts him at a disadvantage.

There are many parallels between tropical forest and coral reef destruction. Both problems are found around the world. Like the forests, the reefs are highly diversified, prolific biologic communities, as yet inadequately understood but with many possible links to existing food production chains as well as great potential for scientific exploitation leading to further practical applications. In both cases there is often conflict between the immediate perceived needs of local communities, whether shifting cultivators or fishermen, and their own long-term well-being. And in both cases, sensible resource management is constantly frustrated by political and administrative difficulties, market pressures, and the exigencies of development.

Opportunities

The environmental picture in island Southeast Asia is not all bleak. The same basic geographic and climatic factors that make the tropical habitat fragile also suggest the possibility of many new or underutilized ways in which man can use his surroundings without destroying them. Only a few examples can be mentioned here.

Geothermal energy holds obvious potential for both Indonesia and the Philippines, comprising as they do a substantial portion of the Pacific "rim of fire." The only major exceptions to a general pattern of widespread volcanism are the underpopulated islands of Borneo and West Irian and some areas of eastern Indonesia and Mindanao. Generally speaking, densely populated areas coincide with volcanic areas. Despite rapidly growing concern in both countries regarding energy supply (Indonesia's domestic oil assets are waning, and the Philippines has only recently started to produce oil on a limited scale) the full implications of this coincidence are not yet realized.

As a general rule, geothermal energy can be developed at costs competitive with conventional energy sources wherever there is active volcanism or heat close to the surface. Rather like old-fashioned radiators, geothermal systems come in two types, hot water and steam. In some places the hot water is under high pressure. In other places there are hot dry rock masses that contain little or no water, and so require introduction and circulation of a heat transfer fluid such as water, if usable power is to be extracted.

Geothermal power has some of the same advantages and disadvantages of hydroelectric power. The source isn't portable, and it won't run an internal combustion engine. In water-based systems dissolved chemicals may cause severe pollution problems, and years of operation may deplete the aquifer (water table), requiring "recharging" or reintroduction of water. Little is known about the life cycle of geothermal systems, since few have been in operation very long, but although none have "run out of steam" thus far it is already clear that there may be limiting factors besides the inexhaustible heat of the earth itself. On the positive side, geothermal plants need not be massive installations and could eventually be relevant to rural needs. On-site industry can be developed using geothermal heat without conversion to electricity, a feature which might be of great importance on Java.[55]

In the Philippines, which unlike Indonesia is heavily

dependent on imported oil, a relatively ambitious start has already been made in the development of geothermal power. At this writing one major field, Tiwi, in southern Luzon is about to become operational. Tiwi is being developed in 55 megawatt stages. Eventually it will generate 560 megawatts, almost as much as the controversial 620 megawatt Bataan nuclear facility (see chapter five) at less than half the latter's $1.1 billion price tag. Several more fields are under development, including one near Manila. By the early 1980s geothermal power will (according to government plans) be supplying 7.5 percent of total national energy needs, and almost 20 percent in another decade.[56]

Indonesia's geothermal capacity is likely to be greater than that of the Philippines, but it remains in the earliest stages of development.[57] New Zealand aid is currently financing a project in West Java which should result in a pioneer 30 megawatt station by 1981. The Union Oil Company, which is developing the Tiwi field in the Philippines under a contract with the National Power Corporation, is at this writing attempting to reach an agreement with Pertamina, which is in charge of Indonesian geothermal resources. The Indonesians have been typically reluctant to allow as much leeway to foreign private enterprise as the Filipinos, while Union, like most multinationals, is wary of committing itself to a major operation in a country with a reputation for corruption, difficult operating conditions, and questionable long-term stability. Given the fact that it took seven years to develop the Tiwi field, it is unlikely that geothermal power, for all its long-run potential, will make much difference to Indonesia for many years to come.[58]

The most dramatic possibilities for balanced, harmonious development of the tropical environment involve the exploitation of underutilized or as yet undiscovered plants. Numerous potentially valuable crops today are grown in restricted areas. The winged bean (Psophocarpus tetragonolobus), for example, is currently important only in Burma and Papua, New Guinea. A soil-enriching legume, it produces edible pods, leaves, and tubers and a protein-rich oil comparable to soya oil. The tubers, containing 20 percent protein, can be eaten like potatoes. Neither pests nor disease appears to be a serious threat, and soil requirements are not demanding. Experiments are already under way to introduce this crop elsewhere in the tropical world.[59]

Regardless of the merits of plantations versus natural forests (discussed earlier), there is a growing need for multipurpose tree crops in areas which have already been ravaged. These amount to at least 6 million hectares in the Philippines and 16 million or more in Indonesia.[60] The best-known success story to date is *Leucaena*, or *ipil-ipil*, originally from Mexico, which attains a height of sixty feet in six years and is a promising source of cattle fodder, firewood, and fertilizer. It can be used to control erosion and in some cases to shade out poisonous weeds that threaten to take over pasture lands.[61] *Leucaena*, already introduced in the Philippines, is only one of many fast-growing leguminous trees which in nature are among the first species to reinvade deforested areas and are hence adaptable to a wide range of sites and nutrient-deficient soils. Some, such as the South Asian shingle tree (*Acrocarpus fraxinifolius*) are spectacular ornamentals as well. Another legume, *Stylosanthes*, has the ability to displace *alang-alang* grass, the normally ineradicable end product of shifting cultivation. Like *Leucaena*, *Stylosanthes* can be used for cattle feed and is well suited for intercropping with plantation tree species. If experiments now under way in Indonesia show that large-scale cultivation of this plant is feasible, it could become the agent of a reclamation effort with revolutionary implications for vast areas of the tropics.[62]

Village-scale energy production from "biomass" also has great potential. Virtually any plant material can be used to make "biogas" in household methane converters. It may also be possible to develop small-scale ammonia factories which would produce fertilizer, currently manufactured primarily from natural gas. In the Philippines a pilot-project jeepney is already operating on distillate fuel manufactured from coconut husks.

The botanical possibilities extend to practically every ecological niche of the variegated tropical environment, as dem-

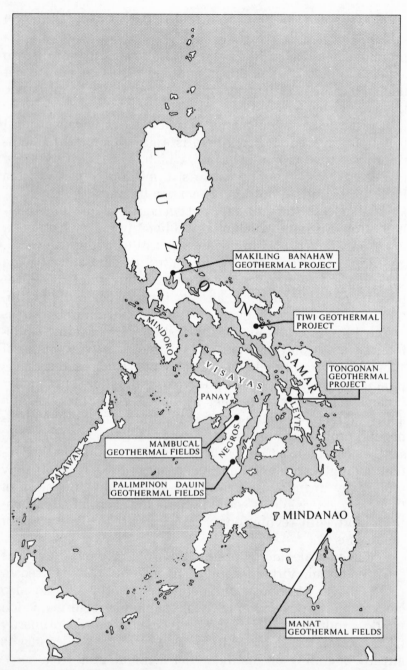

Potential Geothermal Sites: Philippines and Java

SOURCE: Albert Ravenholt, "Energy from Heat in the Earth," American Universities
Field Staff Report AR-1-77 (1977), p. 5.

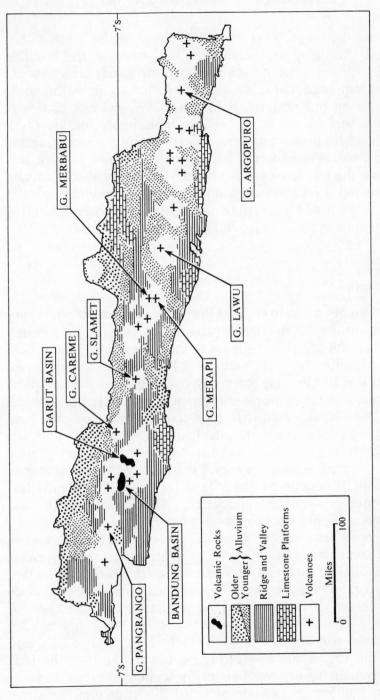

Potential Geothermal Sites (cont.)
SOURCE: E. H. G. Dobby, *Southeast Asia* (London, 1953), p. 217.

onstrated in a series of recent publications by the U.S. National Academy of Sciences. One explores the exciting prospects for farming freshwater aquatic weeds such as water hyacinth, once considered nothing but an impediment to navigation but now recognized as a fast-growing source of human and animal food, fuel, fertilizer, paper, and energy.[63] In the Philippines, among the coral reefs of the rebel-infested Sulu Sea, seaweed farming has become a major activity only within the last few years. Collected by an American firm and processed in Canada, Philippine seaweeds yield extracts which are used for a variety of industrial purposes, including the manufacture of brake fluid for jumbo jet aircraft.[64]

Outlook

I do not mean to suggest that the environment offers easy access to developmental nirvana. It is a truism worth stressing that the primary obstacles to the correct handling of both opportunities and problems are human and institutional. With this in view one can only conclude that the prospects for progress on environmental issues commensurate with the need are bleak. Here it is essential to distinguish between growing concern and its practical consequences. "Environment" is probably the preeminent buzz word of this generation, even more than "energy." In staid institutions scattered through Washington's think-tank belt, researchers now furrow their brows over topics such as Third World erosion and firewood supply that would have been deemed bizarre only a few years ago. The tropical forest issue typifies the awareness explosion. Until recently international aid agencies were solely concerned with devising technology to replace the world's "jungle" with "better" man-made forests, or to consume it more efficiently as particle board, methane, or cattle fodder. Today AID and the World Bank are issuing press releases and sector studies which emphasize balanced use and conservation. Within two months in 1978 the U.S. government sponsored two major conferences on tropical forest problems.[65] Leaders of Third World nations, sensitive to developmental fashions in the West, have been quick to incorporate environmental language into regulations, laws, and five-year plans.

Yet verbiage and good intentions will more often than not continue to bounce off hard political realities. To some extent the very trendiness of the topic encourages cynicism. Awareness alone may provide the policymaker with a false sense of fulfillment. Again, forestry is a good example. The two sides of the Faustian bargain are still unequally perceived. The short-term gain is clear enough, but the long-term damnation is, like Cassandra's prophecy, not wholly credible. As is the case with so many other public policy issues, complexity often leads irresistibly toward immobility. Moreover, awareness has still not proceeded beyond the level of a shallow elite. The deforestation of the tropics may indeed be a greater long-term threat to mankind than the activities of the Soviet Navy. But that is hardly a concept which will be easy to popularize, much less to translate into even a tiny fraction of the bureaucratic attention or budgetary support enjoyed by the U.S. Navy.

Most inhibiting of all is the sobering awareness that, regardless of global consequences, environmental decline in Southeast Asia must remain primarily a responsibility of Southeast Asians. How can foreigners, often unable to make satisfactory progress on similar issues in their own countries, possibly hope to have the slightest effect in alien "soft states" plagued by corruption and skill shortages of all kinds? The sense of frustration is not helped by the fact that existing research on the subject tends to be one-dimensional. There are reams of paper, pro and con, on chipping technology, tree plantations, and sustained yield forestry, but little has been written about the critical interaction between Chinese businessmen, generals, provincial bureaucracies, shifting cultivators, and national research capabilities.

In the long run, cultural factors may be even more important than the more widely recognized panoply of "soft state" administrative inadequacies. It is instructive to observe the completely different patterns of adaptation to the same environment demonstrated by ethnic Chinese and indigenous peoples in western Borneo, one of the few areas of Southeast Asia where there is a significant population of Chinese farmers. The intensive, multicrop activities of the Chinese, including rubber, pepper, fish ponds, vegetables, and livestock, contrast sharply with the monocultural, slash-and-burn rice farming traditional among the indigenous Dayaks. The Chinese produce far more on the same typically impoverished tropical soils without having to move from the same spot. This phenomenon has been recognized for more than a hundred years, as has been the corollary fact that Chinese methods, like new technologies, are easier to admire than to inculcate in others.[66]

Nevertheless, it would be unduly pessimistic to assume that it is impossible to influence Southeast Asian environmental practice. The key lies in making an effective appeal to nationalism, which sooner or later is the determining political force throughout the region, and which is particularly highly developed in Indonesia. This can only be done by convincing a greater number of Indonesians that reckless exploitation of perishable resources will prolong national weakness and vulnerability to external forces.[67] Beyond stressing this point, foreign aid donors should make a strenuous effort to facilitate adequate long-term training for forestry and fisheries staff, to assist generously in developing national research institutions, and to help provide leaders and future government planners with an adequate appreciation of environmental issues. Obviously this is not a short-term prescription.

There are a number of other modest, specific policies which are eminently feasible. Some environmental issues are admirably suited to technical assistance on a regional level. The United States should, as a token of its long-term commitment to Southeast Asia, propose and support a forestry institute under ASEAN auspices. Besides adequate laboratories, library, and staff, it should possess a large enough area of forest to encompass a full range of habitats, from mangrove to high elevation moss forest, with enough acreage to experiment with shifting cultivation, tree farming, and sustained yield logging. It could serve as a base for research and experi-

mentation throughout the region, and to some extent worldwide, much as has the International Rice Research Institute
in the Philippines. Similar facilities are urgently needed for
research on other aspects of tropical botany and on the tropical marine environment as well. In few other fields is the link
between pure science and practical application more significant, or more endangered.

United States embassies could be enlisted in a more considered environmental policy. Diplomats as well as AID personnel should be charged with pointing out, by all means at
their disposal, the serious interest that their government
takes in such issues, somewhat as they were enlisted, albeit
often unwillingly, in the Carter Administration's campaign
for human rights. Embassies in the tropics should strengthen
their currently weak-to-nonexistent scientific reporting capability to allow multidisciplinary analysis of environmental
problems and opportunities. This would require additional
training and in some cases additional staff, which could easily be obtained without expanding existing missions by con-
verting some of the superabundant positions currently devoted, even in countries of slight military importance, to
intelligence and defense-related functions. As in other areas,
it is possible that our policy capabilities may turn out to be
somewhat greater than we realize, once we better understand
the problems.[68]

Multinational corporations are often considered to be the
ultimate villains in the forestry field. Were this so, it might
be easier to devise effective policies. OPIC investment guarantees,[69] for example, could be made contingent on sound
forestry practices, including as an absolute minimum adequate research and cataloging of species before concession
areas are logged. With or without OPIC involvement, the expense of such research efforts should be made tax deduct-
ible as a legitimate business expense. As a first step, President Carter's executive order of January 1979 requiring a
minimal and flexible environmental impact assessment
should apply to all U.S.-funded activities affecting tropical
forests, including OPIC and Ex-Im insurance and financial
guarantees.[70]

Unfortunately, as we have seen, the major multinationals, including both U.S. and Japanese, conduct only a fraction of Southeast Asian logging, nor is it likely that additional American firms will be entering the field in future. The main actors are medium-sized firms, some domestic, others backed by Japanese, Korean, Malaysian, or overseas Chinese capital. Ruthless and resilient, these operators will be the most difficult to deflect from cut-and-run tactics. The larger multinationals, like Weyerhaeuser, have a greater stake in sound, sustained operations. As conspicuous foreigners they are vulnerable and hence more likely to play by the rules, when there are any rules. Some of them are responsive to public opinion in the West. Certainly they should be pressured, coaxed, and cajoled into better conservation practices, but they cannot be expected to reform the industry in the absence of institutional support from host governments. Weyerhaeuser, Georgia Pacific, the Sorianos, and the Japanese firms could also be encouraged to share their expertise more widely, by, for example, contributing to a regional forestry research and development effort, with fair compensation for the expense involved.

The most effective contribution to better forestry practices could be made by alterations in international trade practices. Price stabilization, desirable in itself, would help to subdue the boom-and-bust mentality which, as things stand, militates against long-term planning for more rational utilization. Reversal of the current Japanese practice whereby tariffs are levied on finished timber while logs are admitted duty free would do more than anything else to encourage entrepreneurs in Southeast Asia (both local and foreign) to opt for integrated operations and long-term, sustained yield practices of the PICOP variety. The difficulties involved in persuading the Japanese to adopt such a policy are sufficiently obvious. In fairness, the Japanese should not be expected to bear the whole burden, since they are by no means solely to blame. A substantial proportion of the total Southeast Asian log harvest goes to Taiwan and Korea, where it is used to make plywood for the U.S. market.[71] U.S. importation of processed tropical hardwood has undoubtedly made it easier for

American environmentalists to conserve our own remaining hardwood forests for aesthetic and recreational purposes. It is the ever-growing consumption of the developed nations generally that created and is sustaining the problems. Theoretically, regulating consumption could be accomplished by international agreement to limit importation of tropical hardwoods, in the same manner that quotas have been implemented for the whaling industry. But whales are uniquely appealing. It is not nearly as easy to arouse public opinion on behalf of trees, even though the practical consequences of failure to do so may be more harmful in the long run.

There is more hope of mobilizing effort on utilization issues than on preservation ones. Much is already being done by aid donors to promote renewable energy development both at the village level and beyond. There may be a vital role for the private sector here, as the case of Union Oil and Philippine geothermal development indicates. The governments of both developing and developed nations could stimulate more sharing of technology by encouraging alternative, non-equity investment relationships with foreign entrepreneurs, as I suggested in an earlier chapter.

Third World nations are already facing difficult choices when it comes to the application of environmental standards to industry. The problem has been dramatized in the Philippines by the Bataan nuclear plant and by a massive sintering plant in northern Mindanao which will process iron ore bound from Australia to Japan. This facility, being constructed by Kawasaki, appears to be a classic case of pollution export. Whether economic gain will offset ecological damage in such cases can, of course, only be decided by local governments. Rigid application of developed-country standards would be arrogant, even if agreed-upon standards existed elsewhere, which they frequently do not. Because the consequences of environmental damage are global, international standards and policies are the ultimate answer. But achieving them on a significant scale may await the achievement of world government, which does not appear imminent. In the meantime, many environmental issues will fully justify a degree of American involvement, official and unofficial, including, on occasion, discouragement of specific foreign-funded projects or practices.

The search for an exit from this dilemma will be unending. But it poses the kind of challenge that Americans should enjoy. Nothing in the postwar era thrilled us as much, perhaps, as President Kennedy's first inaugural address. The environment requires another twilight struggle, one which now appears far more significant than the one Kennedy evoked. The amazing degree of popular support for domestic environmental issues, often in the face of well-financed resistance, suggests that such an effort would help to reenlist American idealism and energy in the conduct of foreign affairs as well as help to preserve a habitable world for Americans as yet unborn.

Chapter Eight

Conclusion:
On the Need to Think Ahead

> . . . The old uncertainties about physical sur-
> vival and military safety look simple next to
> the new ones.
> —Stanley Hoffman, *Primacy or World Order*[1]

While this book was being written dramatic events
occurred in Iran. Immediately, parallels were drawn with
practically every authoritarian noncommunist Third World
country. Indonesia was a favorite, being large, Muslim, and
oil producing—if not, sad to say, oil wealthy on an Iranian
scale. As for the Philippines, at least one prominent opposition figure proclaimed on the *Washington Post*'s op-ed page
that his country too might be "another Iran."

There may be some validity in these comparisons, as
chapter two suggests, but they are also easily overdrawn. It
was earlier observed that the most profound political fact
about Indonesian Islam is that, for all its statistical strength,
it is a de facto minority religion. With regard to U.S. policy,
there are obvious and fundamental differences. Since Vietnam, Southeast Asia is no longer for us an area of prime
geopolitical importance in any way comparable with the
Middle East. There has been nothing like the single overwhelming factor of massive oil imports balanced by equally
massive arms exports which in the case of Iran inevitably
dominated and distorted policy. The Philippine bases generate formidable military-bureaucratic pressures but they are
feeble in comparison to the Iranian incubus.

In Iran we remained locked on an obviously hazardous
course in part because the Shah's arms purchases contributed
to the economic viability of American weapons technology,

and hence to our own national defense capability. In island Southeast Asia there are of course analogous linkages between "foreign" and "domestic" policy interests. But the domestic interests at play are diffuse, and do not necessarily point us in a malevolent direction, nor are they, on balance, in conflict with the interests of Southeast Asians. They are, however, reflected in a welter of competing pressures and bureaucracies which tend to produce immobility, until crisis intervenes.

The previous chapters repeatedly suggest that our primary need in the Third World generally is not so much a specific recipe of new policies, designed for immediate impact, as it is a greater capacity for sustained action in the long tedium of noncrisis (or precrisis) situations. Among the many contributing deficiencies are problems relating to public attitudes, bureaucratic structures, and analytic capabilities. In concluding I will dwell at some length on the interplay between foreign affairs analysis and policymaking, partly because it is a subject which has concerned me in my own official career, but also because of the critical relationship between genuine understanding and rational long-term behavior. Before turning to this subject however, it may be useful to summarize the preceding chapters and to identify some common characteristics of specific questions that have been raised, usually without being answered.

The essays have described an island Southeast Asia comprised of maturing authoritarian states with a remarkable record, over the last decade, of national leadership continuity. Although Malaysia and the city state of Singapore were not discussed, this generalization applies to them as well as to Indonesia and the Philippines. At this writing the principal external danger to regional peace emanates from the Southeast Asian mainland, where a tragic process of postcolonial adjustment between ancient antagonists is still under way. For all its cost in suffering, reflected in the exodus of refugees, that conflict does not directly threaten the sea-insulated states to the south.

On balance, the probable short-term outlook for the island world is continued national cohesion and evolving regional détente. Many experts perceive this détente as the result of great power balance, or equilibrium. But there is no discrete regional equilibrium in island Southeast Asia. The United States, with its massive military bases in the Philippines, remains without serious rival as a military actor in this area. Rather, in my view, the détente results from a combination of global, strategic equilibrium and, at the local level, perception by all the relevant external powers, heightened by the Vietnam War, that intervention holds little prospect of profit for anyone. The trend is delicate and it could be upset, most obviously by violent Sino-Soviet rivalry, which is why we must retain a strong interest in a peaceful solution to the continued turmoil in Indochina.

The longer-term internal political outlook for the island states is less certain. Both Indonesia and the Philippines are troubled by profound tensions and inequities, and their political systems lack clear-cut succession mechanisms. Thus, in both states there is a powderkeg factor and next to it one obvious source of sparks. But in both societies there is also an array of constraints against violent political change. One of the most potent is a deep-seated desire to maintain national unity against the constant pressure generated by ethnic divisions. Another is the prevalence of political cultures which are receptive to authoritarian rule. It is time for Americans to give up the illusion that, because of our colonial tutelage, this latter generalization does not apply to the Philippines.

As experience elsewhere should have taught us by now, a bewildering array of variables inhibits accurate prediction of political events in authoritarian Third World states. What can be said with confidence is that social revolution, if it should come, will be driven by profound national forces. As in Vietnam, our capacity to halt political convulsion will be limited, and attempts to oppose or exploit the process will do more harm than good. Particularly in countries like the Philippines, where American support conveys legitimation as well as material benefit, a policy of political detachment will in the end provide the most effective possible stimulus for governments to correct conditions which might otherwise lead to upheaval. Political detachment is not easy to achieve under general conditions of growing interaction in other areas—economic, environmental, and cultural. As a start, however, we should make it clear to Southeast Asians that their internal stability cannot realistically be regarded as a goal or concern of U.S. policy, and we should cease our habitual resort to arms transfers as expressions of political "supportiveness." Such a stance would, as a side benefit, remove one source of virulent hypocrisy from our human rights policy without, under conditions of slowly growing regional détente, affecting our security interests.

More specific key issues in American security policy in the region emerge from a consideration of our bases in the Philippines in chapter three. These facilities, I have argued, are the central element in an anachronistic, postcolonial "special relationship" which is a major obstacle to rational interaction and cooperation on other problems of greater intrinsic significance. So long as the present relationship persists, with the bases as preservative, Americans will continue to be loved, hated, and manipulated simultaneously by Filipino politicians. The relationship guarantees that if social revolution comes to the Philippines (an unlikely prospect in the short run, more likely as time goes by) the bases, and their American population, will be an inevitable target. Under such circumstances it would be impossible for the United States to disengage gracefully. In the worst conceivable case we could in time find ourselves caught up in Asia's last anticolonial war—on the wrong side.

These costs and liabilities are weighed against the declining but still substantial military utility of the bases, mainly as low-cost logistical facilities, and their undeniable value as tangible symbols of continuing U.S. presence in the Western Pacific—a presence which is seen not only by the five nations of ASEAN but also by China, and possibly even by the USSR, as one essential element in the regional détente. The political risks could be reduced if not eliminated by a vigorous reduction of U.S. military personnel at the bases, combined with a gradual process of Filipinization. This process would include transfer of nonoperational functions (logistics and repair) to Filipino and American contractors, the latter subject to the same regulations as other foreign companies, as well as a progressively greater share for the Philippine Armed Forces in the management and use of the facilities. Although intended primarily to preserve the existing relationship, the January 1979 amendment to the 1947 base agreement, with its provision for a complete review after five years, could be a first step toward comprehensive reform along the lines suggested.

As part of a more general revision of our security ties, we should also move to eliminate ambiguities in the Philippine-U.S. Mutual Defense Treaty which were accentuated by the 1979 agreement. Grant military aid, other than training required for the transfer of base functions, should be terminated in line with a regional policy of political detachment. We should get back to the principle that we do not pay compensation (whether as rent or "aid") to allies for base rights, all the more so if genuine reform is under way in order to give the Philippines a greater degree of benefit from the facilities themselves in terms of contract revenues, technology transfer, and utility for national defense. The need to compensate for base rights almost always suggests a lack of shared political values which signals that the military partnership in question rests on an unstable foundation, and the Philippine case is no exception.

Such a policy would in time make the bases "Philippine" in fact as well as in name. Well before full implementation, it would enable the United States to support without qualm the cherished ASEAN goal of Southeast Asia as a Zone of Peace, without foreign bases. Reform and rationalization, if properly presented, would reassure other parties in the region by placing the U.S.-Philippine security relationship in a healthier context and by signaling the definitive end of the postcolonial era with all its accompanying contention and trauma. But as things now stand, the obstacles in the path of such a policy are formidable. Both the U.S. military bureaucracies and the Philippine national leadership, for very different reasons, derive comfort and convenience from the status quo. Above all, Filipinization would require years of carefully planned effort by the United States. It assumes an aptitude for both long-term evaluation and phased execution alien to our foreign policy process.

The essay on human rights (chapter four) compares the initial workings of the Carter policy in Indonesia and the Philippines, both of which have been important testing grounds. The comparison appears at first glance to suggest an intriguing contradiction. While the Indonesian rights record is by most yardsticks worse than that of the Philippines, the administration has been relatively tougher in applying pressures and even a few mild sanctions against Manila, in spite of the fact that our perceived security interests (read bases) in the Philippines might have logically motivated us to soft-peddle human rights there.

The explanation is relatively simple. We have been tougher on the Philippines partly because of a relatively effective anti-Marcos lobby operating in the United States (there is no Indonesian equivalent), and partly because of emotional, "special relationship" factors. We not only expect the Filipinos, our political stepchildren, to do better than others, but also, quite incorrectly, fancy that we retain a special degree of influence over them. As most parents will recognize, this is a dangerous illusion, particularly after children reach adulthood. The American image of Indonesia is quite different. It is perceived as a very large country, perhaps a "new influential" in Brzezinskian terminology, with contradictory overtones of unpredictable violence, peasant poverty, and Indies wealth. Above all, Indonesia's culture is both fascinating and alien to the point of inaccessibility. As with the Saudis, for example, we do not casually presume to influence such people or expect them to meet our standards.

In pressing the Philippines on human rights we have repeatedly extended our disapproval to the very nature of the Marcos regime and authoritarianism per se, although with little success, while in Indonesia our protest has been restricted to specific violations of the person, mainly in connection with the post-1965 political detainees. U.S. human rights initiatives to Indonesia have been only one aspect of an international effort which has evoked, relative to the Philippine case, a greater degree of substantive response and less

paranoia. The comparison suggests that it is unwise to presume too far on old friendships, especially when they are less
than wholly healthy.

Chapter five examines American economic interests in
Indonesia and the Philippines, starting with trade and investment. It further considers that thesis that the United States
has an indirect interest insofar as Southeast Asian economic
relations are vital to our major Pacific ally, Japan. The figures
for trade and investment suggest that the stereotype of a "resource rich" Southeast Asia, a cornucopia of oil, rubber, and
tin critical to developed-nation consumers, is often misleading. With regard to oil, for example, the 8 percent of U.S. imports that came from Indonesia in 1978 do not loom very
large if weighed against other factors, including the long-
term likelihood of declining Indonesian export capacity.
However, from the point of view of ASEAN, or any of its
members, economic relations with the United States and
Japan are a matter of life and death. The Southeast Asian
economies reflect international trends over which local governments can exert little influence, much less control. Short
of rejecting the open market entirely, they have no choice but
to rely on the increasingly interlocking operation of Japanese,
U.S., and European capital and technology. They can be
badly hurt by minute shifts in trade policy, market fluctua-
tions, and the development of synthetic substitutes. They
catch cold when *we* sneeze, and not vice versa.

We cannot be complacent about the implications of our
own lopsided economic power in dealing with this significant portion of the underdeveloped world. The relative prosperity and anticommunist ideology of the ASEAN five have
made them "moderates" in the north-south dialogue thus far,
but unless faster progress is made, they could in time be
driven to more radical tactics. And while the consequences
of failure to make greater tangible progress on north-south
issues may be more political than economic, it is also possible, as the foreign aid lobby keeps telling us, that advanced-
nation progress will sooner or later be dependent on the
progress of the LDCs, particularly middle-income states like
those of ASEAN. From this point of view the Third World is

greater than the sum of its parts, whether they be countries or regional groupings.

We do, of course, retain hope that we can assist the Indonesians and others toward greater national strength through foreign aid. The core of Indonesia's development problem, examined in chapter six, is the overpopulated island of Java, with almost two-thirds of the national population on only 7 percent of the land. In 1977 Javanese overpopulation, plus a problem-ridden agricultural economy, caused Indonesia to import one-third of the rice on the world market.

The Indonesian development debate centers around several issues, including (a) the relative feasibility of a food production versus a labor absorption strategy; (b) the wisdom of concentrating foreign assistance on Java, as opposed to the less populated Outer Islands which have great potential but also severe problems of their own; (c) the role of food imports, including U.S. PL 480 aid, which has been doled out rather unthinkingly up to now; and (d) the Dutch-conceived policy of "transmigration," now the focus of a controversial World Bank effort, whereby Javanese peasants are resettled in the Outer Islands.

The only specific conclusion offered is the eminently safe one that no easy solutions are possible. Above all, the Javanese case dramatizes the long-term nature of major development issues, and suggests that we should reconcile ourselves to an arduous and often unrewarding involvement. It also suggests that the two most critical factors are first, insufficient understanding of the key problems, and second, the institutional capacity of the Indonesians to address them. Large foreign aid programs tend to ride roughshod over the self-help constraint. Such programs are in many ways a response less to Indonesian needs than to donor ideological perceptions, sentiments, and pressure groups. American policymakers perceive Indonesia as big and important, American farmers (and others) want to export more food, and the Congress, quite accurately reflecting American political values, decrees that our aid should go *directly* to the "poorest of the poor" without being siphoned off by professors or officials.

Our world view inclines us to assume that successful programs must display big dollar price tags. But at present Java is more in need of dispersed, small-scale experimentation than massive projects, and quality (defined as long-term self-help capacity) may be inversely proportional to quantity measured in dollars.

Compared to Indonesia, the Philippines has vastly greater human resources, and yet (on a per capita basis) it gets much more aid. One reason is the well-known fact that up to a point aid goes to those who can best absorb, not those who are in most need. A brief comparative postscript to the Java chapter suggests that the Philippine case demands similar restraint, although for entirely different reasons: as things stand, American aid is encouraging the Philippines to export skilled human beings and otherwise to neglect or misuse its own resources. Here it is clearly time for a weaning process to begin, a secondary reason for not using bilateral assistance as a form of compensation for base rights.

Chapter seven looks at some problems and opportunities which are manifest in the tropical, insular, volcanic environment of Indonesia and the Philippines, with emphasis on forestry. Destruction of the world's tropical moist forests (a significant share of them in island Southeast Asia) is a much more serious problem than temperate deforestation because in the tropics the complexity and delicacy of biological communities may preclude regeneration of natural forest. The cost of uncontrolled deforestation extends beyond soil erosion and siltation (e.g., the possible clogging of the Panama Canal within the next few decades) to the probable destruction of a significant proportion of the world's plant species before they can be scientifically discovered, much less investigated for productive applications. The problem is now generating much scientific attention in the developed countries, where consumption patterns and tariff structures continue to encourage the reckless exploitation of tropical hardwood. But outcries of concern are slow to reach the Indonesian planners who see logs primarily as a major source of foreign exchange (second only to oil), not to mention the generals who control logging concessions. At current cutting rates almost half of the world's accessible tropical forests, including Indonesia's, will be gone by the year 2000 or shortly thereafter—and the limits of the accessible are extended yearly. Foreigners could do more to stimulate concern where it will matter by pointing out that permanent loss of what may well turn out to be a nonrenewable resource will prolong national weakness, and by promoting technical assistance to strengthen local forestry research and institutions. As the ultimate consumers of Southeast Asian forests they could also encourage rational exploitation by taxing imported raw timber at higher rates relative to finished wood products.

There are many more environmental problems which should increasingly concern us, as they will concern our children. The forest conservation imperative is matched by the need for reclamation and intelligent utilization of areas already deforested. Solar and geothermal energy, coastal mangrove habitats, and marine resources all offer opportunities for cooperative activity on a scale which may in time significantly effect global welfare.

What are some of the common themes and impressions that emerge from these essays? First and most obvious, our political relations with island Southeast Asia are relatively sound for the time being. The region is no longer, and with luck may not be again, an arena of crisis. The end of the Vietnam War left us in a better position to act effectively in our own long-term interests, just as it stimulated the Southeast Asians toward more substantial regional cooperation, both political and economic, through ASEAN.

Within Southeast Asia (not necessarily everywhere else in the world) traditional security issues are losing much of their relevance. Once regarded as exclusively the product of political conflict and competition, "influence" and "presence" are now clearly linked to a much wider variety of factors, and interaction between the great powers occurs less frequently in the form of the zero-sum game, where the "loser" always suffers at the hands of the "winner." Francis Underhill, former U.S. Ambassador to Malaysia, has noted that the present situation more closely resembles a track meet, with different events going on simultaneously in different arenas, than it does the conventional image of a race. Not all the participants are entered in all the events, some of which are either "no contest" in nature or already over. The United States retains a substantial lead in the conventional (non-nuclear) security event, despite the growing Soviet presence in an otherwise isolated Vietnam. China has a certain moral and cultural eminence, evoking universal respect (not to be confused with love or submission) which no other power can rival. But communism has lost virtually all the sex appeal it enjoyed in the fifties, and now functions mainly, in a negative sense, as a useful if increasingly hollow rationale for authoritarianism.

The United States has enormous impact as a purveyor of desired technology, and as a major source of what is rapidly becoming an international culture, reflected in phenomena from fast foods to modern dance, mass entertainment, elite art forms, and (mainly from our universities) dangerous thought. One side effect has been an ironic role reversal in which Southeast Asian leaders like Lee Kuan Yew and Adam Malik, men who were once themselves regarded by the State Department as dangerous leftists, must now worry about isolating their own youth from the contagious radicalism endemic at places like Berkeley. As for the Japanese, they have achieved a position of economic preeminence, in part the logical consequence of geography, which is unlikely to be challenged by any other external power.

This system is by no means completely harmonious, but it is remarkably free of tension if judged against what would have been predicted only a few years ago. Even where conflict might be deemed inevitable, it frequently appears to be on the wane. American-Japanese commercial relations are a case in point. Increasingly the pattern is one of complementarity and interaction, with American investment dependent on Japanese markets, American and Japanese technology and capital combining in the same projects, and New York, Tokyo, and London banks jointly raising eurodollar funds in offshore markets for syndicated lending which may not directly draw down anyone's national payments account. The element of regional rivalry that does remain in U.S.-Japanese economic relations is not very significant in the context of a relationship which operates worldwide. Moreover, the Japanese know that if they carry their existing economic preponderance too far, it will inevitably arouse serious political reaction. For this reason they do not want to be the only big international capitalists in the game, and welcome a continued healthy share for U.S. and European business.

The absence of mortal rivalry and the diminution of great power conflict in Southeast Asia do not mean that problems are lacking, as should be evident by now. The same growth in global culture and technology which has diminished the relevance of conventional war (at least between major powers) has spawned a host of challenges. New technologies and the demands of the international market are wreaking havoc in the fragile tropical environment at the same time that they contribute to material development. The poorest of the poor may or may not be getting poorer, but it is certainly much easier for them to perceive their poverty. The political maturity of national leaders has heightened their awareness of the overall disparity between north and south. Above all, problems of food and overpopulation have raised the possibility of misery on a scale that risks systemic breakdowns with unforeseeable political consequences.

It is the principal contention of this book that these "new agenda" issues of welfare, trade, and technology are already of primary relevance to U.S. interests in Southeast Asia, and that as time goes by they are likely to become even more important relative to political-military issues. The implications of this assumption are considerable. For one thing, it follows that Southeast Asia is already less significant as a "strategic" regional entity than as one important segment of the Third World. The fact that American officials increasingly see the value of ASEAN in relation to north-south issues is evidence that this perception is already on its way to becoming conventional wisdom.

Conservatives may be inclined to regard strong emphasis on the new agenda as little more than a formula for "withdrawal" or a polite facade for neo-isolationism. If I am correct, however, the changing pattern of American interests will demand more, rather than less, involvement (if not intervention) in the affairs of others. The central challenge facing us in Southeast Asia today may be that although the need for interaction is growing, we will perforce continue to operate in a world where nationalism remains the preeminent political force, a world composed of authoritarian states, making only slow progress toward democracy or even efficiency. It is a sure thing that our mutual compatibility will not increase at the same rate as our shared concerns.

It is easy to be pessimistic about American capability to cope with the new agenda. Many of the prescriptions offered in the preceding pages are negative, and although the essays argue the limitations of traditional political-military force factors, they certainly do not suggest any obvious arsenal of new weapons. Developmental and environmental issues may be paramount, yet if Indonesia and the Philippines are typical, external aid and advice are likely to be effective precisely insofar as they are used with restraint. Multinational private enterprise seems to call for an impossibly dextrous combination of additional regulation in cases where international welfare may be at stake (e.g., the Philippine nuclear case) and the streamlining of existing regulatory procedures (e.g., Indonesian LNG). While it seems increasingly obvious that in the long run trade will be our most effective vehicle for helping the Southeast Asians, it is also palpably the most difficult to maneuver through our own domestic political minefields.

New agenda issues are undeniably frustrating. Merely to appreciate them demands a sophisticated ability to balance "soft" long-term interests against short-term cost and convenience factors. Most solutions, when they can be found, call for sustained·effort, with little hope of immediate, visible results. The new agenda is transnational in character, constantly impinging on areas which were until recently purely internal. This blurring of foreign and domestic concerns has a confusing, debilitating effect in two ways: we are inhibited from intervening on subjects like forest preservation, which under the old agenda was none of our business. And should we wish to do so, the available expertise is rarely found within the traditional foreign affairs community, but rather in domestic agencies (in this case, the USDA's Forest Service). In theory, of course, transnational issues can best be handled in the United Nations and other international organizations. Unfortunately, most decisions are still made in a bilateral context.

These dilemmas are the product of growing interdependence. They have been discussed by others at greater length than is possible here, with reference to a broader range of countries and issues.[2] It is generally agreed that the central problem is less one of declining American power than of increasingly complex circumstances which make the exercise of unilateral power less rewarding. This should be cause for satisfaction insofar as it results partly from our own successful efforts to promote a vigorous, diverse world community. The increasing irrelevance of conventional military and political influence-wielding in countries like Indonesia and the Philippines is a reflection of their progress toward immunity from the simplistic sanctions and interventions of the fifties. Such progress is qualified but hardly nullified by the persistence of economic vulnerability.

The Southeast Asian material presented in the preceding essays suggests that further adjustment on our part to the exigencies of the new agenda is needed in three general areas: structural, concerning the machinery of government; attitudinal, relating to American perceptions of the Third World, and analytical, involving the need to understand increasingly complex issues and the impact of our own behavior upon them.

The need for change in the structures of government follows from the fact that the important actions we take regarding countries like Indonesia and the Phillippines are increasingly taken at home, not abroad. The problem is one of reorienting bureaucracies designed to meet the needs of the previous era. This is a well-worn topic, and I would only mention a few generally recognized specifics. We need a State Department more oriented toward dealing with other Washington agencies, including the Congress, particularly on economic issues. We also need a greater degree of foreign policy sophistication within the other agencies themselves. If it is true that foreign relations are today the result of behavior by an ever wider community of people, it follows that our diplomatic service should place greater emphasis on working and communicating with other actors in American society, and disabuse itself of any lingering pretensions to exclusive foreign affairs responsibility. Yet the need to understand and interact with foreign governments on a growing range of issues will also demand not merely the preservation but the reinvigoration of traditional diplomatic language and area skills, augmented by new functional capabilities.[3] It goes without saying that change in this area is unlikely to be accomplished quickly or completely at a time when shrinking budgets inhibit bureaucratic innovation, yet it is also clear that much could be done by redeploying existing bureaucratic resources, if the need were recognized.

The second kind of change suggested by the essays concerns the manner in which Americans (official and otherwise) regard the authoritarian Third World, and the contradictions that flow from attempts to cooperate on new agenda issues. This dilemma involves more than a reaffirmation of the old-fashioned diplomatic craft of doing business with leaders you may not like. It is a paradox of major policy relevance that the same humanitarian instincts which sustain American support for foreign assistance, including the most enlightened categories of institution building and technology transfer, are repelled by authoritarianism. On balance we shall probably need to face the fact that some degree of contradiction will persist; that one cannot perform the aid function (valuable on its own merits) without lending some political support to dictators. The creative solution is to find the best way between imperatives neither of which can be denied, and to give due emphasis to types of foreign assistance, which, over the long haul, seem most likely to foster liberal politics. It might help to achieve a less schizoid policy mix if we spent more effort exploring the relationship between economic development and human rights. If on balance development erodes authoritarianism, contradiction is diminished. If the answer remains uncertain, as seems likely, risk taking is fully acceptable in American society. The contradiction will also be lessened if our human rights effort can be concentrated on abuse of the person (torture and detainment), leaving anti-authoritarianism in the capable hands of unofficial organizations and pressure groups.

The final category of needed change, and the one I would like to stress, involves the requirement to understand better the kinds of problems we are up against, as a necessary although by no means sufficient prelude to dealing with them. The essays suggest that many categories of questions which are profoundly relevant to American interests are not being systematically asked either within the government or elsewhere. The relationship between human rights and development, the interface between multinational corporations and the Third World, the impact (present and potential) of U.S. trade policies—all these topics constitute entire research agendas which could fruitfully be pursued at regional or individual country level and should be the focus of ongoing efforts. More specific unanswered questions abound, as we have seen: the impact of U.S. surplus food programs in Indonesia, the degree of complementarity/competitiveness between American and Japanese capital in Southeast Asia, the cost-effectiveness of Indonesian transmigration, the dubious relationship between Philippine emigration (encouraged by American law) and Philippine development (encouraged with American aid). In more traditional fields, such as security, the quality of analysis is somewhat higher, although even here, as the question of U.S. bases in the Philippines suggests, there is likely to be insufficient attention to "soft" political and psychological factors of paramount importance.

So far as the government is concerned, there is a critical relationship between bureaucratic structure and analytic capability, and nowhere is this more obvious than in the foreign affairs agencies. Some years ago the American ambassador to a small Asian country was exchanging cables with Washington about the pending elimination of a position in his already miniscule political section. He pointed out that as the Foreign Service diminished in size relative to the entire mass of the U.S. government deployed abroad, it devoted an ever-increasing proportion of its staff to housekeeping functions. When positions were cut, it always seemed easier to do without a small consulate, or to eliminate a political or economic reporting officer, than to trim the administrative support machinery, the more so since the latter served all the other U.S. government agencies, ranging from Agriculture to CIA, to be found at most embassies. The ambassador wanly recalled the brontosaurus, whose brain grew ever smaller in relation to its body, until the species became extinct.

There are several reasons why the lack of analytic capability in government is serious and growing. As the anecdote above suggests, bureaucratic evolution tends to produce a progressive imbalance of thought to bulk, a Gresham's law relationship betwen hard interagency politicking and soft reason. The diffusion of foreign affairs responsibility among many agencies has added to the problem. So, in recent years, has the proliferation of congressional staff and the breakdown of authority patterns within the Congress itself. The Founding Fathers intended a system of government by conflict, embodied in the division of powers, but they cannot have foreseen how much energy would be absorbed internally as the system matured and expanded. Conflict is in many respects a healthy if not always an efficient process. Ideas and programs are tested, publicity is generated, differing points of view find expression. Bureaucratic conflict helps insure that the U.S. executive branch, far from becoming a mandarinate, remains almost as diverse as the national population itself. In one of the wisest books ever written about modern Washington, Charles Frankel observed that "American society is competitive and entrepreneurial; why should American government be different?"[4] But he also noticed the curiously irrational nature of the Washington compost heap, with its many layers and prevalence of heat over light. When a typical decision-producing sequence demands months of arduous negotiation among several executive agencies and Congress, the actors have little choice but to decide first, then to maneuver, and only then, if there is time and energy remaining, to expend some effort on thought.

A second major source of analytical atrophy in foreign

affairs is the time-honored isolation of intelligence from policy. It remains true that operational responsibilities encourage self-serving reports, which was the original reason for the independent evaluation capability concentrated at the CIA. But several things went wrong. First the operational, covert action function of the CIA itself came grossly to overshadow its analytic function. Second, and even more serious, it was until recently a cardinal tenet of intelligence analysis to evaluate only foreign, never American actions; an omission which produced distorted views of a world in which the United States is indeed a major actor. More recently there has been some willingness to take into account the impact of our own presence on foreign behavior, but analysis of U.S. policy is still rigorously excluded on the grounds that this would mix operations and evaluation. The resulting blind spot might be less noteworthy if a serious self-analysis capability existed elsewhere, but it does not. The State Department Inspectorate, for example, is used mainly as a housekeeping tool—to make sure that embassies are being run efficiently— and rarely if ever extended to serious policy issues. The Office of Management and Budget (OMB) is in some ways the nearest thing to what is needed, but its wholly operational character and preoccupation with budgetary restraint preclude anything approaching long-range thought.

Perhaps most serious is the information explosion and the increasing amount of highly technical or otherwise exotic knowledge which bears on foreign relations. The State Department received over a million cables in 1977, and the number goes up by 15 percent yearly. Nevertheless, a growing proportion of the total amount of relevant knowledge never enters official channels, or if it does, is never assimilated. Sheer volume has long since called into question old assumptions about the benign relationship between information and policy formation. Human minds and automated retrieval systems seem equally incapable of coping, and Washington is retrogressing toward the status of an oral-driven community where any paper more than a few pages in length is likely to have a primarily ritual function.[5] In this new postliterate society decisions are necessarily based on interpersonal communication because there is no time for anything else.

But the volume problem is probably less significant than the factor of complexity. As the case of tropical forestry suggests, new agenda issues typically demand a varied mix of analytic skills: diplomatic and foreign area expertise (how can we enlist the cooperation of the Indonesian leadership?), scientific expertise (is regeneration of dipterocarp forest feasible?), as well as, of course, a finely tuned sense of what is possible in American law and politics. Under the circumstances there is a tremendous and ever-growing requirement for cross-disciplinary "translators" whose function is to extract, condense, and interpret, as well as to analyze in the presently accepted sense. Yet the actual trend is in the opposite direction. In the "realistic" action-oriented world of foreign affairs, analytical capability remains acutely vulnerable and is in fact being continually reduced, certainly in quantity and quite possible in quality as well. During the year and a half that this study was under preparation, the CIA did not have a single full-time analyst assigned to Indonesia, the fifth largest country in the world, nor was the omission in any way uncharacteristic of the broader government habit of non-thought.

The difficulties encountered by past efforts to create a "long reach" analytic capability are well known. State's Policy Planning Staff is perhaps the most obvious example. Originally established by George Marshall to work on the broader and longer-range aspects of policy, and famous for its role in the formulation of the Marshall Plan, it gradually became "less and less relevant to top officials' immediate priorities," until, in 1969, its mandate was broadened to include new operational responsibilities. To reflect this change it was rechristened the Policy and Coordination Staff. While it did not notably succeed in its new coordinating function, it did largely abandon the old.[6] Given the prevailing realities of the bureaucratic subculture, policy-oriented planning organizations inevitably feel compelled to choose between immediacy, access to high officials, relevance to current policy, and, on the other hand, writing lengthy papers which no one will read. The American ethos of activism insures that relevance and access will win hands down every time.

This dreary process, repeated at other times and places in government, has led most scholars to doubt whether an institutional solution is possible. Skeptics argue that any new structure will inevitably be perverted by the operators of the next administration, or its product ignored. It is better, many would argue, simply to concentrate on educating officials on the nature of new issues in the hope that they may act in a more enlightened fashion. Yet despite prevailing cynicism, much of it well grounded, the major study groups which periodically poke and probe at the policy process have tended to agree that our planning structures are primitive and need to be improved. (The term "planning" was originally borrowed from the military and, because it suggests the preparation of discrete "plans," is generally agreed by scholars of the subject to be a misnomer; as used with reference to foreign policy it simply means long-range or strategic thinking, an ability to look ahead.)

The most recent major study, the 1976 Murphy Commission, proposed the creation of a small (3–5 man) Presidential Council of International Planning, modeled on the Council of Economic Advisors. The commission further recommended that the State Department appoint an advisory committee of outside scholars, and that a link be established between this and the Policy Planning Staff.[7] A more elaborate proposal by Lincoln Bloomfield, dropped on the commission's cutting-room floor but published in one of its seven volumes of annexes, suggested an expanded State Policy Planning Staff featuring a dual public-private staff with a "dumbbell" shape. Bloomfield proposed that it would conduct cross-sectional, cross-disciplinary analyses of "both political-military-strategic issues and the erstwhile 'low politics' issues of international trade, investment, money, food resources, science, technology, ideology and social change, including issues of balance between foreign and domestic concerns." Crucial to the concept would be, in Bloomfield's words, a "mandated degree of contact with public opinion, including heterodox or dissenting sectors," and involving the right to publish and testify.[8]

The particular institutional solution that Bloomfield advocated may or may not be the right one; judgment on that subject lies far beyond the scope of this book. But there is no question that our long-term interests in Southeast Asia would be better served if we possessed the kind of capability he was talking about. Clearly this capability requires more and better central planning and long-reach analysis within government, even though the locus of the effort (State? White House? CIA?) may be debated. It seems equally obvious, however, given the government's perennial inability to think between the Scylla of irrelevance and the Charybdis of hyperrelevance (or co-optation) that the best place to achieve deep and dispassionate analysis is outside government. The critical structural variable will be (as Bloomfield recognizes) the connection between public and private entities. The problem seems big enough to call for a multidimensional solution, including, at the very least, a central planning staff with connections to such outside entities as the Brookings Institute, the National Academy of Sciences, and the Woodrow Wilson Center for Scholars (Smithsonian), as well as to university area studies programs. The proposed Institute for Scientific and Technological Cooperation, a public entity which will deal in both technology programs and research related to development, should fill part of the gap.

While the government may not be the best place to think deep thoughts, there are a number of other things which only it can do. Abroad, diplomatic missions should conduct far more cross-disciplinary country analysis of new agenda issues and relevant U.S. behavior, public and private. Such analysis simply cannot be conducted in Washington with sufficient attention to local conditions, nor is it likely to be produced by the operational agency involved (such as AID). It could be done by the Foreign Service, although not without major reorientation away from the current pattern of passive political and economical reporting, toward a new format which emphasizes policy analysis. In Washington the government should place priority not on original research but on the collection and "translation" of existing research, leading to policy recommendations. This will demand a much greater degree of professional contact between government analysts and outside experts than currently takes place, and substantially greater staffing resources than are now devoted to analytic functions.

As Bloomfield recommends, those associated with the government's central planning capability should be encouraged to play a vigorous outreach role, teaching, writing, and generally interacting with the entire foreign affairs community, including congressional staffs. They might even be free to undertake studies in response to congressional requests, as the Congressional Research Service and the General Accounting Office (both part of the legislative branch) do at present. Institutionalized openness of this kind would go some distance toward insuring that unpopular opinions or those with long-term implications would not be rejected out of hand or ignored. And while it might be difficult or impossible to deal openly with some traditional political military subjects, public discussion would be an asset both in the analysis of long-range trends and with regard to most major issues of the new agenda. That it would also strengthen our democratic political process goes without saying.[9]

The limitations inherent in these suggestions are obvious. Long-range thought should not be expected to eliminate bureaucratic conflict. For reasons suggested above, research rarely provides final answers and doesn't always reduce controversy. Often it has just the opposite effect. The argument for better planning rests finally on the assumption that as our foreign interests shift toward the long-term and the complex, the present crisis-oriented system is no longer adequate. It is at least possible that a more systematic application of knowledge will reduce the irrationality of the policy process and provide us with better answers in Southeast Asia and elsewhere. We will not know until we make the effort.

There is a parallel here with one of the criticisms that Western theorists level at developing "soft states." It is often said, and has been said earlier in this book, that countries like Indonesia and the Philippines should be doing more to mobilize their own resources, both human and financial, recognizing that this may involve sacrifice for the privileged and perhaps some degree of political risk. But this requirement should not be left solely on the doorstep of the south. Assuming that everyone has an interest in global peace and welfare, the north also has a minimum responsibility to gain some iota of systematic control over intellectual resources, including scientific knowledge, which in the long run may be of paramount value. Such an effort can best be initiated by government, but it will involve ever-broadening sectors of society as the range of disciplines and knowledge relevant to foreign affairs continues to grow. Unlike the kind of effort we are demanding of the south, creating a capacity for systematic long-range thought would cost us next to nothing in terms of sacrifice, and involve no risk at all.

Notes

The following are abbreviations used in the notes:

ABS   Annual Budget Submission (country documents prepared
       by U.S. Agency for International Development)
AID   U.S. Agency for International Development
AWSJ *Asian Wall Street Journal*
BIES *Bulletin of Indonesian Economic Studies*
FEER *Far Eastern Economic Review*

1. U.S. Interests in the Philippines and Indonesia: Context and Content

1. Discussion of geographic factors is based on standard sources, including Charles A. Fisher, *South-east Asia: A Social, Economic and Political Geography* (London, 1964); E. H. G. Dobby, *Southeast Asia* (London, 1948), and Frederick L. Wernstedt and Joseph E. Spencer, *The Philippine Island World: A Physical, Cultural and Regional Geography* (Berkeley, 1967); the term "homelandwater" is borrowed from Donald Emmerson.

2. Figures from the Japan-U.S. Trade Council and the State Department (raw data). See also chapter five.

3. For general background on archipelago peoples and cultures see Hildred Geertz, "Indonesian Cultures and Communities" in Ruth T. McVey, ed., *Indonesia* (New Haven, 1963) and Frank M. Lebar et al., *Ethnic Groups of Insular Southeast Asia*, vol. 1 (Indonesia) and vol. 2 (Philippines and Formosa) (New Haven, 1972 and 1975).

4. Again, historical material in this brief overview is, unless otherwise stated, based on standard sources, including D. G. E. Hall's *A History of South-east Asia* (London, 1968) and David Joel Steinberg, et al., *In Search of Southeast Asia: A Modern History* (New York, 1971).

5. The "plural society" concept was in fact elaborated by J. S. Furnivall in his writings on colonial Burma and Indonesia: see esp. *Netherlands India: A Study of Plural Economy* (Cambridge, 1939).

6. Hall, History of South-east Asia, p. 719.

7. On Chinese society in the colonial Philippines see Edgar Wickberg, The Chinese in Philippine Life (New Haven, 1976); there is no historical work of comparable quality on the Indonesian Chinese, perhaps because they were a more fragmented phenomenon, but see Charles Coppell, "Patterns of Chinese Political Activity in Indonesia" in J. A. C. Mackie, ed., The Chinese in Indonesia: Five Essays (Melbourne, 1976).

8. This key aspect of American colonial policy, frequently overlooked in standard histories, is discussed in Charles J. McCarthy, S.J., "Chinese Coolie Labor Minimal in Philippines," Annals of Philippine Chinese Historical Association (May 1976), pp. 8–20.

9. Quoted in Theodore Friend, Between Two Empires: The Ordeal of the Philippines 1929–1946 (New Haven, 1965), p. 4; the unpublished article by Peter Stanley, "Why Didn't the Americans Tyrannize Them More?" uses the Quezon quotation as the basis for perhaps the best succinct analysis of American colonialism yet written.

10. The independence legislation provided that land reservations (e.g., Clark) would be turned over to the Philippines in 1946, while naval installations would be retained pending negotiations; see Joseph Ralston Hayden, The Philippines: A Study in National Development (New York, 1942), pp. 733, 819.

11. The unwillingness of the United States to use the bases for combat operations in Vietnam, against perceived Philippine reluctance, was discussed in the 1969 Senate (Symington Committee) Hearings; see further discussion in chapter three.

12. U.S. policy toward Indonesia during this period, and the effect it had on enduring Indonesian attitudes toward the United States, is well covered in Franklin Weinstein, Indonesian Foreign Policy and the Dilemma of Dependence, from Sukarno to Soeharto (Ithaca, 1976).

13. Chapter four of Harold Crouch, The Army and Politics in Indonesia (Ithaca, 1978) is by far the best account of the Indonesian coup to date. No work of equivalent depth or even-handedness exists on the advent of Martial Law in the Philippines.

14. For a useful survey of the literature on national interest see Roy Haverkamp, "Is There a National Interest?" Case study for Senior Seminar in Foreign Policy, Department of State (Washington, 1977). Contrary to the widely held view that in the wake of Vietnam and Watergate the United States lost its collective sense of purpose in foreign affairs, research conducted in the fall of 1976 revealed a high degree of consensus among both the public and "experts" as to the nature of U.S. foreign policy goals and interests. See U.S. Foreign Policy: Principles for Defining the National Interest, Public Agenda Foundation Report (Washington, 1977). But it is well to bear in mind that public opinion on foreign policy issues, which are notoriously remote in nature, are often "so soft, volatile and fleeting they barely exist" (George F. Will, "Public Opinion That's Polls Apart," Washington Post, Nov. 10, 1977).

15. That is, the "irreducible" national interests defined by George and Keohane as physical survival, liberty, and economic subsistence, are, rather obviously, not immediately relevant to our dealings with Southeast Asia—although they may indeed be relevant to the southern hemisphere as a whole. Alexander L. George and Robert Keohane, "The Concept of National Interests: Uses and Limitations," Commission on the Organization of the Government for the Conduct of Foreign Policy (Murphy Commission) (Washington, 1977) appendix, 2:67.

16. William P. Bundy, "New Tides in Southeast Asia," *Foreign Affairs* (Jan. 1971), 49:198.

17. See Michael MccGuire, "The Geopolitical Importance of the Strategic Waterways of the Asian Pacific Region," *Orbis* (Fall 1975), 19:1070–71. According to MccGuire, the economic impact on the Japanese of using the longer Australian route would amount to an increase of from 4 to 11 percent in the cost of about 40 percent of Japanese imports, a relatively small factor compared to (say) the OPEC price increases of 1974. MccGuire grants that denial of the use of Southeast Asian straits would greatly hamper U.S. military reactive capability from Guam or Subic Bay to the Indian Ocean, but argues that in the case of Polaris submarines this could be countered by increased forward deployments. The real question, of course, is whether any power, great or small, would gain political benefit by blocking the straits or (in the case of a great power) whether it could be done without involving the immediate threat of nuclear sanction; for more on this see chapter three.

18. See *U.S. Foreign Policy: Principles for Defining the National Interest*, esp. section on "Lessons of Vietnam," pp. 70–72.

19. Hedley Bull, "Foreign Policy Options for Australia," quoted in J. A. C. Mackie, ed., *Australia in the New World Order* (Melbourne, 1976), p. 61. Cf. the public agenda survey finding that "The vision of America as 'a beacon on the hill' remains a powerful symbol for most respondents. They ask the United States to take the lead in making the world a better place, both politically and economically, for others, as well as for Americans." *U.S. Foreign Policy: Principles for Defining the National Interest*, p. 64.

2. The Stability Shibboleth

1. The quotation at head of chapter is from Samuel P. Huntington, *Political Order in Changing Societies* (New Haven, 1968), p. 262.

2. Harry J. Benda, review of Herbert Feith, *The Decline of Constitutional Democracy in Indonesia* in *Journal of Asian Studies* (May 1964), 23:449–56 and Feith's reply in *JAS* (Feb. 1965), 24:305–12.

3. Harry J. Benda, "Decolonization in Indonesia: The Problem of Continuity and Change" in *Continuity and Change in Southeast Asia: Collected Journal Articles of Harry J. Benda*, Yale University Southeast Asia Studies Program Monograph Series no. 18 (New Haven, 1972), p. 220.

4. Ibid.

5. As used in this chapter, the term "revolution" means *social* revolution of the kind that alters institutions and ruling structures, as opposed to interelite coups. Such revolution is inevitably *national* in character, appealing to the dominant ethnic group (lowland Christian in the Philippines; syncretic *abangan* Javanese in Indonesia) as well as, perhaps, to other elements.

6. For a view of trends in Southeast Asia generally, written immediately after the fall of Saigon but accurately foreseeing the pattern of adjustment which has subsequently occurred, see J. A. C. Mackie, "The External Dimension: Regional Problems and Policy Decisions Confronting Australia" in E. P. Wolfers, ed., *Australia's Northern Neighbours: Independent or Dependent?* (Melbourne, 1976), pp. 183–206.

7. For a radical analysis of Indonesia, see David Ransom's crude but influential

essay, "The Berkeley Mafia and the Indonesian Massacre," *Ramparts* (Oct. 1970); Cheryl Payer, "The International Monetary Fund and Indonesian Debt Slavery" in Mark Selden, ed., *Remaking Asia: Essays on the Uses of American Power* (New York, 1972); Rex Mortimer, ed., *Showcase State: The Illusion of Indonesia's Accelerated Modernization* (Sydney, 1973). An excellent introduction to the debate between dependency theory and its critics is Herbert Feith's "South-East Asia and Neo-Colonialism" in Wolfers, ed., *Australia's Northern Neighbors*. For the Philippines, see Robert B. Stauffer, "The Political Economy of Refeudalization" in David A. Rosenberg, ed., *Marcos and Martial Law in the Philippines* (Ithaca, 1979), pp. 180–218; and Thomas C. Nowak and Kay Snyder, "Clientelist Politics in the Philippines," *American Political Science Review* (Sept. 1974), 68:1147–70.

8. Thus Guy Pauker of RAND, a generally conservative Indonesia specialist, is on common ground with the radicals in painting a gloomy picture of the entire region except for the city-state of Singapore: "in most of Southeast Asia today times are not good, raising the question of what forms of government will eventually emerge from the historical crucible after traditional forms of government, democratic-constitutional institutions, and the authoritarian rule of the military will all have failed the pragmatic tests of problem solving." Guy Pauker, Frank Golay, and Cynthia Enloe, *Diversity and Development in Southeast Asia* (New York, 1977), p. 26. For a more optimistic view, see Francis J. Galbraith, *The Importance of Southeast Asia*, University of South Carolina, Institute of International Studies (Columbia, 1977).

9. On this and ethnic tensions generally, see Cynthia Enloe, "Ethnic Diversity, the Potential for Conflict," in Pauker, Golay, and Enloe, *Diversity and Development*, pp. 137–81, esp. p. 151.

10. For recent background on Irian unrest and the Papua New Guinea connection, see Ralph R. Premdas, "Papua New Guinea in 1977: Elections and Relations with Indonesia," *Asian Survey* (Jan. 1978), 18:58–67.

11. An enormous subject is oversimplified here. The classic work on the religious background is Clifford Geertz, *The Religion of Java* (Glencoe, 1960). While the distinction between *abangan* Javanese and fervent Muslim (or *santri*) is difficult to appreciate at a distance, it is a recognized fact of life in Indonesia which makes the ethnic divisions of American ward politics look feeble by comparison. Indonesian politics are often categorized in terms of ethnoreligious "streams" (*aliran*) related to the Geertzian categories but with the addition of other variables, such as nationalism: see Herbert Feith and Lance Castles, *Indonesian Political Thinking, 1945–1965* (Ithaca, 1970).

12. The year 1977 saw a renewal of Islamic unrest in the northern Sumatran province of Aceh, long renowned for fundamentalist intransigence, as well as the discovery of an Islamic conspiracy at the center, the Komando Jihad (Holy War Command): R. William Liddle, "Indonesia 1977: The New Order's Second Parliamentary Election," *Asian Survey* (Feb. 1978), 18:181.

13. While there is a substantial literature on the Indonesian Communist Party of the Sukarno era, little has been written about the post-1965 remnants of communism. Harold Crouch, *The Army and Politics in Indonesia* (Ithaca, 1978), fills the gap somewhat; see esp. chapter eight onwards.

14. On the recent history of the Muslim rebellion see Lela Garner Noble, "The Moro National Liberation Front in the Philippines," *Pacific Affairs* (Fall 1976), 49:405–24.

15. Donald Smythe, *Guerilla Warrior: The Early Life of John J. Pershing* (New

York, 1973). More general background on U.S. "Moro" policy is in Peter Gowing's *Mandate in Moroland: The American Government of Muslim Filipinos, 1899–1920* (Quezon City, 1977).

16. For the history of communist insurgency in the Philippines, see David R. Sturtevant, *Popular Uprisings in the Philippines, 1840–1890;* (Ithaca, 1976); Sturtevant sees a gradual transition from "mysticism to relative sophistication" during this period.

17. One typical problem has been the government's harsh handling of the controversial Chico River hydroelectric project, which would inundate rice terraces of the Kalinga tribe. The issue has troubled other members of the various "Igorot" minorities, who collectively number about 500,000 in the former Mountain Province; this, in turn, has provided some basis for NPA activities, including participation by lowland dissidents. The Chico controversy was well documented in the Church newsletter, *Signs of the Times* (published by the Association of Major Religious Superiors), banned in 1976.

18. The New Peoples Army is the military wing of the Communist Party of the Philippines, Marxist/Leninist (CPP/ML), which broke from the older Soviet-oriented party (of which the Huks were the main field faction) in 1969. Tilman Durdin, "Philippine Communism," *Problems of Communism* (May–June 1976), pp. 40–48, is a good, concise survey of Philippine communist parties and the transition from Huk to CPP/ML (or NPA); for the former see also Eduardo Lachica's *HUK: Philippine Agrarian Society in Revolt* (Manila, 1971). Huk (or HUK) is an abbreviation of the Tagalog phrase meaning "People's Army against the Japanese." The brief interpretation of the NPA here is my personal judgment. Press accounts of the NPA typically sound alarming unless the reader realizes that comparable accounts have been appearing for years: for example, see Rodney Tasker, "Learning the Lesson of Iran," *FEER*, June 29, 1979, pp. 24–25.

19. The association of Senator Aquino and other politicians with NPA guerillas/private armies was the justification for President Marcos' charge that the Philippines was (and still is) threatened by a "rightist-leftist" conspiracy. More recently, ex-NPA elements have been recruited into the security forces (e.g., the late Commander Pusa of Tarlac) in a manner which, with other evidence, suggests that the old symbiotic pattern is not dead.

20. President Marcos did not quite drop the Philippine claim to the Malaysian state of Sabah at the 1977 meeting of ASEAN heads of state in Kuala Lumpur. As a result, Malaysian suspicion and resentment remained alive.

21. On this affair see Harold Crouch, "The '15 January Affair' in Indonesia," *Dyason House Papers* (Aug. 1974); but my view is based primarily on personal observation.

22. Two major mechanisms of social mobility have been the tradition of godparenthood and the central importance in Filipino society of dyadic, one-to-one ties between political actors; good discussions of both are found in the essays by Fred Eggan and Carl Lande in George M. Guthrie, ed., *Six Perspectives on the Philippines* (Manila, 1968).

23. Emma Porio, Frank Lynch, and Mary Hollnsteiner, *The Filipino Family Community and Nation: The Same Yesterday, Today and Tomorrow?* (Manila, 1975), p. 85.

24. Nor would this be a wholly new development. On traditional revolutionary themes in Tagalog folk,religion, see Reynaldo Ileto, "Pasion and the Interpretation of Change in Tagalog Society, 1840–1912," Ph.D. diss., Cornell University, 1974.

25. David Wurfel, "Indonesia and the Philippines: Prospects of Convergence?" MS, 1978, pp. 15–16.

26. Many observers are baffled by the long-term political implications of a pattern, discernible in both Indonesia and the Philippines, in which village elites, as well as urban middle classes, are to some (debatable) extent sharing in the proceeds from national economic growth, while the "poorest of the poor" appear to be getting poorer. For example, a recent commentary on Indonesia by Herbert Feith notes evidence that the informal sector of Jakarta hawkers, etc., is swelling as a result of "trickle-down" from enclave development: see Feith, "Political Control, Class Formation and Legitimacy in Suharto's Indonesia," *Kabar Seberang Sulating Maphilindo* (June 1977), 2:3–4 (North Queensland: James Cook University). On the growing prosperity of rural elites, and possible worsening condition of the "poorest," see Masri Singarimbun, "Sriharjo Revisited," *BIES* (July 1976), 12:117–25; also Lea Jellinek, "The Life of a Jakarta Street Trader" and "The Life of a Jakarta Street Trader—Two Years Later," Centre of Southeast Asian Studies, Monash University, Working Papers nos. 9 and 13 (Melbourne, 1976–77). Welfare trends and their political implications in the Philippines are equally uncertain; see Emma Porio, Frank Lynch, and Mary Hollnsteiner, *The Filipino Family, Community and Nation* (Manila, 1975) and Mahar Mangahas, *Measuring Philippine Development: Report of the Social Indicators Project* (Manila, 1976).

27. Mackie emphasizes this kind of thing as a primary risk: see "The External Dimension," pp. 196–97.

28. Writing primarily of the mainland, Alexander Woodside notes that "the outlook is one of instability within a context of nondemocratic politics, but of instability which threatens no one but Southeast Asians themselves. Foreign military and political involvement in such a landscape is the greatest 'destabilizer' of all." "Progress, Stability and Peace in Mainland Southeast Asia" in Donald Hellman, ed., *Southern Asia: The Politics of Poverty and Peace* (New York, 1976), p. 152.

29. Southeast Asian leaders themselves sometimes emphasize the possibility of revolution and other dire happenings as a spur to action. No one has done this more consistently than the Singaporeans, who are fond of speculating in public about instability, proxy wars, and regional cataclysm. But these are sermons intended less as predictions of the future than as warnings of what is likely to happen *unless* the ASEAN powers help themselves, both by more effective development policies and (especially) more regional cooperation. For an excellent example see Foreign Minister Rajaratnam's interview, "Is Asia Vital to Western Interests?" (His answer was "no."), Embassy of the Republic of Singapore, Manila, *Singapore Newsletter*, Apr. 20, 1976.

30. See, for example, A. Doak Barnett, *China and the Major Powers in East Asia* (Washington, 1977), esp. pp. 288–94. Barnett uses the equilibrium concept in an Asia-wide framework. There is debate as to whether it automatically extends to Southeast Asia; see J. A. C. Mackie, "United States Interests in Southeast Asia," paper prepared for Seventh National Conference, Australian Institute of International Affairs, Apr. 1977.

31. See Donald Zagoria, "The Soviet Quandary in Asia," *Foreign Affairs* (Jan. 1978), 61:306–23. Zagoria lists four basic factors behind the Soviet lack of success in Asia at large. I would reword his categories slightly, insofar as noncommunist Southeast Asia is concerned, as follows:

(a) Persistent fear and suspicion of the Soviets, aggravated by their aggressive intelligence tactics and general heavy-handedness.

(b) Reluctance of Southeast Asian leaders to offend the Chinese, reflecting China's bigger-than-life political and cultural prestige throughout the region.

(c) The low prestige and nonexistent popular appeal of Soviet goods, technology, and mass culture.

(d) Generally weak and unimaginative tactics (both diplomatic and economic) by the Soviets themselves. The aggressive development of Soviet merchant shipping is an important but unique exception to the general trend.

32. The latter possibility was once cited as a justification (thin, in my opinion) for U.S. arms aid to Indonesia; U.S. House of Representatives, *Security Assistance to Asia for Fiscal Year 1978: Report of a Special Study Mission to Asia, April 8–21, 1977, by Members of the Committee on International Relations*, 95th Cong., 1st sess., 1977, p. 8.

33. For an overall view of Soviet maritime activity, which concludes that it is primarily the result of economic factors, see Richard T. Ackley, "The Merchant Fleet" in Michael MccGwire and John McDonnell, eds., *Soviet Naval Influence: Domestic and Foreign Dimensions* (New York, 1977), pp. 291–310.

34. On this point see Franklin Weinstein, "U.S.-Vietnam Relations and the Security of Southeast Asia," *Foreign Affairs* (July 1978), 61:842–56.

35. It is sometimes argued that U.S. involvement in Vietnam bought time for the noncommunist regimes of Southeast Asia to consolidate themselves, and that earlier American acceptance of a communist Vietnam would have resulted in a rash of communist regimes throughout the area. The question will never be settled, but in my view it is much more likely that, at enormous cost in blood, money, and national dissension, the United States missed an opportunity to work with, rather than against, Vietnamese nationalism. Such a policy might (in theory) have produced something very similar to the geopolitical situation which now prevails, but twenty years earlier. It would not have involved withdrawal, but continuing cooperation with regimes (e.g., Thailand, the Philippines) whose national movements were not, as in Vietnam, captured by communism in the process of anticolonial struggle. The Vietnamese would have perhaps more easily dominated Cambodia, and at an earlier date, but the Cambodian terror of Pol Pot et al. (arguably a by-product of the war) might have been avoided. Of course, such a relatively sophisticated approach was never a possibility in the cold war climate of the times, and indeed could never have been considered until the implications of Sino-Soviet schism became obvious in Washington.

36. William R. Henderson, "Some Reflections on U.S. Policy in Southeast Asia," in Henderson, ed., *Southeast Asia: Problems of United States Policy* (New York, 1963), p. 263.

37. General Lansdale's role is described in the Pentagon papers and in his autobiography, *In the Midst of Wars: An American's Mission to South-East Asia* (New York, 1975); for the post-Lansdale era see Joseph Burkholder Smith, *Portrait of a Cold Warrior* (New York, 1976).

38. While it is true that radical dependency theory originated in the Third World, especially Latin America, it has been amplified and transmitted to Southeast Asia largely by European and American universities. The notion that the West is now the wellspring of most dangerous thought is not alien to the region, as witness Lee Kuan Yew's well-known reservations about Western social science generally. The same awareness underlies the Indonesian government's ambivalent attitude toward the Western-oriented intelligentsia formerly associated in politics with the defunct Indonesian Socialist Party (PSI); this group has been a major source of tech-

nocratic expertise, yet it has also produced the loudest criticism of government policy, and its younger members have continued to play an especially active role in student unrest.

39. President Ford's "Pacific Doctrine" referred to "our continuing stake in the security and stability of Southeast Asia"; State Department Bulletin, Dec. 29, 1975. More recent examples include the following: "We feel our security assistance is an appropriate contribution to the preservation of the independence of these countries [recipients of military aid in Asia] and to regional stability in the still-uncertain post-Vietnam period. . . . I believe the Administration's economic and security assistance proposals for FY 1978 represent an appropriate contribution on the part of our government to peace, stability and development in East Asia"—Statement of Richard C. Holbrooke before House Subcommittee for East Asian and Pacific Affairs, Mar. 10, 1977; "Although the deep involvement of the United States in Southeast Asia has lessened, we retain an interest in insuring the stability and independence of the friendly nations of the region which have long looked to us for support"— remarks of Lucy Wilson Benson, Under Secretary of State for Security Assistance, before the Subcommittee on International Security and Scientific Affairs of the House International Relations Committee, Mar. 30, 1977; "the United States remains very interested in the stability and development of Southeast Asia"—interview by Richard Holbrooke with Milton Chase of the Singapore Straits Times, published June 5, 1977. Vice President Mondale's speech in Hawaii on May 10, 1978, emphasizing a "new agenda" for Asia, did not explicitly list stability as an American interest, but argued that "only in an environment of security can human rights flourish."

40. U.S. Senate, Subcommittee on United States Security Agreements and Commitments Abroad of the Committee on Foreign Relations, Republic of the Philippines, Part I, 91st Congress, 1st sess., 1969, p. 13.

41. The term "detachment" is also used by Harrison; see The Widening Gulf, Asian Nationalism and American Policy (New York, 1978), esp. ch. 10, "The Future of U.S. Military Policy in Asia," pp. 361–394.

42. Military aid in fiscal year 1979 for the two countries was as follows (in millions of U.S. $):

	Indonesia	Philippines
Military Assistance Program (MAP) grants	0.75	15.6
International Military Education and Training (IMET)	2.0	0.65
Foreign Military Sales (FMS) credits	32.0	15.6

U.S. State Department, Security Assistance Programs Summary, Fiscal Year 1980 (Washington, 1979), p. 43.

43. The A-4 sale, widely reported in press accounts of the trip, came on top of earlier approval of sale of a squadron of another type of jet aircraft (F5Es) worth $121 million.

44. As far as I am aware, the degree of correlation between U.S. training and political behavior during the coup period has not been studied. Several of the high-ranking generals who were killed by the communists were U.S. trained. U.S. trained officers who sided with the PKI included police General Sudirgo, army General Supardjo (later killed by government forces in Kalimantan) and intelligence Colonel Suherman (the latter freshly returned from Fort Leavenworth: see Harold Crouch, The Army and Politics in Indonesia [Ithaca, 1978], p. 114.) See also the mixed reac-

tion of Indonesian trainees to their U.S. experience cited in Franklin B. Weinstein, *Indonesian Foreign Policy and the Dilemma of Dependence: From Sukarno to Soeharto* (Ithaca, 1976), p. 65. For an opposing view on military training as an effective agent of U.S. influence (without specific reference to Indonesia), see Ernest W. Lefever, "The Military Assistance Program," *Annals of the American Association of Political Science* (Mar. 1976), 424:85–89.

45. Similarly, in the case of the Philippines it is sometimes argued that since the military are the most likely eventual heirs to the Marcos regime, expanded training programs are of critical importance in order to maintain the American connection, all the more so as memories of wartime camaraderie fade and a younger generation of relatively nationalistic officers comes of age. Again the analysis tends to be self-fulfilling prophecy: while the political future remains in doubt, increased American attention to the military would, in the "special" Philippine context, greatly enhance their prospects for political dominance.

3. The U.S.-Philippine "Special Relationship" and American Military Bases

1. Quotations are from U.S. Senate, Subcommittee on United States Security Agreements and Commitments Abroad of the Committee on Foreign Relations, *Republic of the Philippines*, Part 1, 91st Cong., 1st sess., 1969 (hereafter referred to as Symington Hearings), p. 109; Peter Stanley, "Why Didn't the Americans Tyrannize Them More?" MS, n.d., p. 12; for the Nixon statement, see Department of State Bulletin, Aug. 25, 1969.

2. "Philamerica: End of a Chapter," *FEER*, July 1, 1972.

3. Total 1976 immigration figures were: Mexico, 57,863; Philippines, 37,821; and Korea, 30,803. U.S. Immigration and Naturalization Service figures quoted in Zero Population Growth, *ZPG Looks at Immigration* (Washington, 1978).

4. Per capita U.S. bilateral aid levels (resource flows) in 1978 were as follows: Thailand, $0.10; Indonesia, $1.15; Philippines, $1.28. Agency for International Development, *Congressional Presentation, Fiscal Year 1980* (Washington, 1979).

5. General Accounting Office, "Veterans Administration Benefits Programs to Philippines Need Reassessment," GAO Graybook to Senator Proxmire, HR D78-26, Jan. 18, 1978.

6. George J. Viksnins, "Economic Aspects of the Philippine Bases," MS, 1978, p. 3.

7. *New York Times*, Aug. 25, 1976, p. 3.

8. U.S. Senate, Subcommittee on Foreign Assistance of the Committee on Foreign Relations, *U.S.–Philippine Base Negotiations*, 95th Cong., 1st sess., 1977, (hereafter cited as Mantel Report), p. 4.

9. Diosdado Macapagal, *Democracy in the Philippines* (Manila, 1976), esp. p. 162.

10. "Old Political Zest Reborn in Philippines," *Washington Post*, Mar. 9, 1978.

11. For example, "A CIA Coup in Manila?" *Philippine Liberation Courier*, Sept. 8, 1978.

12. Facts and figures on the bases are from unclassified briefings at the facilities plus the following sources: Symington Hearings and Mantel Report, passim; A. S. Britt, "U.S. Military Bases in the Philippines: Strategic Bastion or Pacific Trap?" (Washington: Research Directorate, National Defense University, April 1978); Alvin

J. Cottrell and Thomas H. Moorer, U.S. Overseas Bases: Problems of Projecting American Military Power Abroad (Washington: Center for International and Strategic Studies, 1977); Lawrence E. Grinter, "The Philippines Bases: Continuing Utility in a Changing Strategic Context" (Washington: Research Directorate, National Defense University, June 1978); "Philippine Bases: How Important to U.S. Interests in Asia?" Issue Brief, Congressional Research Service, Library of Congress, May 23, 1979; Harvey Stockwin, "Philippines: Basis for the Bases," FEER, May 13, 1977; Arnold Zeitlin backgrounder, "U.S. Bases—Philippines," Associated Press Wire, May 24, 1975.

13. On the Huks and the bases see Robert Shaplen, Time Out of Hand: Revolution and Reaction in Southeast Asia (New York, 1969), pp. 250–51; Symington Hearings, pp. 226 ff., p. 355 ($1 million figure is from latter); Eduardo Lachica, HUK (Manila, 1971), esp. pp. 141–54.

14. In a recent moderate expression of the antibase position, former Foreign Affairs Secretary and University of the Philippines President Salvador Lopez wrote, "For the Philippines the consequences of American withdrawal from military bases here would be almost magical. The Filipinos would know at last what it is to live in pride and dignity of independence. The incubus of national humiliation that has blighted Filipino feeling toward America since Dewey came uninvited in 1898 would be lifted, and the relations between the peoples would become more natural and healthy." "U.S. Bases: A Philippine View . . . ," AWSJ, Oct. 6, 1978.

15. David Wurfel, "Martial Law in the Philippines: The Methods of Regime Survival," Pacific Affairs (Spring 1977), p. 28.

16. For example, Raul Manglapus' Movement for a Free Philippines has cautiously avoided attacking the bases, claiming only that the Marcos regime is illegal and has no right to negotiate on the issue. The MFP clearly feels that only with American help can Marcos be ousted, and it is therefore eager not to cause us offense on the bases. Manglapus argues that "most Filipino leaders only wanted the United States to withdraw military aid, an item separable from the bases question. . . ." Manglapus, "The Philippines: Going the Way of Iran?" Washington Post, Apr. 17, 1979. Some exile opposition groups, such as the Anti–Martial Law Coalition and Friends of the Filipino People, have opposed the bases. In the Philippines, both Senator Jovito Salonga and the respected Civil Liberties Union of the Philippines have taken strong antibase positions.

17. Symington Hearings, pp. 137, 348 n; Nixon-Magsaysay joint statement of July 3, 1956, in Republic of the Philippines, Official Gazette, 52:7:3550; for postwar history of base-related issues see George E. Taylor, The Philippines and the United States: Problems of Partnership (New York, 1968) esp. pp. 233–49; Fred Greene, U.S. Policy and the Security of Asia (New York, 1968), esp. pp. 99–100, 150–52; Claude Buss, The United States and the Philippines (Washington, 1977), pp. 119–26.

18. United States High Commissioner to the Philippine Islands, Third Annual Report, 1938–39 (Washington, 1943), pp. 13–14.

19. "Report of Statistics on the Exercise of Criminal Jurisdiction in Foreign Tribunals Over United States Personnel, 1 December 1975–30 November 1976" (Washington: Department of Defense, 1977), cited in Grinter, "The Philippine Bases," p. 98.

20. Samuel Eliot Morison, History of United States Naval Operations in World War II, vol. III, The Rising Sun in the Pacific, pp. 167–70.

21. The question of U.S.-Philippine consultation on the B-52 raids came up in the Symington Hearings; see pp. 29, 40, 352; text of the Bohlen-Serrano Agreement is on p. 24. The State Department maintained, not convincingly, that the fact that the

Philippine government had been consulted, and that "prior consultation" was specified in the Bohlen-Serrano agreement for all combat operations not related to the Mutual Defense Treaty, "does not give the Filipinos a veto over matters to which consultations relate." Ibid., p. 352; see also Grinter, "The Philippines Bases," p. 13.

22. Symington Hearings, pp. 60–61.

23. U.S. House of Representatives, Subcommittee on Asian and Pacific Affairs of the Committee on International Relations, *Our Commitments in Asia*, 93rd Cong., 2d sess., 1975, pp. 25–26.

24. Franklin B. Weinstein, "The United States and Southeast Asia: New Perspectives on Security," MS, 1978, p. 16.

25. U.S. Embassy Manila fact sheet, 1972.

26. Interview with Lee Kuan Yew in *U.S. News and World Report*, Oct. 31, 1977. Among the ASEAN states Singapore is exceptional for its ardent espousal of neutrality based on the "all in" concept (i.e., the balanced presence of *all* the great powers rather than their withdrawal). Cynics have observed that as a small, ethnic Chinese city-state, Singapore has reason to prefer maximum great power involvement to an alternative which might leave her alone among her much larger Malay neighbors.

27. Dwight Perkins' testimony, *Our Commitments in Asia*, p. 82.

28. Guy J. Pauker, *Military Implications of a Possible World Order Crisis in the 1980s* (Santa Monica: Rand Project Air Force Report, Nov. 1977), esp. p. 94.

29. Philippines-Vietnam Communiqué of July 12, 1976 (text from State Department). This language was widely interpreted as indicating Hanoi's tacit acquiescence to the continued existence of the bases, because quite different language in an earlier communiqué, negotiated during a Philippine mission to Hanoi in August 1975 but never accepted by President Marcos, had referred in much more specific and hostile terms to the U.S. presence, stipulating that "The Philippine side will not let the United States use Philippine territory to oppose the Vietnamese people and peoples of the other Indochinese countries." Also, and contrary to provisions in U.S. law, the earlier communiqué had provided that ex-U.S. aircraft, ships, etc., taken from Vietnam to the Philippines should be immediately returned to Vietnam. Although Marcos never publicly repudiated the August 1975 communiqué, the diplomat who negotiated it in Hanoi, Ambassador Mangila, subsequently resigned from the Foreign Service, and diplomatic relations were not in fact established until the later (July 1976) mission of Phan Hien. (The text of the Mangila Communiqué as broadcast by Radio Hanoi is from the State Department.)

30. "Marcos on U.S. Bases Discussions with Mondale," Agence France Press from Foreign Broadcast Information Service (FBIS), 8 May, 1978; Romulo-Murphy letter of Jan. 7, 1979, para. 2 (part of the "Exchange of Notes" revising the base agreement; see note 33 below).

31. See testimony of Francis T. Underhill: "We have, in effect, hired for the next five years a very expensive fire extinguisher. It still looks good and provides psychological reassurance, but in time of need I believe we would find it nailed securely to the wall." Edited version of testimony in U.S. House of Representatives, Subcommittee on Foreign Operations of the Appropriations Committee, *Foreign Assistance and Related Programs, Appropriations for 1980, Part 1*, 1979, p. 304.

32. Symington Hearings, p. 68.

33. The main documents constituting the amended base agreement consist of the following: Exchange of Notes Amending the Philippine-U.S. Military Bases Agreement of 1947, Jan. 7, 1979; Carter-Marcos letter of Jan. 4, 1979; Vance-Romulo letter of Jan. 6, 1979; "Arrangements Regarding Delineation of United States Facili-

ties at Clark Air Base and Subic Naval Base; Powers and Responsibilities of the Philippine Base Commanders and Related Powers and Responsibilities of the United States Facility Commanders; and the Tabones Training Complex," undated; all from State Department.

34. During his election campaign from jail Aquino endorsed Marcos' position on the bases (see his statement at a March 11, 1978 news conference) but after it was clear that the negotiations would succeed he signed the bitterly antibase letter of December 25, 1978, from various opposition leaders, since then widely circulated by anti-Marcos groups in the U.S.

35. Ibid., p. 348; for text of treaty see 3 UST 3947.

36. Article V, North Atlantic Treaty.

37. Symington Hearings, p. 16.

38. On Marcos' concern over the Spratly islands and the U.S. position see "Philippines to Link Bases Pact with U.S. Defense Pledge," *Washington Post*, Jan. 25, 1977; on the legal dispute itself, see Selig S. Harrison, *China, Oil, and Asia: Conflict Ahead?* (New York, 1977), esp. pp. 196–98; Martin H. Katchen, "The Spratly Islands and the Law of the Sea: 'Dangerous Ground' for Asian Peace," *Asian Survey* (Dec. 1977), 17:1167–81.

39. The phrase "of equal validity" is found in the Vance-Romulo letter of Jan. 6. The same letter defines "metropolitan territory" in accordance with the Treaty of Paris of 1898 (i.e., excluding the South China Sea islands) but specifies that attacks on "armed forces, public vessels or aircraft in the Pacific," or on "island territories under its [Philippine] jurisdiction" need not be within the Treaty of Paris line to be covered by the treaty.

40. "SEATO's Flags are Coming Down for the Last Time," *Washington Post*, June 29, 1977. The United States, Britain, Australia, New Zealand, the Philippines, and Thailand remain as active Manila Pact signatories.

41. For the text of the Manila Pact see Oliver E. Clubb Jr., *The United States and the Sino-Soviet Bloc in Southeast Asia* (Washington, 1962), pp. 151–56.

42. On this subject see in particular Weinstein, "The United States and Southeast Asia."

43. Britt, "U.S. Military Bases," discusses shipyard capability in Singapore and cites following comparative costs per man-day:

West Coast naval shipyards	$179.55
SRF—Guam	151.00
SRF—Yokosuka (Japan)	107.20
U.S. Naval Office, Singapore	30.00
SRF—Subic	23.26

44. See, for example, George McT. Kahin's discussion in "The Need to End Our Risky Military Ties to Manila," *Washington Post*, Outlook Section, Aug. 27, 1978.

45. See esp. the Kuala Lumpur Declaration, Nov. 27, 1971, on the "Zone of Peace, Freedom and Neutrality," *Facts on ASEAN*, Ministry of Foreign Affairs, Malaysia.

46. Salvador P. Lopez, "U.S. Bases, a Philippine View, . . ." *AWSJ*, Oct. 6, 1978.

4. U.S. Human Rights Policy in Indonesia and the Philippines

1. Robert A. Packenham, *Liberal America and the Third World* (Princeton, 1973). As Packenham notes (p. 101) Title IX, formally "Utilization of Democratic In-

stitutions in Development," aroused "indifference, skepticism or vigorous opposition" among critical foreign affairs professionals, much as human rights policy has done. Title IX remains on the books but is no longer a major focus of AID attention, or rather has been subsumed under the more recent congressional mandate to aid the "poorest of the poor."

2. Emphasis in original: Donald M. Fraser, "Human Rights and United States Foreign Policy—The Congressional Perspective," paper prepared for American Bar Association Conference on Human Rights and International Law (Washington, Apr. 1978). This policy is qualified by the fact that no one in either the Congress or the Executive Branch attempts to render categorical judgments as to which countries are "gross violators."

3. "Human Rights and U.S. Policy," issue brief prepared by Vita Bite, Congressional Research Service, in U.S. House of Representatives, *Human Rights and United States Foreign Policy: A Review of the Administration's Record, Hearings before Subcommittee on International Organizations, Committee on International Relations, October 2, 1977, 95th Cong., 1st sess., 1978, pp. 47–74; see also Donald Fraser, "Freedom and Foreign Policy," Foreign Policy* (Spring 1977), 26:140–56.

4. Elizabeth Drew, "Human Rights" (A Reporter at Large), *New Yorker*, July 18, 1977.

5. See, for example, Secretary Vance's speech before the University of Georgia Law School, Apr. 30, 1977. He used "vital" rather than "basic" needs. The latter term is more commonly employed in relation to aid issues, but the meaning is the same and to avoid semantic confusion I have used "basic" in both human rights and AID contexts (see chapter six).

6. In Indonesia emergency powers were contained in the famous March 11 Order ("Super Semar") extracted from Sukarno on Mar. 11, 1965, and subsequently reaffirmed by the Indonesian Congress (Provisional People's Consultative Assembly—MPRS). In the Philippines, the emergency powers which Marcos assumed in the original Martial Law decree of Sept. 21, 1972 were later ratified in the palace-manipulated Transitory Provisions approved by the Constitutional Convention. These powers have since been reaffirmed by referenda, and more recently, on Sept. 1, 1976, by the National Advisory Council (Batasang Bayan). In both countries the rulers have been extremely careful to make sure that the emergency powers remain in force, and in neither case has legislative ratification involved genuine choice. See Peter Polomka, *Indonesia Since Sukarno* (Victoria, 1971), p. 88; and for the 1976 Philippine developments, see Lela Garner Noble, "Philippines 1976: The Contrast between Shrine and Shanty," *Asian Survey* (Feb. 1977), 17:134.

7. The Indonesian prisoners are the subject of a voluminous literature. Much information is provided in two Fraser Committee hearings, U.S. House of Representatives, *Human Rights in Indonesia and the Philippines,* and *Human Rights in Indonesia: A Review of the Situation with Respect to the Long-Term Political Detainees, Hearings before the subcommittee on International Organizations of the Committee on International Relations, December 18, 1975–May 3, 1976 and October 8, 1977, 94th Cong. 2d sess. and 95th Cong. 1st sess.* For the Amnesty position see *Indonesia: An Amnesty International Report* (London, 1977) and the updating contained in Amnesty's introduction to the Indonesian translation of this report (MS, Oct. 1978).

8. Jusuf Wanandi, "Human Rights: An Indonesian View," *FEER*, Dec. 2, 1977, p. 23.

9. David Jenkins, "The Give and Take of Freedom," *FEER*, May 18, 1979, reported new arrests of 1965–66 suspects and shifting of prisoners between Category

A (senior Communist Party leaders awaiting trial) and Category B (other Party functionaries believed involved in the Coup attempt of 1965 but without sufficient evidence for trial). Category C was formerly the most numerous and was supposed to include the least involved Party and Party-front members. For a report on recent prisoner releases see Raphael Pura, "Indonesia Sets Free Most Prisoners from '65 Uprising," *AWSJ*, Dec. 10, 1979.

10. The estimate of 500 is from the 1978 Philippine 502(b) report: U.S. Congress, *Country Reports on Human Rights Practices, Joint Committee Report*, February 3, 1978, 95th Cong., 2d sess. (hereafter cited as *Country Reports*), p. 261. The situation had not changed appreciably as of mid-1979.

11. On torture see ibid.; *Report on an Amnesty International Mission to the Republic of the Philippines, November 22–December 9, 1975*, 2d ed. (London, 1976), pp. 22 ff.; William J. Butler, John Humphrey, and G. R. Bission, *The Decline of Democracy in the Philippines* (Geneva: International Commission of Jurists, 1977); and on "disappearances," see Association of Major Religious Superiors, *Political Detainees in the Philippines* (Manila, 1976), esp. chapter 2, "Torture, Deaths and Disappearances," and George McT. Kahin, "Testimony on the Philippines before Fraser Subcommittee" (MS, Apr. 27, 1978). The question of why torture persists in the Philippines, in a human rights climate which is in many ways relatively benign, is difficult to answer. The most common theory is that President Marcos, rather like old-fashioned city bosses in the United States, relies on ties of personal loyalty which transcend all shortcomings, including brutality and inefficiency. The same theory explains why the President reversed the civil service purge inspired by Executive Secretary Alejandro Melchor in late 1975; he belatedly recognized the reform principle to be fundamentally subversive of his system of rule. In my view it is also possible that the President personally resents the pressure which the U.S. government has exerted in torture cases, and that this has further motivated him to resist it even at the cost of strained relations.

12. Based primarily on personal observation. Cf. Lela Garner Noble's comment, "Outside of Manila there are only the military and bureaucratic and 'representative' structures which sometimes have new forms but *seldom new people*. Where there are new people they have been delegated little authority; they lack the traditional bases of the old elites and have no confidence that they are trusted by any elites. As a result the system lacks integrity, in the general sense of wholeness or in the more limited sense of honesty." (Emphasis added.) "Emergency Politics in the Philippines," *Asian Survey* (Apr. 1978), 18:361–62. I am not aware of any lengthier analysis of Marcos' local government policies which penetrates the fog of government rhetoric about largely meaningless New Society institutions, or unemotionally evaluates the as yet generally feeble role of the military except in the relatively few areas of active insurgency (Muslim Mindanao and Sulu; Samar, the northern Sierra Madre, etc.)

13. Based mainly on personal experience, but see also *Indonesia: An Amnesty International Report*, pp. 113 ff.

14. Constantino is the biographer of Recto and the author of *The Philippines: A Past Revisited* (Manila, 1975), a major Marxist-revisionist reinterpretation of Philippine history. His books are in print in Manila and command a wide following among educated Filipino youth. In Indonesia or Singapore he would be regarded as an intolerably dangerous character.

15. Mostly from the otherwise highly critical 1978 Philippine 502(b) report, *Country Reports*, p. 267.

16. *Human Rights in Indonesia and the Philippines*, p. 94.

17. Like my comments on academic freedom, remarks on foreign press freedom are based on experience in the Philippines 1974–76.

18. For general background on the press and Martial Law, see David Rosenberg, "Liberty Versus Loyalty: The Transformation of Philippine News Media under Martial Law," in David A. Rosenberg, ed., *Marcos and Martial Law in the Philippines* (Ithaca, 1979), pp. 145–79. Rosenberg emphasizes the unfavorable contrast with pre–Martial Law conditions.

19. *Manila Daily Express*, Sept. 12, 1976.

20. Figures on refugees and civilian casualties are those used by President Marcos; see *FEER*, Oct. 28, 1977, p. 5; Nov. 18, 1977, p. 23.

21. For examples of human rights reports which make no mention of the Muslim south, see the Philippine 502(b) report in *Country Reports*; the Amnesty International and ICJ reports cited above; also National Resource Center on Political Prisoners in the Philippines, *Human Rights and Martial Law in the Philippines* (Oakland, 1977). Recently Mindanao has started to attract a bit more attention as a human rights problem.

22. The brief summary of East Timor developments contained in this paragraph and the two that follow is drawn from material in the Fraser hearings, U.S. House of Representatives, *Human Rights in East Timor and the Question of the Use of U.S. Equipment by the Indonesian Armed Forces*, and *Human Rights in East Timor, Hearings before the Subcommittee on International Organizations of the Committee on International Relations, March 23 and June 28–July 10, 1977*, 95th Cong., 1st sess.; also Center for International Policy, *Human Rights and the U.S. Foreign Assistance Program, Fiscal Year 1978*, Part 2 (East Asia) (Washington, 1977), pp. 18–30; testimony of Benedict O'Gorman Anderson before the Fraser Subcommittee, Feb. 15, 1978, (MS). Judgment expressed on the likelihood of Indonesia's accepting an independent East Timor is my own.

23. See speech of Deputy Secretary of State Warren Christopher before the American Bar Association, Feb. 13, 1978, State Department *Bulletin* Mar. 1978, p. 22; also interview with Zbigniew Brzezinski, *U.S. News and World Report*, Feb. 13, 1978, p. 32.

24. *New York Times*, Mar. 13, 1977, p. 1.

25. *Country Reports* on Philippines, p. 260.

26. Ibid., p. 237.

27. U.S. House of Representatives, Subcommittee on International Organizations, *The Status of Human Rights in Selected Countries and the U.S. Response*, July 25, 1977, 95th Cong., 1st sess., p. 51.

28. The Lopez family–controlled *Philippine News* (San Francisco) of May 6–12, 1978, reported preliminary efforts by the House International Relations Committee to cut $5 million from the total Philippine MAP appropriation of $19.1 million under the headline "Another Lesson for Marcos."

29. *FEER*, May 27, 1977; see also *Christian Science Monitor* editorial of May 20.

30. "Mondale, ending Debate, will include Manila on trip," *New York Times*, Apr. 29, 1978. Conservative commentators flaunted this episode as an example of human rights zealotry in the State Department; see Evans and Novak, "Clout on Human Rights Policy," *Washington Post*, May 11, and John Roche's "State Department a Disaster Area," *Washington Star*, May 12. Roche reached the wonderfully confused conclusion that since the Indonesian rights record is worse than that of the Philippines, Jakarta should have been the candidate for boycott, but ". . . Manila

was first on [Ms. Derian's] list precisely because our huge bases there trigger her McGovernite-conditioned reflexes. . . . [Marcos] is a Bad Man and we should take our bases and go home."

31. *Washington Post*, Nov. 22, 1977; *New York Times*, Dec. 18, 1977.

32. For details of Philippine MAP, including types of aircraft, see U.S. House of Representatives, *Human Rights in South Korea and the Philippines: Implications for U.S. Policy, Hearings before the Subcommittee on International Organizations,* May–June 1975, 94th Cong., 1st sess., pp. 317–20; on the Indonesian OV-10s, see *Human Rights in East Timor and the Question of the Use of U.S. Equipment . . . ,* pp. 64 ff.

33. *Human Rights and the U.S. Foreign Assistance Program*, pp. 19–20.

34. *Human Rights in East Timor*, p. 48. The State Department legal adviser testified that under a June 1976 change in the security assistance law (coinciding approximately with the resumption of U.S. arms aid to Indonesia) an automatic cutoff of aid was no longer required in the event that U.S. equipment was used to cross international boundaries, but merely notification to the Congress by the President; ibid., p. 62.

35. Report by Allan S. Nanes in *Human Rights in East Timor*, p. 80.

36. Fraser, "Human Rights . . . The Congressional Perspective."

37. *Human Rights in Indonesia and the Philippines*, pp. 39 ff.

38. *Human Rights and United States Foreign Policy: A Review of the Administration's Record*, p. 16.

39. The phrase is reportedly favored by Brzezinski: Elizabeth Drew, "Brzezinski" (A Reporter at Large), *New Yorker*, May 1, 1978, p. 110. Other "new influentials" are Saudi Arabia, Nigeria, Iran (presumably no longer) and Venezuela (all like Indonesia oil exporters), plus India and Brazil.

40. Manila *Bulletin Today*, Oct. 1977.

41. *FEER*, Sept. 22, 1977.

42. This view was cited constantly during U.S. press coverage of the May elections; see, for example, Jay Matthew's story in the May 3 *Washington Post*.

43. *New York Times*, Mar. 5, 1978.

44. *New York Times*, May 4, 1978.

45. "First Lady in Distress," *FEER*, Aug. 11, 1978, p. 23.

46. "Bitter Battle over Bases," *Time*, Oct. 9, 1978.

47. Personal communication.

48. The phrase is from Ernest W. Lefever's article "The Trivialization of Human Rights," *Policy Review* (Winter 1978), pp. 11–26.

49. Stanley Hoffman, "The Hell of Good Intentions," *Foreign Policy* (Winter 1979), 29:3–26.

50. Fraser, "Human Rights . . . The Congressional Perspective."

5. American Prosperity and the Island World: Investment, Trade, and the North-South Agenda

1. On American economic policy in the Philippines see Frank H. Golay, "The Philippine Economy" in George M. Guthrie, ed., *Six Perspectives on the Philippines* (Manila, 1971); Taft's policies are covered in Peter Stanley, *A Nation in the Making* (Cambridge, 1974), esp. pp. 89 ff. The $160 million figure is calculated from Helmut G. Callis, "Capital Investment in Southeastern Asia and the Philippines," *Annals of*

the American Academy of Political and Social Science (Mar. 1943), 226:23; it does not include some $37 million in U.S.-held Philippine government bonds.

2. Center for Strategic and International Studies, U.S. Philippine Economic Relations (Washington, 1971) p. 101; the role of U.S. investment in the first postwar decade is thoroughly discussed in Frank H. Golay, "Economic Collaboration: The Role of American Investment" in Golay, ed., The United States and the Philippines (Englewood Cliffs, 1966), pp. 95–124.

3. The nationalist case is most forcefully developed by Alejandro Lichauco in his "Imperialism and the Security of the State," a memo to fellow delegates at the 1972 Constitutional Convention; see also his Nationalism, Economic Development and Social Justice (Manila, 1967). For the view that the exchange control system exhausted its potential for encouraging entrepreneurship and became little more than an incentive to corruption see Robert E. Baldwin, Foreign Trade Regimes and Economic Development: The Philippines (New York, 1975) esp. ch. 3.

4. Frank H. Golay, "An American Interest in the Philippines: Magnitude, Distribution and Recent Changes in United States Direct Investment" (MS, Oct. 1975), p. 27.

5. Frank H. Golay, "United States Interests and Philippine Policy," (MS, Oct. 1976), p. 7.

6. Tony Patrick, "Banking on the Marcos Method," FEER, Sept. 27, 1974, p. 67.

7. Laura Jeanne Henze, "U.S.-Philippine Economic Relations and Trade Negotiations," Asian Survey (Apr. 1976), 4:329.

8. Leo Gonzaga, "Manila's Sluggish Inflow," FEER, Sept. 30, 1977, p. 47.

9. FEER, Asia Yearbook 1978, p. 296.

10. For background see Alex Hunter, "The Indonesian Oil Industry" in Bruce Glassburner, ed., The Economy of Indonesia, Selected Readings (Ithaca, 1971); Leon Howell and Michael Morrow, Asia, Oil Politics and the Energy Crisis (New York: International Documentation, 1974); Sevinc Carlson, Indonesia's Oil (Washington: Center for Strategic and International Studies, 1976).

11. Business Asia, Oct. 14, 1977, p. 324.

12. David Jenkins, "Indonesia: Going Down, Down, Down," FEER, July 29, 1977, p. 59.

13. Embassy of the United States, Jakarta, "Foreign Economic Trends and Their Implications for the United States," Mar. 1978, p. 9.

14. Jenkins, "Indonesia: Going Down, Down, Down," p. 59.

15. Embassy of the United States, Jakarta, "Industry Outlook Report: Indonesia's Petroleum Sector," July 1, 1977, p. 49.

16. On production sharing see Robert Fabrikant, "Production-sharing contracts in the Indonesian Oil Industry" in Howell and Morrow, Asia, Oil Politics and Energy Crisis.

17. Mark Johnson, "Oil: Recent Developments," BIES (Nov. 1977), 13:40.

18. U.S. Embassy, "Indonesia's Petroleum Sector," pp. 50–51.

19. Another set of figures that in some respects more accurately reflects the globalized economy of today is the "Capital Expenditures by Majority-owned Foreign Affilates of U.S. Companies" series which appears every March and September in the Department of Commerce publication Survey of Current Business. These figures are not kept cumulatively and are gross (i.e., do not reflect sales or other dispositions). They cover "expenditures that are made to acquire, add to or improve property, plant and equipment, and that are charged to capital accounts," regardless of the source of the money; i.e., including funds raised locally and in

eurodollar markets. Figures are as follows for Indonesia and the Philippines (in millions of dollars):

Year	Indonesia	Indonesia (oil)	Philippines	All LDCs (in billions)
1966	D	D	65	1.7
1967	D	D	61	2.3
1968	57	48	46	2.9
1969	81	71	40	3.3
1970	144	106	D	3.5
1971	264	177	73	3.6
1972	257	170	60	3.8
1973	278	224	65	4.2
1974	506	424	98	5.4
1975	776	713	120	6.4
1976	318	271	102	5.4
1977	280	237	102	5.9
1978	342	288	174	6.6
Total	3,303	2,729	1,008	55.0

(D = suppressed; figures for 1977–78 are for "latest plans"; totals are my calculations.)

20. Calculated from International Monetary Fund, Direction of Trade, passim.

21. For recent developments in this area see "Star Performer: Electronics Industry in Philippines Boosts Exports at Rapid Pace," AWSJ, Aug. 24, 1978; "Philippines Signs Textile Pact with U.S., Calls it Among the Most Generous in Asia," AWSJ, Sept. 18, 1978; "Philippine Move to Vary Exports Shows Success," AWSJ, Aug. 9, 1978.

22. All commodity percentages are calculated from U.S. Commerce Department annual trade figures (raw data).

23. Larry A. Niksch, "United States Relations with the Association of Southeast Asian Nations (ASEAN): A Background Document for the Second U.S.-ASEAN Conference in Washington, August 3–4, 1978" (Washington: Congressional Research Service, 1978), p. 19. However, recent press accounts report large discoveries of chromium ore in Indonesia and Papua New Guinea: see "Kawasaki Steel, Amax of U.S. Join in Asian Chromium Search Venture," AWSJ, July 28, 1978.

24. Wijarso, "Oil II: A Doomsday Scenario: —and Alternatives," BIES (Nov. 1977), 13:49. Other Indonesian officials subsequently disputed the "doomsday scenario." Pertamina's new chief, Piet Haryono, told a group of foreign businessmen that "I can say for sure that the amount of oil to be discovered is much larger than the amount that has been discovered during the past century" (AWSJ, Sept. 15, 1978). U.S. government energy experts, however, are inclined to agree with Wijarso that Indonesia's oil supply and demand curves will cross sometime in the next decade.

25. U.S. Senate, Subcommittee on Foreign Economic Policy of the Committee on Foreign Relations, International Debt, the Banks, and U.S. Foreign Policy, 95th Cong., 1st sess. (Aug. 1977), p. 9; statement on number of officers employed in bank international divisions is based on an informal survey by Carnegie Endowment staff.

26. Ibid.; see also the remark by the Citibank president referring to his overseas profits, "Around here it's Jakarta that pays the check"; "Why They Call It Fat City," Fortune, Mar. 1975, p. 110; quoted in Raul S. Manglapus, Japan in Southeast Asia: Collision Course (Washington, 1976), p. 74.

27. For background on developing country eurocurrency borrowing see P. A. Wellons, *Borrowing by Developing Countries on the Euro-Currency Market* (Paris, 1977).

28. Federal Reserve Bank of Chicago, *International Letter*, June 23, 1978.

29. Senate Foreign Relations Committee, *International Debt, the Banks, and U.S. Foreign Policy*, p. 43.

30. World Bank, *World Debt Tables: External Public Debt of Developing Countries* (Sept. 2, 1977), 1:176.

31. Marilyn Seiber, "The Philippines: Land of the Morning, Child of Debt" in Seiber and Larry Franko, eds., *Developing Country Debt* (forthcoming).

32. Ibid.; "Philippines Will Continue as Major Borrower in 79," *AWSJ*, Dec. 7, 1978.

33. Federal Reserve Bank of Chicago, *International Letter*.

34. Robert S. McNamara, *Address to the Board of Governors* (Washington: World Bank, 1977), p. 20.

35. "Surveying ASEAN's Foreign Debt," *AWSJ*, Sept. 18, 1978.

36. Trade figures calculated from IMF *Direction of Trade* and Japan Tariff Association, *Japanese Exports and Imports*, (Dec. 1977).

37. In 1976, 47.6 percent of Japanese official aid went to ASEAN; *FEER* Mar. 10, 1978, p. 35 (table).

38. Japanese-ASEAN economic relations are summarized in Niksch, "United States Relations with ASEAN," p. 51–52. For more recent developments, see "Japan to Carry Out ASEAN Aid Pledge Even if Projects Change, Foreign Minister Says," *AWSJ*, Sept. 12, 1978. As the Niksch study suggests, ASEAN economic demands on the United States and Japan have been similar in substance, but they have been presented to us in more muted tones, since ASEAN leaders have regarded the problem of encouraging U.S. presence in the region (both economic and political) as a more fundamental concern.

39. The firm was Bechtel, and the interview took place in late 1977.

40. It is noteworthy that U.S.-Japan economic rivalry for Southeast Asian (or other regional) markets is simply not mentioned in many scholarly studies—see, for example, Franklin Weinstein, *U.S.-Japan Relations and the Security of East Asia* (Boulder, 1978)—nor does the subject receive much mention at such gatherings as the annual Japan-U.S. Businessmen's Conference (see report of the fifteenth conference held in Tokyo, June 16–17, 1978, published by the United States Chamber of Commerce, Washington, D.C.).

41. For LNG developments, see U.S. Embassy, "Indonesia's Petroleum Sector," pp. 39 ff.; Ken Kahn, "Indonesia's LNG Ventures," *Pacific Research* (Nov.–Dec. 1976), vol. 8; "Indonesia's Challenging New Frontier," *FEER*, Aug. 4, 1978, p. 36.

42. On Southeast Asian interest in north-south issues, see Frank Golay, "National Economic Priorities and International Coalitions" in G. Pauker, F. Golay, and C. Enloe, *Diversity and Development in Southeast Asia: The Coming Decade* (New York, 1977).

43. On GSP see Peter Ginman and Tracy Murray, "The Generalized System of Preferences" in K. Sauvant and H. Hasenpflug, eds., *The New International Economic Order: Conflict or Cooperation Between North and South?* (Boulder, 1977), ch. 12.

44. Michael Richardson, "Only Sympathy for ASEAN," *FEER*, June 9, 1978, p. 81.

45. The U.S. position on commodity price stabilization was well spelled out in

Fred Bergsten's testimony in U.S. House of Representatives, Subcommittee on Economic Stabilization of the Committee on Banking, Finance and Urban Affairs, *International Commodity Agreements*, 95th Cong., 1st sess. (June 8, 1977).

46. Text of Joint Press Statement, ASEAN-U.S. Dialogue, released Aug. 4, 1978. For reaction see "ASEAN Gets No New Concessions in Talks with U.S. Despite Common Fund Pledge", in *AWSJ*, Aug. 8, 1978.

47. Seiber, "Land of the Morning, Child of Debt"; for recent concern about the Philippine debt level see "Philippines: Troubles Closing In," *FEER*, June 29, 1979, p. 55.

48. John Sewell, Overseas Development Council, "Can the Rich Prosper Without Progress by the Poor?" (MS, Mar. 1978).

49. The request was made in a memo from ASEAN members to the United States in early 1977 and later repeated at the first ASEAN–U.S. dialogue. *Business Asia*, June 10, 1977, p. 178.

50. Discussion of Pertamina is based primarily on the following sources: "Ambivalent Borrower: Indonesia" in Wellons, *Borrowing by Developing Countries on the Euro-Currency Market*, pp. 196–232; Bruce Glassburner, "In the Wake of General Ibnu: Crisis in the Indonesian Oil Industry," *Asian Survey* (Dec. 1976) 16:1099–1112; Donald K. Emmerson, "The Bureaucracy in Political Context," in Karl D. Jackson and Lucian Pye, eds., *Political Power and Communications in Indonesia*, Berkeley, 1978 esp. pp. 113–16; "A Lesson for Lenders," *FEER*, Dec. 23, 1977, and various other press coverage, plus the Senate hearing cited below (note 55).

51. Wellons, "Ambivalent Borrower: Indonesia," pp. 210, 213.

52. Ibid., p. 218. Wellons' study, while by far the most valuable material published on the Pertamina affairs thus far, is at times exasperatingly oblique.

53. Glassburner, "In the Wake of General Ibnu," p. 1110.

54. For a slightly different version of the same opinion (and a generally excellent account of the Pertamina affair) see Seth Lipsky and Raphael Pura, "Indonesia: Testing Time for the 'New Order', *Foreign Affairs* (Fall 1978), 17:189.

55. Testimony of Erland H. Heginbotham, U.S. Senate, Subcommittee on Foreign Economic Policy of the Committee on Foreign Relations, *The Witteveen Facility and the OPEC Financial Surpluses*, 95th Cong., 1st sess. (Sept.–Oct. 1977).

56. Manglapus, *Japan in Southeast Asia*, esp. pp. 77–78.

57. On these points see Franklin B. Weinstein, "Multinational Corporations and the Third World: The Case of Japan and Southeast Asia," *International Organizations* (Summer 1976), 30:400–3. Weinstein's article is the best nonpolemic discussion I have seen both of social costs relating to foreign investment in Southeast Asia generally, and the special problems of the Japanese variant.

58. Material on the Philippine reactor case is drawn primarily from interviews in Washington, D.C.; see also S. Jacob Scherr, "Safety Review for U.S. Nuclear Exports—Proposals for Change" (MS, May 1978, Natural Resources Defense Council, Washington, D.C.); Constance Holden, "Environmental Assessment Sought for Federal Actions Abroad," *Science* (Aug. 18, 1978), 201:598–600; "Martial Law Benefits Marcos Friends," *Washington Post*, Dec. 19, 1977; "Westinghouse–Manila Deal Studied," *New York Times*, Jan. 20, 1978; and other press coverage.

59. "Environmental Group and Ex-Im Bank Sign Agreement Ending Suit," *Washington Post*, Feb. 24, 1979; Evans and Novak, "Missing an A-Plant," *Washington Post*, July 2, 1979.

60. Both quotations are from "Indonesia: Tangling with U.S. Red Tape," *AWSJ*, Sept. 23, 1978.

61. "Why the Multinational Tide is Ebbing," *Fortune*, Aug. 1977, pp. 111–120.

62. The kind of educational effort needed is illustrated by the activities of the Corporate Consultation Program of the Carnegie Center for Transnational Studies; see, for example, Louis T. Wells, *Appropriate and Applicable Technology: The Indonesian Case Study* (New York: Carnegie Center for Transnational Studies, 1976).

63. See Overseas Private Investment Corporation, *Investment Insurance Handbook* (Washington, 1978).

6. Malthus in Eden: The Land-Labor-Food Crisis of Inner Indonesia

1. I have used "Outer Indonesia" and "the Outer Islands" interchangeably.

2. Statistics on Indonesian and Bangladesh food aid are from the U.S. Agency for International Development (hereafter AID) *Annual Budget Submission* (hereafter cited as *ABS*) for the respective countries for FY 1978.

3. Clifford Geertz, *Agricultural Involution* (Berkeley, 1963), p. 89.

4. Ibid., pp. 69–70; Widjojo Nitisastro, *Population Trends in Indonesia* (Ithaca, 1970), pp. 31, 163.

5. Geertz, *Agricultural Involution*, p. 97.

6. Figures on farm size are debatable, as are virtually all other statistics relating to Javanese agriculture. The World Bank estimates that 30 percent of Javanese farms are less than 0.25 hectares. The 1973 Agricultural Census indicated that 57.4 percent of farms on Java are less than one-half hectare, compared to 28 percent elsewhere in Indonesia; Ann Booth and R. M. Sundrum, "The 1973 Agricultural Census," *BIES* (July 1976), 13:92. According to Sajogyo, 20 percent of all farm households averaged less than 0.1 hectares in 1963: "Modernization Without Development in Rural Java," contribution to U.N./FAO study (MS, n.d.), p. 7.

7. AID says that the Indonesian tenancy rate is only 3.2 percent, compared to 39.9 percent for the Philippines (Indonesia *ABS* FY 1980 Annex F, p. 12). Sajogyo's figures show that if one includes partial tenancy on the part of the near landless, whose own holdings are insufficient to support them, the figure for "tenant farmers" on Java rises to about 40 percent ("Modernization Without Development," p. 4). But as the work of Gillian Hart and others suggests, the real problem on Java is not the "high" rate of tenancy but the fact that as effective consolidation of land holdings progresses, tenants are losing their use rights and being pushed out of the agricultural labor force. Hence, an apparent recent *decrease* in tenancy and increase in wholly owned farms may correlate with *declining* welfare.

8. Geertz, *Agricultural involution*, p. 97.

9. William Collier estimates that "in Java perhaps as much as one half of the villages in these densely populated areas had no land and one-fourth had very little land": see "Food Problems, Unemployment, and the Green Revolution in Rural Java," *Prisma* (Mar. 1978), 9:39.

10. Terence H. Hull, Valerie J. Hull, and Masri Singarimbun, *Indonesia's Family Planning Story: A Success and Challenge* (Washington: Population Reference Bureau, 1977); Indonesia *ABS* FY 1980, Annex C. For more on Indonesian family planning efforts, see chapter seven.

11. Total U.S. bilateral economic aid for Indonesia in FY 1978, including PL 480, was $164 million; see table 6.2.

12. Field studies conducted by the Agro Economic Survey are the major source of knowledge about the labor and institutional implications of shifts in rice technology. Much of this work is summarized in William L. Collier and Suntoro, "Rural Development and the Decline of Traditional Village Welfare Institutions in Java," paper presented at Western Economics Association's 1978 conference in Honolulu (MS, June 1978). Figures on increase in seasonal harvesters are from Gary E. Hansen, "Rural Local Government and Agricultural Development in Java," cited in David Rosenberg et al., "Indonesia: Country Profile," (MS, June 1978), p. 242.

13. William L. Collier and Rudolf F. Sinaga, *Social and Regional Implications of Agricultural Development Policy*, Agricultural Development Council Staff Paper 75-3 (New York, 1975), p. 29.

14. C. Peter Timmer, "Choices of Technique in Rice Milling on Java," *BIES* (July 1973), 9:57–76; William L. Collier et al, "Choice of Technique in Rice Milling—A Comment" and Timmer's reply in *BIES* (Mar. 1974), 10:106–26.

15. Rudolf F. Sinaga, "Employment, Income Distribution and Policy Implications of Agricultural Mechanization in Java" (MS, 1977).

16. William L. Collier and Harjadi Koesworo, "Aquaculture and Sea Fisheries, the Village Economy in Coastal Java" (MS, 1977).

17. Donald K. Emmerson, "Order of Meaning: Understanding Political Change in a Fishing Community in Indonesia," paper presented at annual meeting of the American Political Science Association (MS, Sept. 18, 1975).

18. This is Rosenberg's estimate: "Indonesia: Country Profile," p. 247.

19. Total increase in the labor force is estimated at 5.7 million over the next five years: Indonesia *ABS* FY 1980, Annex C, p. 1.

20. Another researcher has concluded that the number of villagers living below the poverty line increased from 52 percent to 61 percent between 1969 and 1976: Prijono Tjiptoherijanto's review of Sritua Arief, *Indonesia: Growth, Income Disparity and Mass Poverty* (Jakarta, 1977) in *Prisma* (Mar. 1978), 9:81.

21. On declining real wages in certain rural areas see William L. Collier, "Agricultural Evolution in Java: The Decline of Shared Poverty and Involution," chapter in Gary Hansen, ed., *Agricultural Development in Indonesia* (in press); Achmad T. Birowo, "Technology and Employment in Agriculture," *Prisma* (Nov. 1975), 2:41. AID concludes cautiously that "over the past 10 years real per capita income for the poorest 40 percent of the population has probably remained constant or increased only marginally, although the statistics are not accurate on this point." Various scholars have sharply challenged more optimistic World Bank conclusions: see esp. David Dapice, "Some Notes on Income Distribution in Indonesia," paper prepared for Carnegie/State Department seminar on Indonesian Rural Development (MS, Nov. 1978); Benjamin White, "Political Aspects of Poverty, Income Distribution and Their Measurement: Some Examples from Rural Java" (MS, 1978). Finally, a recent study of plantation workers' wages indicated that real wages, while generally correlating with the overall state of the economy, have never recovered to pre–World War II levels: Gustav Papenek, "The Effect of Economic Growth and Inflation on Workers' Income" (MS, Carnegie/State Department seminar, Nov. 1978).

22. Figures are from office of U.S. Agricultural Attaché, Jakarta, and from Leon A. Mears, "Problems of Supply and Marketing of Food in Indonesia—Repelita III" (MS, Carnegie/State Department seminar, Nov. 1978, esp. p. 5).

23. Collier, for example, notes research of colonial era scholars suggesting that

the Geertzian pattern of shared poverty was a natural byproduct of hard times, whereas in times of prosperity burden-sharing was deemphasized if not abandoned: "Agricultural Evolution."

24. Two excellent studies of this critical period are Margo L. Lyon, *Bases of Conflict in Rural Java*, Research Monograph no. 3 (Berkeley: Center for South and Southeast Asia Studies, University of California, 1970); and Rex Mortimer, *The Indonesian Communist Party and Land Reform*, Monash Papers on Southeast Asia, no. 1 (Canberra: Centre of Southeast Asian Studies, Monash University, 1972). Contrary to some popular accounts, the 1965 killings were not directed primarily against the ethnic Chinese, most of whom had been forced to leave the rural areas of Java under Sukarno. On the Hindu island of Bali the main source of stress appears to have been (as on Java) politically inflamed tension between smallholders and landless peasants.

25. Leon A. Mears, "Indonesia's Food Problems—Repelita II/III" (MS, 1976), p. 2.

26. On BUUD's and BIMAS see Gary E. Hansen, "Bureaucratic Linkages and Policy-Making in Indonesia: BIMAS revisited" in Karl D. Jackson and Lucian Pye, eds., *Political Power and Communications in Indonesia* (Berkeley, 1978); for an earlier critique of Indonesia's green revolution see Richard William Franke, "Miracle Seeds and Shattered Dreams in Java," *Natural History* (Jan. 1974), 83:11 ff., and David Penny's review of Franke's Ph.D. thesis in *BIES* (Nov. 1973), 9:109–12.

27. World Bank estimate. There are in fact seven subcategories of INPRES program operating at various levels of local government and for specialized purposes, including forestry or "greening," health, and the construction of primary schools and markets.

28. Personal communication with AID advisers.

29. On the military in local government, see Donald K. Emmerson, "Bureaucracy in Political Context" in Jackson and Pye, *Political Power and Communications*, p. 103; on the trend toward increasing top-down authority, one-way communication, and other problems in the bureaucracy, see ibid. pp. 123 ff., esp. p. 136, where Emmerson concludes with an eloquent summary of the contradiction between coercion, repression, centralization, and control on the one hand, and, on the other, the goals which they are often employed to achieve—efficiency, growth, justice, and social change.

30. *ABS*, FY 1980, Annex F, p. 3.

31. For an account of the Kentucky program see Howard Beers, *An American Experience in Indonesia: The University of Kentucky Affiliation with the Agricultural University of Bogor* (Lexington, 1971).

32. AID, "United States Economic Assistance to Indonesia" (MS, n.d. [1966?] in Cornell University Library).

33. William L. Collier et al., "Renting of Farmers' Rice Fields by Sugar Cane Factories—A Case Study in East Java," Agro Economic Survey Report (MS, Mar. 1973).

34. Donald K. Emmerson, "The Bureaucracy in Political Context" in Jackson and Pye, *Politica! Power and Communication*, pp. 117–20. According to stories circulating in Indonesia at the time, Bank President McNamara was informed in the course of a 1974 visit to Indonesia that farmers' interests would probably be hurt by the sugar project. He replied that the loans should be considered from the viewpoint of Indonesia's macroeconomic needs. The problem is now rather universally recognized, and there have been no more major sugar loans to Indonesia by IBRD or ADB.

35. For an example of recent land reform discussion, see interview with Minister of Agriculture Soedharsono, *Kompas*, Mar. 29, 1977; a report of President Suharto's reference to the need to "regulate ownership of land" in his 1978 Independence Day address was in *AWSJ*, Aug. 18, 1978. On the existing land reform law (for which implementing regulations were never written) see Mortimer, *Indonesian Communist Party and Land Reform*, esp. pp. 15 ff. William Collier notes that the law has actually facilitated land sales, and suggests some corrective measures: "Food Problems," p. 51.

36. Gillian Hart, "The Processes of Poverty in Rural Java" (MS, Carnegie/State Department seminar, Nov. 1978).

37. "Diperlukan Proyek-Proyek Sederhana," *Kompas*, Nov. 10, 1978.

38. See Boediono, "An Economic Survey of North Sulawesi," *BIES* (Nov. 1972), 8:74.

39. See Kai Bird, "Food for Peace—or Politics," *Washington Post*, Jan. 4, 1978; James Morrell, "The Big Stick: The Use and Abuse of Food Aid," *Food Monitor* (Dec. 1977), vol. 2; also Cheryl Payer, "Food is Rice," *Pacific Research* (Mar.–Apr. 1976), vol. 8; for a worldwide critique which focuses on the disincentive problem, see Francis Moore Lappe and Joseph Collins, *Food First: Beyond the Myth of Scarcity* (Boston, 1976), esp. pp. 329 ff. A 1975 GAO study developed the disincentive argument for Indonesia and seven other countries; *Disincentives to Agricultural Production in Developing Countries* (Washington: United States General Accounting Office, Nov. 26, 1975). Cf. evidence that U.S. food aid retarded Taiwanese agriculture in the fifties and early sixties, and that its termination in 1965 was a critical factor in improving per capita production: Keith Griffin, "An Assessment of Development in Taiwan," *World Development* (June 1973), 1:32–33.

40. Donald F. McHenry and Kai Bird, "Food Bungle in Bangladesh," *Foreign Policy* (Summer 1977), 7:72–88.

41. Collier, "Food Problems," p. 47.

42. World Bank sources; see also Saleh Affif and C. Peter Timmer, "Rice Policy in Indonesia," pamphlet, Food Research Institute (Stanford, 1971), p. 145.

43. Cf. Bruce Glassburner, "Indonesia's New Economic Policy and its Sociopolitical Implications," in Jackson and Pye, eds., *Political Power and Communications*, p. 148; Glassburner notes that Japanese surplus rice has played a supplementary role.

44. *P.L. 480 Concessional Sales, History, Procedures, Negotiating and Implementing Agreements*, Economic Research Service, U.S. Department of Agriculture (Washington, 1977), p. 23.

45. Ibid., p. 33; see also testimony of John Sullivan, Assistant Administrator of the Bureau for Asia, AID, in U.S. House of Representatives, *Foreign Assistance Legislation for Fiscal Year 1979* (Part 6), Hearings before Subcommittee on Asian and Pacific Affairs, Committee on International Relations, 95th Cong., 2d sess., 1978, pp. 31–32.

46. For background on transmigration, see J. M. Hardjono, *Transmigration in Indonesia* (Kuala Lumpur, 1977); Colin Andrews, "Transmigration in Indonesia: Prospects and Problems," *Asian Survey* (May 1978), 18:458–72. A review of Hardjono's book which stresses the desirability of moving laborers (as opposed to agriculturalists) to the Outer Islands and takes a generally optimistic view of the program is H. W. Arndt and R. M. Sundrum's "Transmigration: Land Settlement or Regional Development?" in *BIES* (Nov. 1977), 13:72 ff., and Hardjono's reply in the following issue.

47. Andrews, "Transmigration in Indonesia," p. 463.

48. Ibid., p. 463.

49. World Bank estimate. For earlier and apparently less inclusive (hence lower) estimates see ibid., p. 465; also Ron Trostle, Indonesia's Transmigration Program: A Background Paper (MS, AID Jakarta, 1977).

50. Barry Newman, "Missing the Mark: In Indonesia, Attempts by World Bank to Aid Poor Often Go Astray," AWSJ, Nov. 10, 1977. Newman's article goes beyond transmigration to the more general criticism that the new poverty-oriented projects demand a slower, less technocratic, more field-oriented approach than the Bank's traditional modus operandi; for more recent developments see Raphael Pura, "Policy Rift Within World Bank Threatens Vast Indonesia Plan," AWSJ, Dec. 12, 1978.

51. Jusuf E. Wanandi, "An Indonesian View of Human Rights," FEER Dec. 2, 1977.

52. "Jet Makers Perk Up as Indonesia Studies Resettlements by Air," AWSJ, Aug. 4, 1978.

53. Seth Lipsky and Raphael Pura, "Indonesia: Testing Time for the New Order," Foreign Affairs (Fall 1978), 57:191–92.

54. This was the Agro Economic Survey's Five-year Rice Intensification Survey; see Benjamin White, "Notes on Agricultural Employment and Rural Labour Utilization in Java," (MS, 1977) p. 3.

55. Former Indonesian Ambassador to the United States Soedjatmoko has pointed out the problems associated with the "basic human needs" strategy, expressing some doubt that donors will be able to sustain the level of persistence and sophistication which will be needed to fulfill present levels of rhetorical commitment. He also observes that real progress in meeting basic human needs will involve "fundamental change in the redistribution of economic and political power." Although he does not say so, this is something which might alarm authorities in both Washington and Jakarta should it take place with perceptible speed. Soedjatmoko, "National Policy Implications of the Basic Needs Model," Prisma (Mar. 1978), 9:3–25.

56. For multilateral aid (about 25 percent of which is from U.S. sources), the disparity is much greater. In FY 1978 per capita disbursements in Indonesia and the Philippines from the World Bank, the Asian Development Bank, and U.N. agencies were $4.87 and $14.52 respectively: AID, Congressional Presentation, Fiscal Year 1980, Annex II (Asia) (Washington, 1979).

57. For statistics see table 1.1, on basic indicators.

7. Environmental Problems and Opportunities

1. Quotation from paper presented at USDA Conference on Improved Utilization of Tropical Forests, Madison, Wisconsin, May 1978; see also the same author's "A Faustian Dilemma," Unasylva (1978), 29:13.

2. "Deforestation—Death to the Panama Canal" in Proceedings of the U.S. Strategy Conference on Tropical Deforestation, Department of State (Washington, 1978), pp. 22–24.

3. Quotation is from Terence H. Hull, Valerie J. Hull, and Masri Singarimbun, "Indonesia's Family Planning Story: Success and Challenge," Population Bulletin (Nov. 1977), vol. 32. Growth rates and national goals are more recent information from AID. U.S. officials involved in the program note that if the Chinese accomplish-

ment is matched, it will have been done with much less coercion, which is not to say that there hasn't been any; on that point see Donald Emmerson, "Bureaucracy in Political Context," in Karl D. Jackson and Lucian Pye, *Political Power and Communications in Indonesia* (Berkeley, 1978), p. 120. Emmerson also suggests that heavy bureaucratic pressure to meet family planning targets may have skewed "acceptor" figures; however, the weight of expert opinion seems to be that the distortion has not been serious; see Terence H. Hull, "Rapid Fertility Decline: A Comment," *BIES* (July 1976), 12:106–7.

4. Discussion of Philippine family planning is based partly on personal observation and discussion with AID offficials in Manila and Washington, but see also Family Health Care, Inc., *A Review of the Philippines Population Program* (Washington, 1977).

5. Statistics from ibid., AID, and Population Reference Bureau.

6. Jac P. Thysse, "A Plea for Immediate Activities to Control the Menacing Deforestation and Erosion in Mountain Areas on Java," Simposium Pencegahan dan Pemulihan Tanah-tanah Kritis Dalam Rangka Pembangunan Wilayah (MS, Jakarta, Oct. 1975): the figure on arable land lost is from Achmad Soemitro, "Critical Points in Watersheds," AID translation from *Prisma* (Sept. 1978).

7. Erik P. Eckholm, *Losing Ground: Environmental Stress and World Food Prospects* (New York, 1976), p. 132.

8. "Greening" comes under the INPRES program (see chapter six).

9. Ross Marlay, *Pollution and Politics in the Philippines*, International Studies, Southeast Asia Series, no. 43, Ohio University Southeast Asia Program (Athens, 1977).

10. Jakarta information based on personal observation.

11. See studies by Robert Hackenberg on Davao, esp. *Fallout from the Poverty Explosion: Economic and Demographic Trends in Davao City, 1972–74* (Davao, 1975).

12. For background on the Indonesian timber industry in East Kalimantan and elsewhere, see the following: Gale Dixon, "Some Questions Regarding Timber Exploitation in East Kalimantan," Working Paper no. 2, Centre of Southeast Asian Studies, Monash University, 1974; Chris Manning, "The Timber Boom with Special Reference to East Kalimantan," *BIES* (Nov. 1971), 7:30–60; Willem Meijer, *Indonesian Forests and Land Use Planning* (Lexington, 1975); chapter by Willem Meijer in Gary Hansen, ed., *Agricultural Development in Indonesia* (in press); Norman Myers, *The Sinking Ark; A New Look at the Problem of Disappearing Species* (New York, 1979), pp. 148–52; and Kuswata Kartawinata, et al., "East Kalimantan and the Man and Biosphere Program," *Borneo Research Bulletin* (Apr. 1978) 10:28–40. Total foreign investment in forestry as of 1975 was $568 million, of which $306 million was Philippine (almost 30 percent consisting of the recently divested Soriano holding). Other leading investors were South Korea ($62 million), Japan and Malaysia ($49 million each), Hong Kong ($38 million) and the United States ($34 million). U.S. Department of Commerce, *Indonesia: A Survey of U.S. Business Opportunities* (Washington, 1977), p. 114.

13. FAO, *Yearbook of Forest Products 1964–76* (Rome, 1978), p. 51.

14. Maijer, *Indonesian Forests*, p. 16; Anthony Rowley, "Forests: Save or Squander?" *FEER*, Dec. 2, 1977, p. 65. See also Paul Gigot, "The Fall of the Forests," *FEER*, Nov. 30, 1979, pp. 52 ff. which reports a developing commercial hardwood shortage in Southeast Asia partly as the result of "Klondike mentality" logging in recent years.

15. Background on tropical moist forests worldwide, including statistics on areas, is from Myers, The Sinking Ark; see also J. G. Bene, J. W. Beall, and A. Cole, The Tropical Forest—Overexploited and Underused (Ottawa, 1976). The figure on estimated depletion by the turn of the century is from Council on Environmental Quality and U.S. Department of State, Entering the Twenty First Century; The Global Year 2000 Report to the President (Washington, D.C., in preparation).

16. Based on Myers, The Sinking Ark, and extract entitled "Garden of Eden to Weed Patch" in Natural Resources Defense Council Newsletter, (Jan.–Feb. 1977), vol. 6.

17. Myers, The Sinking Ark, pp. 117–8.

18. Paul Richards, "The Tropical Rain Forest," Scientific American (Dec. 1973), p. 64.

19. "Garden of Eden to Weed Patch," p. 12.

20. Myers, The Sinking Ark, p. 119.

21. For effect on local climate, see J. Ewell and L. Conde, "Potential Ecological Impact of Increased Intensity of Tropical Forest Utilization," final report to National Forest Service, U.S. Department of Agriculture (mimeograph, 1976), an extremely useful survey of technical literature. On the CO_2 question, see George Woodwell, "CO_2 Deforestation Relationships," in Proceedings, U.S. Strategy Conference on Tropical Deforestation, pp. 34–38.

22. For a spirited attack on multinational logging and Weyerhaeuser in particular for ignoring the plight of indigenous peoples, see George Appell, "The Multinationals in Borneo: General Custer as CEO," paper presented at the Workshop on the Social Consequences of Development sponsored by Cultural Survival Inc., Cambridge, Mass., Apr. 5, 1976. Appell's paper charges that logging operations have had a debasing effect on local villagers and threaten the existence of some members of the hunting-and-gathering Punan group. Weyerhaeuser's reply, quoted in the paper, argues that, far from constituting "ethnocide," its logging operations are helping local people adjust to the modern world and providing jobs, housing, schools, medical care, and so forth. Weyerhaeuser stresses that its concession area has "almost no tribal population," aside from shifting cultivators attracted to the area by logging operations.

There is no question that logging has violently disrupted so-called primitive societies in some areas of both Indonesia and the Philippines; for another example, see Robin Hanbury-Tenison, A Pattern of Peoples (London, 1975), p. 58–60. For a discussion of the threat posed by logging to tribal societies in the South Cotabato area of the Philippines, see John Nance, The Gentle Tasaday: A Stone Age People in the Philippine Rain Forest (New York, 1977) passim.

23. Myers, The Sinking Ark, p. 135.

24. Eric Eckholm, Disappearing Species: The Social Challenge, Worldwatch Paper 22 (Washington, 1978), p. 7.

25. Norman Myers, "An Expanded Approach to the Problem of Disappearing Species," Science (1976), vol. 193, quoted in Ewell and Conde, "Potential Ecological Impact," p. 39.

26. Current sustained-yield regulations for these three countries are discussed in Rowley, "Save or Squander?" Meijer notes that Indonesian forestry regulations call for a 60 centimeter minimum girth, but "in the agreements with the timber companies this figure is reduced to fifty centimeters and in actual practice even smaller sizes are logged." He also argues that thirty-five years is much too short a cycle to allow natural regeneration (Hansen volume—see note 12). Clear cutting (that is,

without girth limit) is allowed in Indonesia *if* tree plantations are to be established (communication with Weyerhaeuser).

27. The argument for regeneration is found in J. E. D. Fox, "Constraints on the Natural Regeneration of Tropical Forests," *Forest Ecology and Management* (1976), 1:37–65; also Willem Meijer, "Devastation and Regeneration of Lowland Dipterocarp Forests in Southeast Asia," *Bio Science*, Sept. 1973, pp. 528–33.

28. A classic anthropological study of the Ibans of Sarawak calculated that, in one area, a population of up to 46 people per square mile could be supported on the basis of shifting or slash-and-burn cultivation (more correctly known as "swidden") without doing permanent damage to the land: J. D. Freeman, *Iban Agriculture* (London, 1955), pp. 134–36. The figure would vary from place to place; as noted above, some Borneo rainforest soils are so poor that they won't grow rice at all.

29. Personal observation in Ilongot area of Luzon in the company of Stanford University anthropologists Renato and Michelle Rosaldo, 1974.

30. Again the generalization does not apply universally. Sarawak's Ibans, for example, formerly demonstrated a well-documented appetite for primary forest which stimulated their migration across vast areas in the nineteenth century. But the Iban case is exceptional, and widely recognized as such by neighboring Borneo societies. Robert Pringle, *Rajahs and Rebels: The Ibans of Sarawak under Brooke Rule* (London, 1970), esp. chapter 8.

31. Meijer, *Indonesian Forests*, pp. 61, 68.

32. National Environmental Protection Council, *First Annual Report* (Manila 1977), pp. 91–92.

33. Myers, *The Sinking Ark*, p. 151.

34. On the interrelationship between logging and politics in Sabah, see Edwin Lee, *The Towkays of Sabah* (Singapore, 1976).

35. On Tri Usaha Bhakti holdings see Richard Robison, "Toward a Class Analysis of the Indonesian Military Bureaucratic State," *Indonesia* (Apr. 1978) 25:28.

36. Details on Weyerhaeuser are drawn partly from Myers' *The Sinking Ark*, pp. 194–202, and communication with company officials; see also Meijer, *Indonesian Forests*, esp. pp. 39–43. Weyerhaeuser is not only the largest but also by far the most widely discussed of the U.S. timber firms in Indonesia, largely because the company, in line with its reputation for corporate enlightenment, has proved unusually willing to talk about its operations with scholars and critics.

37. In 1970 a commission appointed by President Suharto to investigate corruption criticized timber policy for undue liberality to foreigners and inadequate conservation practices. Supposedly confidential, the report was leaked to the Jakarta daily *Sinar Harapan*. J. A. C. Mackie, "The Commission of Four Report on Corruption," *BIES* (Nov. 1970) 4:89–90. While such officially sanctioned criticism has been rare, corruption associated with the military role in business has been a primary target of every wave of student protest since the advent of the New Order in 1966.

38. According to Robison, the military partners in most timber joint ventures contribute only on the order of 0.5 percent of the capital, but end up with a 20–25 percent interest in the operational logging company. "The central feature of the joint venture is the exchange of politically controlling economic concessions for financial reward." The conservative Indonesian publication *Business News* has observed that this pattern of nonactive partners or "local puppets . . . enrich[es] a small group of persons without creating any possibilities for the emergence of bona fide entrepreneurs in the future." Robison, "Indonesian Military Bureaucratic State," p. 29. For

the history of the military role in business, see "The Army's Economic Interests" in Harold Crouch, *The Army and Politics in Indonesia* (Ithaca, 1978), pp. 273–303.

39. Alf Leslie, "Where Theory and Practice Contradict," *Unasylva* (1977) vol. 29, no. 115, concludes that both "natural regeneration" and "sustained yield" are dead as the dodo, and that developing countries are unlikely to be impressed by the need to preserve gene pools in the face of massive economic incentives to rapid exploitation.

40. Brochure (untitled) by P.T. International Timber Corporation, Indonesia, 1977. See also Norman Johnson, "Biological Opportunities and Fast Growing Plantations," *Journal of Forestry* (Apr. 1976), 206–11. (The author is now President of Weyerhaeuser's Indonesian joint venture.)

41. Communication with Weyerhaeuser.

42. Letter from H. H. Itlis and colleagues to Dr. Robert L. Youngs, Director, Forest Products Laboratory, U.S. Forest Service, Apr. 13, 1978, circulated to participants at the Forest Service–sponsored International Conference on Improved Utilization of Tropical Forests, Madison, Wisconsin, May 21–26, 1978. For a balanced discussion of the pros and cons of plantation forestry in the tropics see Eric Eckholm, *Planting for the Future: Forestry for Human Needs*, Worldwatch Paper 26 (Washington, 1979).

43. S. D. Richardson, "A Faustian Dilemma."

44. Details on PICOP are from Roberto Abeleda's presentation at the Madison conference (see note 42) and material supplied by the company, especially brochure entitled "A Vision of Enterprise" (1977); PICOP is also discussed briefly in Myers, *The Sinking Ark*, and in *Forestry*, Sector Policy Paper, World Bank (1977), esp. p. 43.

45. Bowring and Tasker, "Philippines in Decline," *FEER*, Dec. 2, 1977, p. 60.

46. On the general dimensions of the problems see "The Other Energy Crisis," ch. 6 in Eckholm, *Losing Ground*.

47. Wijarso, "Oil II: A Doomsday Scenario: And Alternatives," *BIES* (Nov. 1977), 13:56.

48. Statement by Minister of State for Research Sumitro Djojohadikusumo, Joint Publications Research Service, Feb. 20, 1978.

49. A significant amount of Indonesian interisland trade is still carried by Madurese and Buginese sailing craft. "Development" in the years ahead will probably eliminate most of this labor-intensive, energy-conserving, but inefficient traffic, adding to Indonesia's domestic oil consumption in the process. See Barry Newman, "Cargo Ships Powered Only by Monsoons Thrive in Indonesia," *Wall Street Journal*, Sept. 7, 1977; also "Prahu Shipping in Indonesia," parts I and II, *BIES* (July–Nov. 1975), vol. II.

50. Rowley, "Save or Squander," p. 63; information on Bali from personal observation.

51. This paragraph is mainly drawn from Donald K. Emmerson, "The Case for a Maritime Perspective on Southeast Asia" (MS, 1979).

52. Bernard H. Oxman, "The Third United Nations Conference on the Law of the Sea: The 1977 New York Session," *American Journal of International Law* (Jan. 1978), 72:63–66. For the archipelago provisions in the draft treaty see Part IV, "Informal Composite Negotiating Text/Revision I" (MS, U.S. Department of State, 1978); and, for an Indonesian view, Mochtar Kusumaatmadja, "The Legal Regimes of Archipelagoes: Problems and Issues," in Lewis M. Alexander, ed., *The Law of the Sea:*

Needs and Interests of Developing Countries (Kingston, 1973), pp. 166–77. Since this article was written, its author, Indonesia's leading authority on law of the sea, has succeeded Adam Malik as Foreign Minister.

53. Republic of the Philippines, National Environmental Protection Council, *Philippine Environmental Quality* (Manila, 1977) p. 125.

54. Personal observation.

55. For general background on geothermal power see *Energy: Global Prospects 1985–2000*, Report of Workshop on Alternative Energy Strategies, Massachusetts Institute of Technology (New York, 1977); National Academy of Sciences, *Energy for Rural Development: Renewable Resources and Alternative Technologies for Developing Countries* (Washington, 1976).

56. On Philippine geothermal plans see National Research Council of the Philippines, *Proceedings of the Symposium on Energy Resources of the Philippines* (Manila, 1976), pp. 14–23; Albert Ravenholt, "Energy from Heat in the Earth," *American Universities Field Staff Reports*, Southeast Asia Series (Philippines, 1977), vol. 25, no. 5.

57. Pertamina has estimated geothermal resources on Java and Bali alone at 1,078 megawatts (*Indonesia Times*, May 29, 1978) but this is probably far too low.

58. Conversation with Union Oil and AID officials; on the role of Union in geothermal power development generally, see "Union Oil Gets Up Steam for Geothermal Energy," *Fortune*, July 31, 1978.

59. National Academy of Sciences, *The Winged Bean: A High Protein Crop for the Tropics* (Washington, 1975).

60. The figure on Indonesian deforestation is from Johnson, "Biologic Opportunities," but is almost certainly low; the Philippine figure is an AID estimate.

61. National Academy of Sciences, *Leucaena: Promising Forage and Tree Crop for the Tropics* (Washington, 1977).

62. Personal communication with AID adviser.

63. National Academy of Sciences, *Making Aquatic Weeds Useful: Some Perspectives for Developing Countries* (Washington, 1976).

64. Personal observation.

65. Typically, one conference was oriented toward exploitation, the other toward conservation; see notes 1 and 2 above.

66. The most famous ancestors of today's West Borneo Chinese arrived before Dutch rule, originally as gold miners. The descendants are found in both Malaysian (Sarawak) territory and in the adjoining Indonesian province of West Kalimantan. There is an extensive historical literature on this community, but so far as I am aware, no modern study of their agriculture has been published. For an excellent sociological study see T'ien Ju-k'ang, *The Chinese of Sarawak: A Study of Social Structure* (London, 1953).

67. There is already growing public concern in Indonesia about deforestation both on Java and in the Outer Islands as evidenced by the appointment (in April, 1978) of a highly respected senior official, Emil Salim, as Minister of State for Environment and Development, as well as by some excellent press reporting. See for example "Semua Ingin Hidup, Tapi Hutan Dihantam" ("Everyone Wants to Live, but the Forest is Annihilated") in the popular Jakarta news weekly *Tempo*, June 9, 1979.

68. A start has already been made in this direction, as indicated by the participation of CIA analyst Bruce Ross as consultant for the forestry section of the Council on Environmental Quality's Global Year 2000 study, commissioned by President Carter (not yet available at this writing). See *Tropical Moist Forests Conservation*

Bulletin (May 1978), 1:23. (This publication of the Natural Resources Defense Council is a useful guide to individuals and programs concerned with tropical deforestation.)

69. OPIC guarantees are not a major factor in Indonesian timber exploitation. Weyerhaeuser's Indonesian investment was originally insured under OPIC in 1971, but the company canceled its policy recently, apparently because it feels that its relationship with the Indonesian government, as well as its profit position in Indonesia, is sufficiently secure.

70. The January 1979 Executive Order is briefly discussed in chapter four in connection with Philippine nuclear power. Its extension to OPIC and Ex-Im forestry activities is among the recommendations of the Natural Resources Defense Council-chaired Tropical Forest Working Group organized to follow up the State Department's conference of 1978.

71. In 1976 Japan took 65 percent of Southeast Asian log exports, compared to 15 percent and 11.9 percent for Korea and Taiwan, respectively. Fifty-five percent of Korean and Taiwanese plywood exports went to the United States. See Sudikin Djajapertjunda, *The Utilization of Tropical Hardwood from Indonesia* (Jakarta, 1978), pp. 35–36.

8. Conclusion: On the Need to Think Ahead

1. Stanley Hoffman, *Primacy or World Order: American Foreign Policy Since the Cold War* (New York, 1978), p. 133.

2. See, for example, ibid., also Miriam Camps, *The Management of Interdependence* (New York, 1974).

3. Cf. the Murphy Commission's emphasis on more effective "foreign assessment" and "advocacy" roles for the State Department: U.S. Government, *Commission on the Organization of the Government for the Conduct of Foreign Policy* (Washington, 1975) (hereafter cited as Murphy Commission report) and my essay, "Creeping Irrelevance at Foggy Bottom," *Foreign Policy*, (Winter 1977–78), 29:128–39.

4. Charles Frankel, *High on Foggy Bottom: An Outsider's Inside View of the Government* (New York, 1968), p. 92.

5. The "oral-driven" concept is from Chester L. Cooper's comment on Bloomfield's essay cited in note 8 below, also in vol. 2 of the Murphy Commission appendices, p. 229.

6. I. M. Destler, *Presidents, Bureaucrats and Foreign Policy: The Politics of Organizational Reform* (Princeton, 1974), pp. 214–18, 224–28, quotation p. 214; an excellent brief history of the Policy Planning Staff and its successors.

7. Murphy Commission report, p. 149.

8. Lincoln P. Bloomfield, "Organizing for Policy Planning," Appendix F, vol. 2 of appendices, *Commission on the Organization of the Government for the Conduct of Foreign Policy*, pp. 214–15 (includes a short guide to recent writing on the subject). The kind of capability that he advocates would not obviate the need for the more immediate brand of policy analysis currently performed by State's Policy Planning Staff, or the desirability of a specifically aid-related research arm such as the proposed Institute for Scientific and Technological Cooperation; for some of the thought behind the latter see U.S. House of Representatives, Committee on International Relations, *Rethinking United States Foreign Policy Toward the Developing*

World, 95th Cong., 1st sess. (Aug.–Nov. 1977), particularly testimony of Lester E. Gordon, pp. 53 ff., p. 61. It now appears that Congress will approve the ISTC only as an office within AID rather than the separate entity originally contemplated.

9. On the need for greater sharing of executive branch information with the Congress and academia, see G. McT. Kahin, "A Polarization of Knowledge—Specialization on Contemporary Asia in the United States," *Journal of Asian Studies* (Aug. 1974), 33:515–22.

Index